T0214059

Lecture Notes in Computer Science 11931

More information about this series at http://www.springer.com/series/7411

Falko Dressler · Christian Scheideler (Eds.)

Algorithms for Sensor Systems

15th International Symposium on Algorithms and Experiments
for Wireless Sensor Networks, ALGOSENSORS 2019
Munich, Germany, September 12–13, 2019
Revised Selected Papers

 Springer

Editors
Falko Dressler (iD)
Paderborn University
Paderborn, Germany

Christian Scheideler (iD)
Paderborn University
Paderborn, Germany

ISSN 0302-9743   ISSN 1611-3349   (electronic)
Lecture Notes in Computer Science
ISBN 978-3-030-34404-7   ISBN 978-3-030-34405-4   (eBook)
https://doi.org/10.1007/978-3-030-34405-4

LNCS Sublibrary: SL5 – Computer Communication Networks and Telecommunications

This Springer imprint is published by the registered company Springer Nature Switzerland AG
The registered company address is: Gewerbestrasse 11, 6330 Cham, Switzerland

Preface

The papers in this volume were presented at the 15th International Symposium on Algorithms and Experiments for Wireless Sensor Networks (ALGOSENSORS 2019), held during September 12–13, 2019, as part of the ALGO 2019 event in Munich, Germany.

ALGOSENSORS is an international symposium dedicated to the algorithmic aspects of wireless networks. Originally focused on sensor networks, it now covers algorithmic issues arising in wireless networks of all types of computational entities, static or mobile, including sensor networks, sensor-actuator networks, and autonomous robots. The focus is on the design and analysis of algorithms, models of computation, and experimental analysis.

This year the Program Committee (PC) was organized into two tracks: an Algorithms and Theory track headed by Christian Scheideler and an Experiments and Applications track headed by Falko Dressler.

The 11 full papers presented in this volume were carefully selected from 16 submissions. We would like to thank all the authors who submitted their work to ALGOSENSORS 2019 and the PC members for their valuable and insightful reviews and comments. Finally, we also thank the Steering Committee chair Sotiris Nikoletseas for his valuable advice and the Organizing Committee of ALGO 2019 for their time and effort to ensure a successful meeting.

September 2019

Falko Dressler
Christian Scheideler

Organization

Program Committee

Matthew Andrews	Nokia Bell Labs, USA
Amotz Bar-Noy	City University of New York, USA
Aaron Becker	University of Houston, USA
Naveed Anwar Bhatti	RISE Stockholm, Sweden
Costas Busch	Lousiana State University, USA
Ioannis Chatzigiannakis	Sapienza University of Rome, Italy
Yingying Chen	Rutgers University, USA
Bogdan Chlebus	Augusta University, USA
Shantanu Das	Aix-Marseille University, France
Falko Dressler	Paderborn University, Germany
Sándor Fekete	Braunschweig University of Technology, Germany
Jie Gao	Stony Brook University, USA
Bernhard Haeupler	CMU, USA
Taisuke Izumi	Nagoya Institute of Technology, Japan
Irina Kostitsyna	Eindhoven University of Technology, The Netherlands
Evangelos Kranakis	Carleton University, Canada
Olaf Landsiedel	Kiel University, Germany
Mo Li	Nanyang Technological University, Japan
Marina Petrova	KTH Royal Institute of Technology, Sweden
Christian Scheideler	Paderborn University, Germany
Michael Segal	Ben Gurion University, Israel
Tigran Tonoyan	Reykjavik University, Iceland

Additional Reviewers

Shibata, Masahiro
van Renssen, André
Wang, Haotian

Contents

Faulty Robots

Mobility Management

Evacuation of Equilateral Triangles by Mobile Agents of Limited Communication Range

Iman Bagheri, Lata Narayanan$^{(\boxtimes)}$, and Jaroslav Opatrny

Department of Computer Science and Software Engineering,
Concordia University, Montreal, Canada
imanbag@gmail.com, {lata,opatrny}@cs.concordia.ca

Abstract. We consider the problem of evacuating $k \geq 2$ mobile agents from a unit-sided equilateral triangle through an exit located at an unknown location on the perimeter of the triangle. The agents are initially located at the centroid of the triangle and they can communicate with other agents at distance at most r with $0 \leq r \leq 1$. An agent can move at speed at most one, and finds the exit only when it reaches the point where the exit is located. The agents can collaborate in the search for the exit. The goal of the *evacuation problem* is to minimize the evacuation time, defined as the worst-case time for *all* the agents to reach the exit. We propose and analyze several algorithms for the problem of evacuation by $k \geq 2$ agents; our results indicate that the best strategy to be used varies depending on the values of r and k. For two agents, we give four algorithms, the last of which achieves the best performance for all sub-ranges of r in the range $0 < r \leq 1$. We also show a lower bound on the evacuation time of two agents for any $r < 0.336$. For $k > 2$ agents, we study three strategies for evacuation: in the first strategy, called X3C, agents explore all three sides of the triangle before connecting to exchange information; in the second strategy, called X1C, agents explore a single side of the triangle before connecting; in the third strategy, called CXP, the agents travel to the perimeter to locations in which they are connected, and explore it while always staying connected. For 3 or 4 agents, we show that X3C works better than X1C for small values of r, while X1C works better for larger values of r. Finally, we show that for any r, evacuation of $k = 6 + 2\lceil(\frac{1}{r} - 1)\rceil$ agents can be done using the CXP strategy in time $1 + \sqrt{3}/3$, which is optimal in terms of time, and asymptotically optimal in terms of the number of agents.

1 Introduction

Consider the situation where several mobile agents/robots are located inside a closed region, that has a single exit point on the perimeter of the region at a location unknown to the agents. Due to some emergency, the agents all need to

This research was supported by NSERC, Canada.

© Springer Nature Switzerland AG 2019
F. Dressler and C. Scheideler (Eds.): ALGOSENSORS 2019, LNCS 11931, pp. 3–22, 2019.
https://doi.org/10.1007/978-3-030-34405-4_1

leave this region as quickly as possibly. Thus the agents need to collaboratively search for the exit and minimize the time that is needed for *all of them* to reach the exit. This *evacuation problem* has already been considered for several different regions and agents of different capabilities.

Two models of communication between the agents have been considered in the context of group search and evacuation. In the first model, called the *face-to-face* model, the agents can communicate only when they are in the same place at the same time. In the second model, called the *wireless* model, the agents can communicate at any time and over any distance. The algorithms for evacuation in the wireless and face-to-face models are in general, quite different. It is natural to ask how the agents would perform evacuation if their communication range was limited to some r with $0 \leq r \leq \infty$ where the diameter of the region is assumed to be 1. Note that $r = 0$ gives the face-to-face model, and $r = \infty$ corresponds to the wireless model. In any region of diameter 1, since agents never need to be at distance greater than one to communicate with other agents, a communication range of $r > 1$ confers no advantages. Thus the wireless model is equivalent to the case $r = 1$.

In this paper we study the problem of evacuating an equilateral triangle whose sides are of size 1 with agents located initially in the centroid of the triangle, and whose communication capabilities are limited to a given, fixed distance $0 < r < 1$. To the best of our knowledge, the case of limited range communication of agents in evacuation problems has not been considered yet. Since the evacuation of the equilateral triangle was previously studied for the face-to-face model [10] and the wireless model [15], it will allow us to evaluate the impact of the limited transmission range on the evacuation algorithms. When there are three or more agents, then an agent can act as a *relay* between two other agents, thereby increasing the *effective communication range* of the agents. Indeed a *virtual meeting* can occur between many agents, even when they are not co-located, so long as the network of communication they create is connected. This suggests that the interplay between the communication range r and the number of agents k should be considered in the design of evacuation algorithms.

1.1   Our Results

We first study in detail the case of $k = 2$ agents. In Sect. 3 we propose four evacuation algorithms for two agents, parametrized by r, each subsequent algorithm improving evacuation times. As shown in Table 1, throughout the entire range $0 \leq r \leq 1$, our algorithms take advantage of increased communication range to achieve lower evacuation time. Our first algorithm uses a simple fast exploration of the perimeter strategy in which agents move together to the midpoint of an edge, and then move in opposite directions to explore the boundary of the triangle. In [10], it was shown that for $r = 0$, the evacuation time is improved by making several *detours* into the interior of the triangle. Our second and third algorithm for two agents and $r > 0$ uses the same type of detours as that of [10]. We show here that in this algorithm a detour is useful only for $r < 0.7375$, while using more than one detour is not useful for $r > 0.4725$. Our last two-agent algorithm employs a *new* kind of detour that attempts to balance better the evacuation time at different possible locations of the exit. We show that our new algorithm achieves the best evacuation time for all values of $r > 0$. Finally, we show a lower bound of $1 + 2/\sqrt{3} - r$ on the evacuation time of two agents for any $r < 0.366$.

For $k > 2$ agents, we investigate three different strategies for evacuation. In the first strategy, called *Explore 3 sides before Connecting* (X3C), the perimeter of the triangle is partitioned into $k + 1$ segments. The agents move to explore k segments on all three sides, subsequently entering the interior of the triangle to form a connected network in order to communicate the results to the other agents, after which they either move to the exit or they all explore the remaining segment. In the second strategy, called *Explore 1 Side before Connecting* (X1C) only one of the sides of the triangle is partitioned into multiple segments, each to be explored by an agent. At the end of the exploration of the edge, two of the agents explore the remaining two sides of the triangle, while the other agents move inside to create and maintain connectivity of all agents. As soon as the exit is found, all agents can move to the exit. In the final strategy (which is only possible if the number of agents is large enough relative to r), called *Connected Exploration of Perimeter* (CXP), the agents move to positions over two sides of the perimeter to ensure that the agents are connected *before* they start exploration, and they stay connected during the entire exploration.

We study in detail the case of 3 and 4 agents in Sect. 4. Note that the CXP strategy cannot apply in these cases, and thus we study only the X3C and X1C strategies. Our results show that X3C works better than X1C for smaller values of r and X1C is better for larger values of r; see Table 1.

Finally we consider in Sect. 5 the problem of the optimal evacuation of k agents. It was shown in [15] that for any r, regardless of the number of agents, evacuation cannot be done in time less that $1 + \sqrt{3}/3$; on the other hand, this time can be achieved by 6 agents and $r = 1$. In this paper we show that for any $r > 0$, evacuation can achieved in the optimal time of $1 + \sqrt{3}/3$ if the number of agents is $6 + 2\lceil(\frac{1}{r} - 1)\rceil$. Indeed for $r = 1/2$, eight agents suffice, and for $r = 1/3$, ten agents suffice, for $r = 1/4$, twelve agents suffice. We also show that $\Omega(1/r)$ agents are required to evacuate in time $1 + \sqrt{3}/3$.

We conjecture that for any $k \geq 6$ agents, there exist r_1, r_2 with $0 < r_1 < r_2 < 1$ such that X3C is the best strategy of the three for $0 \leq r \leq r_1$, X1C is the best strategy for $r_1 < r \leq r_2$, and CXP is the best strategy for $r_2 < r \leq 1$.

All omitted proofs can be found in [3].

1.2 Related Work

The evacuation problem was introduced in [12] for agents inside a disk in both the wireless and face-to-face communication models. The authors gave optimal algorithms for 2 agents in the wireless model, and proved upper and lower bounds for the evacuation time for 2 agents in the face-to-face model. They also considered the problem for 3 agents and showed asymptotically tight bounds for k agents in both models. The problem for the face-to-face model was revisited

Table 1. A summary of the evacuation times of our algorithms.

	Two agents		Three agents		Four agents	
r	Evac. time	Algorithm	Evac. time	Algorithm	Evac. time	Algorithm
0	2.3367	See [10]	2.0887	see [10]	1.98157	See [10]
0.1	2.23473	1-Detour-new	2.08871	X3C	1.96199	X3C
0.2	2.15903	1-Detour-new	2.07642	X3C	1.88392	X1C
0.3	2.09612	1-Detour-new	1.93620	X1C	1.67649	X1C
0.4	2.04052	1-Detour-new	1.78880	X1C	1.62573	X1C
0.5	1.99003	1-Detour-new	1.68958	X1C	1.61912	X1C
0.6	1.94355	1-Detour-new	1.67532	X1C	1.61302	X1C
0.7	1.90049	1-Detour-new	1.66666	X1C	1.61050	X1C
0.8	1.86047	1-Detour-new	1.66666	X1C	1.61050	X1C
0.9	1.82326	1-Detour-new	1.66666	X1C	1.61050	X1C
1	1.78867	See [16]	1.66666	See [15]	1.61050	See [15]

in [13], and the results further improved in [7]. The evacuation of an equilateral triangle with agents in the wireless model was considered in [15], and in the face-to-face communication model in [10]. We should also mention the work on polygons [20], evacuation of circle with faulty agents [13], and the case of multiple exits on a circle [11,26].

The evacuation problem is related to many other problems that have been considered previously. It can be seen as a variation of a search problem. In this context we should mention the classical *cow-path* problem, i.e., a problem of searching on a line [2,4,5], several of its versions [17,24,25], a group search on a line [9], and a search on a line with faulty agents [14]. There are many studies involving mobile, autonomous agents in the plane [21]. The problem of search [8,19], gathering of agents [1,18] in the plane, pattern formation [22], etc., have been done. The cop-and robber games [6], and graph searches [23] are also related.

2   Model and Notation

The search domain considered in this paper is the perimeter of an equilateral triangle with side 1. We denote the triangle by T, with vertices A, B and C starting at the top of the triangle, going counter-clockwise, and the centroid of the triangle by O, as in Fig. 1a. Point M is the midpoint of the segment BC. The *height* of the triangle is denoted by h and $y = h/3$. The line segment connecting any two points P and Q is denoted by PQ and its length by $|PQ|$. Agents are initially located at the centroid O of the triangle. Each agent can move at speed at most 1, and it has a wireless transmitter/receiver with range $r \leq 1$. Unless specified otherwise in the algorithm, agents always move with speed 1. Agents are able to carry out simple computations, e.g., if an agent finds the exit it can calculate the path to follow in order to inform other agents about the exit. In this paper agents are assumed to be non-faulty, meaning that they: follow their assigned trajectory, recognize the exit if they reach its location, and they can always exchange information if their distance is less than or equal to r.

Each agent follows a path, called its *trajectory*, assigned to it before the exploration begins. We specify each evacuation algorithm by specifying a trajectory of each agent and its actions. An agent may leave its predetermined trajectory only if either it has found the exit point, or it has been notified by another agent about the location of the exit. For each of these two situations the algorithm specifies the action to be followed.

We denote the time that point x is seen for the first time by either of the agents by t_x. By $E_{\mathcal{A}}(k, r)$ we mean the worst-case evacuation time of algorithm $\mathcal{A}$ with k agents, $k \geq 2$ and communication range of r, $0 \leq r \leq 1$. We denote the optimal evacuation time by k agents by $E^*(k, r)$, that is:

$$E^*(k, r) = min_{\mathcal{A}} E_{\mathcal{A}}(k, r)$$

We define an *r-interception* to be the action of moving to a point in which the agent is at distance at most r of the other agent(s). In all our algorithms, the trajectory of each agent is a sequence of line segments. To analyze the algorithms, we identify on each segment a *critical point*, defined to be the point or the immediate neighbourhood of a point where the evacuation time on the segment is maximized. In order to minimize the maximum evacuation time, after identifying these critical points, we optimize the algorithms by adjusting some parameters in the trajectories.

3   Evacuation of Two Agents

In this section we give upper and lower bounds on the evacuation time for two agents with $0 < r < 1$. Recall that the best known algorithm described in [10] for the face-to-face model ($r = 0$), evacuates two agents in time 2.3367 and employs two detours per agent. In [16], an optimal algorithm for the wireless model ($r = 1$) with evacuation time of $3/2 + y \approx 1.78867$ is described. Hence if the agents are capable of communication within a certain range $0 < r < 1$, it is clear that the evacuation time should lie between these two values. We divide the triangle into two halves by a vertical line through A and O, as shown in Fig. 1a. The trajectories of the two agents presented in this section are *symmetric* with respect to line AO. Thus the trajectory of the first agent R_1 includes exploration of the left half of the perimeter, and the second agent R_2 is responsible for exploration of the right half of T. Therefore, without loss of generality, in the analysis of algorithms we will assume that the exit is located in the right half of the triangle throughout this section.

The evacuation algorithms for two agents presented in this section use the same generic Algorithm 1 given below. They only differ in the trajectories of the agents.

Algorithm 1. Generic 2-agent Evacuation Algorithm Followed by an Agent.

function EXPLORATION
    found← false
    while not<found> and not<msg_recd > **do**
        move along the predetermined trajectory
    ACTION
function ACTION
    if found **then**
        P ← current location
        if the other agent is not within communication range **then**
            calculate the closest point U, where the other agent can be r-intercepted
            go to U
        send(P) to the other agent
    go to P and exit

Let S_1 and S_2 be points on the sides AB and AC at distance r from A, shown in Fig. 1a. Points S_1, S_2, A form an equilateral triangle at the top of T with side r. If the agents do not find the exit outside $\Delta S_1 A S_2$ and enter this smaller triangle, they are always within communication range with each other, and the evacuation time for the three algorithms described in this section, is independent of the exit position and will always be $t_{S_1} + r$.

3.1 The No-Detour Algorithm

The trajectories of both agents are shown in Fig. 1a and defined in Trajectories 1. The trajectory of R_1 is shown in blue, the green trajectory is for R_2. Clearly, these trajectories do the fastest possible exploration of the perimeter of T, and these trajectories are known to give the optimal time of $y + 1.5$ for the wireless evacuation of T by two agents starting in O.

Trajectories 1. No-Detour
    R_1 follows the trajectory :$< O, M, B, A >$
    R_2 follows the trajectory :$< O, M, C, A >$

The Algorithm No-Detour uses the generic Algorithm 1 with respect to Trajectories 1. For the analysis of this algorithm, we assume the exit is found by R_2. Then we show that the maximum evacuation time is when the exit is located at point C.

In order to determine the critical point of some segments in T we use the following lemma, which is a simple generalization of Theorem 1 in [7] for the case $r > 0$.

Lemma 1. *[7] Suppose R_1 and R_2 with $r > 0$ are looking for an exit on lines L_1 and L_2 respectively, as on Fig. 2. Assume the exit is found by R_2 at point N, and Q be the point where R_1 is r-intercepted. Let S be the line connecting N and Q, β be the angle between L_2 and S, and γ be the angle between L_1 and S by γ.*

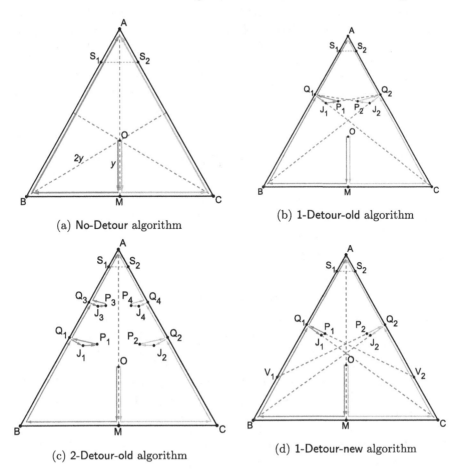

(a) No-Detour algorithm

(b) 1-Detour-old algorithm

(c) 2-Detour-old algorithm

(d) 1-Detour-new algorithm

Fig. 1. Trajectories for 2 agent exploration (Color figure online)

If $2\cos\beta + \cos\gamma < 1$ then shifting the exit in the direction of the movement of R_2 yields a larger evacuation time, while if $2\cos\beta + \cos\gamma > 1$, then shifting the exit in the opposite direction of the movement of R_2 yields a larger evacuation time.

Proof. Omitted.

Lemma 2. *Vertex C is the critical point on segments MC and CA.*

Proof. Omitted.

Theorem 1. $E_{\text{No-Detour}} = y + 0.5 + r + \frac{2(1-r^2)}{2r+1}$.

Proof. We established that C is the critical point for MC and CA. When the exit is located at C, the evacuation time will be $t = y + 0.5 + |BQ| + |QC|$ where

Q is the point that R_1 is r-intercepted. Since both agents travel equal distances at the point of interception, we get $|BQ| = |QC| - r$. On the other hand by using the Cosine Rule we have $|QC| = \sqrt{BQ^2 + 1 - BQ}$. By solving for $|BQ|$ we obtain $t = y + 0.5 + r + \frac{2(1-r^2)}{2r+1}$. ∎

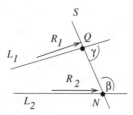

Fig. 2. Illustration for Lemma 1.

3.2 Trajectories with Detours as in [10]

In Theorem 1 we showed that placing the exit at point C causes the maximum evacuation time when using the No-Detour algorithm. In this section we generalize the detour trajectories given in [10] for the face-to-face model to arbitrary $r > 0$, with the goal of improving the evacuation time by decreasing the evacuation time at C. The inclusion of a detour in the trajectories of each agent consist of the agent stopping exploration at some point of the perimeter and moving inside the triangle to improve the evacuation time when the exit is located in some segments around C or B. When the agents realize that the exit was not found in these segments, they return to the same point on the boundary where they left off and resume the exploration of the perimeter. We first consider the inclusion of one detour in the trajectories.

The 1-Detour-old Algorithm: The trajectories are symmetric and thus we define the detour for R_1 only. We fix point Q_1 on the side AB, see Fig. 1b. The exact location of this point will be specified later. Point J_1 is on segment Q_1C such that it satisfies the equation $|BQ_1| + |Q_1J_1| = |CJ_1| - r$. Point P_1 is located on segment J_1Q_2 such that P_1 satisfies the equation $|Q_1J_1| + |J_1P_1| = |Q_2P_1| - r$. Points Q_2, J_2 and P_2 are located symmetrically with those of points Q_1, J_1 and P_1 respectively, with respect to line AM.

The trajectory of each agent is defined in Trajectories 2, see also Fig. 1b.

We show below that if R_1 reaches point P_1 and it is not notified about the exit by the other agent, then it realizes that the exit has not been found yet. Thus it returns to point Q_1 where it started the detour and resumes the exploration of the perimeter. Algorithm 1 with respect to Trajectories 2 is referred to as the 1-Detour-old algorithm.

Trajectories 2.   1-Detour-old
$R_1 :< O, M, B, Q_1, J_1, P_1, Q_1, A >$
$R_2 :< O, M, C, Q_2, J_2, P_2, Q_2, A >$

Lemma 3. *If the exit is located at some point N on segment MC, then R_1 will be r-intercepted at or prior to reaching J_1.*

Proof. Omitted.

Lemma 4. *Suppose the exit is located at some point N on segment CQ_2, then R_1 will be r-intercepted while moving on segment J_1P_1.*

Proof. We know that if the exit is located at Q_2, then R_1 will be r-intercepted when it is at point P_1. In order to show that if the exit is before Q_2, agent R_1 can be intercepted before reaching P_1 it is enough to prove $|CN| + |NP_1| - r \leq |CQ_2| + |Q_2P_1| - r$. For the purpose of contradiction suppose not, meaning $|CN| + |NP_1| - r > |CQ_2| + |Q_2P_1| - r = |CN| + |NQ_2| + |Q_2P_1| - r$ and we get $|NP_1| > |NQ_2| + |Q_2P_1|$ which according to the triangle inequality is impossible. Hence a contradiction.   ∎

We now split the trajectory of R_2 into segments MC, CQ_2, Q_2S_2, S_2A, and determine the critical point for each segment and the evacuation time of the critical point for each segment.

Lemma 5. *On segments MC and CQ_2 point C is the critical point, and the evacuation time for this segment is at most $y + 0.5 + |BQ_1| + |Q_1C|$.*

Proof. Omitted.

Lemma 6. *Assume the exit is located at point N inside segment Q_2S_2 and let Z be a point on segment Q_1A such that $Q_1Z + r = Q_2Z$. Then the evacuation time for this exit is at most $y + 0.5 + |BQ_1| + |Q_1J_1| + |J_1P_1| + |P_1Q_1| + |Q_1Z| + |ZQ_2|$.*

Proof. Omitted.

As mentioned before, the evacuation time for an exit in segment S_2A is $t_{S_1} + r$, which is less than the evacuation time for exit located in segment Q_2S_2. Thus, combining the results of the previous lemmas we can now give a value for $E_{\text{1-Detour-old}}(2, r)$.

Theorem 2. *Let $t_1 = y + 0.5 + |BQ_1| + |Q_1C|$ and $t_2 = y + 0.5 + |BQ_1| + |Q_1J_1| + |J_1P_1| + |P_1Q_1| + |Q_1Z| + |ZQ_2|$, where point Z is the point that if the exit is located right after Q_2, agent R_1 will be r-intercepted at or before Z. Then $E_{\text{1-Detour-old}}(2, r) = max\{t_1, t_2\}$.*

Observe that by increasing the size of segment BQ_1, time t_1 increases, and on the other hand, decreasing length of BQ_1, increases t_2. Best value for $|BQ_1|$ is obtained when $t_1 = t_2$. Clearly, there is exactly one value of Q_1 which equates t_1 and t_2. However, because of the complexity of the equations, we do not have an explicit solution for Q_1 as a function of r. As shown there, the 1-Detour-old algorithm with one detour has a lower evacuation time than the No-Detour algorithm for $0 < r < 0.7$.

Observation: The 1-Detour-old algorithm does not allow a detour for $r \geq$ 0.7375: As can be seen from Table 2, the improvement provided by using 1-Detour-old algorithm diminishes when r increases, and it does not give any improvement for $r = 0.7375$. This is because the values r and $|Q_1 J_1|$ are inversely related. Increasing r will decrease the value of $|Q_1 J_1|$ up to a point when $|Q_1 J_1|$ is equal to zero. At this point we would have $r = \sqrt{|BQ_1|^2 + 1} - |BQ_1| - |BQ_1|$. By substituting this value in $f(r, |BQ_1|) = g(r, |BQ_1|)$ and solving that equation we get the values of 0.1843512042 and 0.7374048168 for $|BQ_1|$ and r respectively. If we increase r, we get negative value for $|Q_1 J_1|$ which is invalid.

The 2-Detour-old Algorithm: It is shown in [10], that for $r = 0$, i.e., the face-to-face communication, the evacuation time can be improved by using more than one detour. We now show that for *smaller* values of r, a further improvement in evacuation time can be similarly achieved by making more detours. Consider the situation in the execution of the 1-Detour-old algorithm when R_1 and R_2 reach vertices B and C respectively, assuming no agent have found the exit so far. The remaining search problem will be a triangle with two unexplored sides of length 1, call this problem $\mathcal{P}_1$. Now consider the time when the two agents finish their detour and get back to points Q_1 and Q_2 with no exit found. Call the remaining search problem $\mathcal{P}_2$. It is obvious that $\mathcal{P}_2$ is a scaled down version of $\mathcal{P}_1$, however with proportionally larger r.

Thus, if r is not too large yet for problem $\mathcal{P}_2$, another detour could be done in the upper part of the triangle. The trajectory of two agents with two detours shown in Fig. 1c is specified in Trajectories 3.

Trajectories 3.   2-Detour-old
$$R_1 :< O, M, B, Q_1, J_1, P_1, Q_1, Q_3, J_3, P_3, Q_3, A >$$
$$R_2 :< O, M, C, Q_2, J_2, P_2, Q_2, Q_4, J_4, P_4, Q_4, A >$$

Algorithm 1 with respect to Trajectories 3 is called 2-Detour-old algorithm. In the case of two detours, similarly as in the case of one detour, it can be shown that there exists three critical points, namely C, and the points right after Q_2 and Q_4. The evacuation times for these points will be as follows:

1. $t_1 = y + |MB| + |BQ_1| + |Q_1 C|$
2. $t_2 = y + |MB| + |BQ_1| + |Q_1 J_1| + |J_1 P_1| + |P_1 Q_1| + |Q_1 Q_3| + |Q_3 Q_2|$
3. $t_3 = y + |MB| + |BQ_1| + |Q_1 J_1| + |J_1 P_1| + |P_1 Q_1| + |Q_1 Q_3| + |Q_3 J_3| + |J_3 P_3| + |P_3 Q_3| + |Q_3 V| + |V Q_4|$

where V is a point on segment $Q_3 S_1$, such that $|Q_3 V| = |V Q_4| - r$.

By equating these three values we obtain an optimized two detour evacuation algorithm.

It has been shown in [10] that for the face-to-face communication model, detours can be recursively added to improve the evacuation time, though the improvement obtained by successive detours decreases rapidly. In contrast, we showed above that for $r > 0.7374$, not even one detour improves the evacuation time. Similarly it can be shown that a second detour is not helpful for $r >$ 0.472504.

3.3   A New Kind of Detour Trajectory

In this section, we propose and analyze a different detour. Since 1-Detour-old trajectories have been shown in the previous subsection not to be applicable for r greater than 0.7375, we consider now trajectories with a new type of a detour that will be shown to be applicable to any value of r. The trajectories are again symmetric and thus we only describe the detour for R_1 in detail.

We fix point Q_1 on the side AB, see Fig. 1d. The exact location of this point will be specified later. Point J_1 is on segment Q_1C such that it satisfies the equation

$$|BQ_1| + |Q_1J_1| = |CJ_1| - r$$

This is similar to the 1-Detour-old algorithm, and ensures that if agent R_2 finds the exit at C, it can intercept the agent R_1 at J_1. We differ from the 1-Detour-old algorithm in the definitions of point V_2 located on segment CQ_2, and point P_1 located on the segment Q_1V_2. The locations of V_2 and P_1 are determined by the following equations.

$$|BQ_1| + |Q_1J_1| + |J_1P_1| = |CV_2| + |V_2P_1| - r$$
$$|Q_1J_1| + |J_1P_1| + |P_1Q_1| + |Q_1V_2| = |Q_1C|$$

The first equation ensures that if the exit is found by agent R_2 at V_2, it can intercept agent R_1 at point P_1. If however, agent R_2 finds the exit after point V_2, it can only intercept agent R_1 after R_1 finishes its detour. The second equation ensures that the time taken by agent R_1 to reach V_1 from Q_1 *after* the detour is the same as the time taken by agent R_1 to reach point C *before* the detour.

Points V_1, Q_2, J_2 and P_2 are located symmetrically with points V_2, Q_1, J_1 and P_1 respectively, with respect to line AM. The trajectories of the two agents are defined in Trajectories 4 and shown in Fig. 1d. Algorithm 1 with respect to Trajectories 4 is referred to as the 1-Detour-new algorithm.

Trajectories 4.   1-Detour-new
$$R_1 :< O, M, B, Q_1, J_1, P_1, Q_1, A >$$
$$R_2 :< O, M, C, Q_2, J_2, P_2, Q_2, A >$$

The following lemmas are implied by the definitions of the trajectories.

Lemma 7. *If the exit is located at some point N on segment MC, then R_1 will be r-intercepted at or prior to reaching J_1.*

Lemma 8. *Suppose the exit is located at some point N on segment CV_2, then R_1 will be r-intercepted while moving on segment J_1P_1.*

Lemma 9. *Suppose the exit is located at some point N on segment V_2S_2, then R_1 will be r-intercepted while moving on segment Q_1S_1.*

We now split the trajectory of R_2 into segments MC, CV_2, V_2Q_2, Q_2S_2, S_2A, and determine the critical point for each segment and the evacuation time of the critical point for each segment.

Lemma 10. *On segments MC and CV_2 point C is the critical point, and the evacuation time for this segment is at most $y + 0.5 + |BQ_1| + |Q_1C|$.*

Lemma 11. *On segment V_2Q_2 the evacuation time is maximal in the immediate neighbourhood of point V_2 and the evacuation time for this segment is at most $y + 0.5 + |BQ_1| + |Q_1C|$.*

Lemma 12. *Assume the exit is located at point N inside segment Q_2S_2 and let Z be a point on segment Q_1A such that $Q_1Z + r = Q_2Z$. Then the evacuation time for this exit is at most $y + 0.5 + |BQ_1| + |Q_1J_1| + |J_1P_1| + |P_1Q_1| + |Q_1Z| + |ZQ_2|$.*

Proof. Omitted.

Clearly, the evacuation time for an exit in segment S_2A is $t_{S_1} + r$, which is less than the evacuation time for exit located in segment Q_2S_2. Thus, combining the results of the previous lemmas we can now give a value for $E_{1\text{-Detour-new}}(2, r)$.

Theorem 3. *Let $t_1 = y + 0.5 + |BQ_1| + |Q_1C|$ and $t_2 = y + 0.5 + |BQ_1| + |Q_1J_1| + |J_1P_1| + |P_1Q_1| + |Q_1Z| + |ZQ_2|$, where point Z is the point that if the exit is located right after Q_2, agent R_1 will be r-intercepted at or before Z. Then $E_{1\text{-Detour-new}}(2, r) = max\{t_1, t_2\}$.*

As for 1-Detour-old algorithm, by increasing the size of segment BQ_1, time t_1 increases, and on the other hand, decreasing length of BQ_1, increases t_2, and we establish the best value for $|BQ_1|$ when $t_1 = t_2$. We obtained values of Q_1 for which $t_1 = t_2$ for specific values of r by numerical calculations. We remark that we can further improve the evacuation time by doing more detours, but have not done any calculations for this.

Our results for two agents are summarized in Table 2 below. It can be seen that even with one detour, the performance of our new algorithm is very close to that of 2-Detour-old, the old detour algorithm with 2 detours.

3.4   A Lower Bound for Evacuating Two Agents

We say two points have opposite positions if one point is a vertex of T and the other point is located on the opposite edge of that vertex. To prove a lower bound for two agents we need the following lemma.

Lemma 13. (Meeting Lemma for $r > 0$). *Assume that points $p_1, p_2 \in T$ have opposite positions. In any algorithm in which one of the agents visits p_1 in time $t' \geq 0.5 + y$ and the other visits p_2 in time t with $t' < t < 0.5 + h + y - r = 0.5 + 4y - r$ the two agents cannot exchange any information between times t' and t.*

Proof. Omitted.

Theorem 4. *Assume that two agents with transmission range $r \leq 3y - 0.5 \approx$ 0.366 are initially located at a centroid of an equilateral triangle with sides 1. The evacuation time of any algorithm for two agents is at least $1 + 4y - r = 1 + 2\sqrt{3}/3 - r$.*

Proof. For the purpose of contradiction assume there exists algorithm $\mathcal{A}$ such that $E_{\mathcal{A}}(2,r) < 1 + 4y - r$. Initially we focus on the set of points $S = \{A, B, C, M_1, M_2, M_3\}$. We give an adversary argument. There exists some input I in which the exit is the last point visited by an agent. Suppose time t is the time that the fifth point from set S is visited; call the point v. Wlog assume that v is visited by R_1. Since at time t, at least five of the points in S have been visited, at least 3 points should be visited by one of the agents and $t \geq y + 1$. On the other hand because the algorithm should satisfy $E_{\mathcal{A}}(2,r) < 1 + 4y - r$, then $t < 0.5 + 4y - r \leq 0.5 + 4y$ since the adversary can place the exit at the sixth point, and then R_1 would need additional time 0.5 to get to the exit.

Now, by considering the exhaustive cases of v being one of the midpoints or the vertices of the triangle, it is tedious but straightforward to establish the lower bound, using arguments similar to the case for $r = 0$ given in [10]. ■

The following table shows the evacuation time of two agents for different values of r and different algorithms.

Table 2. Evacuation times of 2 Agents algorithms.

	Evacuation times				Lower bound
r	1-Detour-new	2-Detour-old	1-Detour-old	No-Detour	Theorem 4
0.00	2.34433	2.3367	2.3838	2.78867	
0.10	2.23473	2.25424	2.27422	2.53867	2.0547
0.20	2.15903	2.18584	2.19427	2.36010	2.0447
0.30	2.09612	2.12325	2.12651	2.22617	2.0347
0.40	2.04405	2.06506	2.06593	2.12200	N/A
0.50	1.99003	N/A	2.01050	2.03867	N/A
0.60	1.94355	N/A	1.95926	1.97049	N/A
0.70	1.90049	N/A	1.91169	1.91367	N/A
0.80	1.86047	N/A	N/A	1.86559	N/A
0.90	1.82326	N/A	N/A	1.82438	N/A

4   Evacuation of Three or Four Agents

Algorithms for the evacuation of three agents from the centroid have been previously proposed for both $r = 0$ in [10], and $r = 1$ in [15]. These two algorithms use very different trajectories. The X3C and X1C strategies described in Sect. 1 can be considered generalizations of the algorithm for 3 agents for the $r = 0$ case in [10] and the $r = 1$ case in [15] respectively. However, the best partitioning of the perimeter into segments is non-trivial to find, and requires significant experimentation. Additionally, the positions where the agents should connect after their initial exploration is also not obvious for arbitrary r, while it should clearly be the centroid for the $r = 0$ case and no meeting is required for the $r = 1$ case.

We describe the X3C algorithm for 3 agents for the case $r > 0$ in Sect. 4.1 and the X1C algorithm for three agents in Sect. 4.2. Finally in Sect. 4.3, we briefly describe the algorithm for 4 agents. An important consideration in the design of algorithms for three agents is the fact that we can use one of them as a *relay* which can extend the range at which an agent can send a message with the location of the exit. Both algorithms that are proposed in the following subsections follow the generic Algorithm 2, but they differ in the trajectories assigned to each agent.

Algorithm 2. Evacuation Algorithm for Three and Four Agents.

---

function EXPLORATION
    found← false
    while not<found> and not<msg_recd> **do**
        move along the predetermined trajectory
    ACTION
function ACTION
    if found **then**
        P ← current location
        while the other two agents are not in effective communication range **do**
            continue moving on the trajectory
    broadcast $< P >$
    go to P and exit

4.1 Explore 3 Sides Before Connecting (X3C)

The *Explore 3 sides before Connecting (X3C)* Trajectories of the three agents are defined in Trajectories 5 and shown in Fig. 3a. We partition the perimeter of T into 4 segments. Three of the segments are assigned to individual agents for exploration. After the exploration of these segments are finished, they move inside T to *distributed meeting points* J_1, J_2 and J_3. These points have the following properties:

- They are at distance r from each other.
- Their distances to point O are equal.
- Points J_1, J_2 and J_3 are located on line segments OM_2, OM_3 and OM_1 respectively.

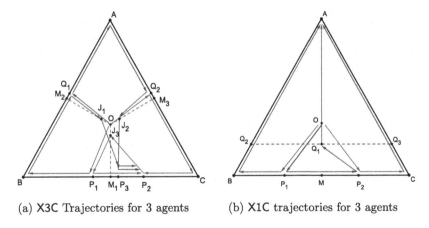

(a) X3C Trajectories for 3 agents   (b) X1C trajectories for 3 agents

Fig. 3. Trajectories for 3 agents.

After the information is exchanged at the distributed meeting points, if the exit is not found, they all move toward the fourth segment.

> **Trajectories 5.**
> $$R_1 :< O, P_1, B, Q_1, J_1, P_3 \text{ and wait for } R_3, P_2 >$$
> $$R_2 :< O, Q_1, A, Q_2, J_2, P_3 \text{ and wait for } R_3, P_2 >$$
> $$R_3 :< O, Q_2, C, P_2, J_3, P_1, P_2 >$$

From the above it follows that $|J_1C| = |J_2B| = |J_3A|$. At this point, due to the difference between the distance of each agent to point P_1, they don't move together. Only R_3 moves toward point P_1 and both R_1 and R_2 move toward P_3, the midpoint of segment P_1P_2 and wait there for R_3. If R_3 has found the exit, they move back toward point P_1 and if not, they move toward point P_2 together. It is obvious that R_1 and R_2 moving to P_3 does not have any negative effect on the worst case evacuation time, since if the exit is close to point P_1, agent R_3 from P_1 has to travel $\frac{|P_1P_2|}{2}$ to inform the other two agents and it takes another $\frac{|P_1P_2|}{2}$ for them to get to the exit, and if the exit is located near P_2, it again takes $|P_1P_2|$ for R_3 to get to the exit from P_1.

We design the trajectories so that agents arrive at the distributed meeting points at the same time. Therefore we have:

1. $t_1 = |OP_1| + |P_1B| + |BQ_1| + |Q_1J_1|$
2. $t_2 = |OQ_1| + |Q_1A| + |AQ_2| + |Q_2J_2|$
3. $t_3 = |OQ_2| + |Q_2C| + |CP_2| + |P_2J_3|$

On the other hand, at the end of the first phase when information is exchanged, there will be two critical points: (1) for R_2 to reach point B, and (2) for R_3 to finish the unexplored part of the triangle. Putting the constraints together, we obtain the following equations:

1. $t_1 = t_2 = t_3$ and
2. $|J_2B| = |J_3P_1| + |P_1P_2|$

Solving these equations with Maple software, we achieve the results.

Notice that if $r = 0$, algorithm X3C converges to Equal Travel Early Meeting algorithm in [10] and our result for $r = 0$ is identical to their results. This algorithm has the lowest evacuation time for $r = 0.1761$, and from then on the total evacuation time starts to increase.

4.2   Explore 1 Side Before Connecting (X1C)

As r increases, the evacuation time in the X3C algorithm starts to get larger. The X1C strategy yields a lower evacuation time than X3C for larger values of r. The trajectories of agents are illustrated in Fig. 3b and defined in Trajectories 6.

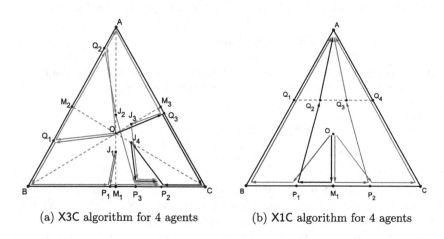

(a) X3C algorithm for 4 agents   (b) X1C algorithm for 4 agents

Fig. 4. Trajectories for 4 agents.

Trajectories 6.
R_1 follows the trajectory: $< O, P_1, B, A >$,
R_2 follows the trajectory: $< O, P_1, P_2, Q_1, A >$,
R_3 follows the trajectory: $< O, P_2, C, A >$,
where P_1 and P_2 are located at the same distance from M.

The locations of points Q_2, Q_1 and Q_3 are selected so that agents R_1, R_2 and R_3 reach them at the same time, say t, and after that, they will be in effective communication range with each other.

The location of point Q_1 depends on the value of r:

Case 1: $(0 \le r < 0.5)$ Point Q_1 is the midpoint of segment Q_2Q_3, where Q_2 and Q_3 are chosen so that $|AQ_2| = |AQ_3| = 2r$. Since at time t agents R_1 and R_2 should be at points Q_2 and Q_1 respectively, we have $|OP_1| + |P_1B| + |BQ_2| = |OP_1| + |P_1P_2| + |P_2Q_1|$. Using $|P_2Q_1| = \sqrt{|Q_1M|^2 + (|P_1P_2|/2)^2}$ and $|Q_1M| = 3y - |AQ_1|$, we get $(1 - |P_1P_2|)/2 + (1 - 2r) = |P_1P_2|+$

$\sqrt{(3y - \sqrt{3r^2 - 4r + 1})^2 + (|P_1P_2|/2)^2}$ from which $|P_1P_2|$ can be obtained as a function of r. Evacuation time for this case is $|OP_1| + |P_1B| + |BQ_2| + |Q_2C|$.

Case 2: $(0.5 \le r < 2/3)$ Point Q_1 is positioned on segment MP_2 such that $|BP_1| = |P_1P_2| + |P_2Q_1|$ and $|BQ_1| = r$ By solving these two equations we get $P_1P_2 = r/2$. The evacuation time is $|OP_1| + |P_1B| + |BC| = \sqrt{y^2 + (r/4)^2} + (1/2 - r/4) + 1$.

Case 3: $(r \ge 2/3)$ Point Q_1 is at distance $2/3$ from B. Then we have $|P_1P_2| = 1/3$ and the evacuation time is $|OP_1| + |P_1B| + |BC| = \sqrt{y^2 + (1/6)^2} + 1/3 + 1$.

As seen from Table 3a, algorithm X1C has better evacuation time than X3C for $r > 0.22589$, and for $r \ge 0.7$ it achieves the same evacuation time as the algorithm in [15] that uses $r = 1$.

4.3   Evacuation of Four Agents

X3C and X1C can be generalized for 4 agents, with the difference that the communication range for small value of r can now be extended to $2r$ in X3C algorithm employing two agents as relays. See Fig. 4a and b for the trajectories and Table 3b for evacuation times;

Table 3. A comparison of evacuation times of Algorithms X3C and X1C for (a) three agents and (b) four agents.

r	X3C	X1C
0	2.08872	2.64971
0.1	2.07849	2.37052
0.2	2.07642	2.13056
0.22589	2.07714	2.07572
0.25	2.07828	2.02747
0.3	2.08210	1.93620
0.4	2.09689	1.78880
0.5	2.13037	1.68958
0.6	N/A	1.67532
≥ 0.7	N/A	1.666667

(a)

r	X3C	X1C
0.0	1.98157	2.59944
0.1	1.96199	2.19408
0.11619	1.95993	2.13688
0.1721	1.95993	1.95993
0.2	1.95993	1.88392
0.3	N/A	1.67649
0.4	N/A	1.62573
0.5	N/A	1.61912
0.6	N/A	1.61302
0.7	N/A	1.61050
1.0	N/A	1.61050

(b)

5   Evacuation of $k > 4$ Agents

It is shown in [15] that $1 + 2y \approx 1.5773$ is a lower bound on the evacuation time of k wireless agents (i.e., $r = 1$) from the centroid of the triangle, for any number k of agents. It follows that this is also a lower bound for any $0 \le r \le 1$. It is shown in [15] that this time can be achieved with 6 agents with $r = 1$. We show below that for any $0 < r < 1$, evacuation can be done in time $1 + 2y$ using the CXP strategy, however, the minimum number of agents needed is inversely proportional to r.

First, we show that for $0 < r < 1$, the lower bound on the evacuation time of $1 + 2y$ cannot be achieved with a constant number of agents.

Theorem 5. *Given transmission range r, the number of agents needed to achieve the optimal evacuation time $1 + 2y$ is at least $1/r + 1$.*

Proof. Let t be the time the first agent, say R_1, reaches a vertex, say A. Clearly, $t \geq 2y$. Since the adversary can place the exit at either B or C, for the evacuation time to be exactly $1 + 2y$, it must be that $t = 2y$, and furthermore, another agent must have reached either B or C or both, and must be able to instantly communicate the presence of the exit to R_1. For this communication to happen, an additional $1/r - 1$ agents are needed, for a total of $1/r + 1$ agents.   ∎

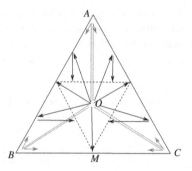

Fig. 5. Trajectories of 12 agents, 6 red agents are exploring, 6 agents form a relay network. (Color figure online)

Next we show that for any $0 < r < 1$, the CXP strategy can achieve this lower bound with a sufficient number of agents.

Theorem 6. *For any $0 < r < 1$, the evacuation of $k = 6 + 2\lceil(\frac{1}{r} - 1)\rceil$ agents of transmission range r from the centroid of an equilateral triangle can be done in time $1 + 2y \approx 1.5773$, which is optimal.*

Proof. Let $i = \lceil\frac{1}{r} - 1\rceil$. The trajectories of the agents are as shown in Fig. 5. Each vertex is reached by two agents and they explore the perimeter of the triangle from that vertex until the mid-point on each edge. Notice that the exploration terminates at time $2y + 0.5$, and if an agent finds the exit at time $2y + t$, other exploration agents are at distance at most $1 - t$ from it.

Furthermore, $2i$ agents go to edges AB and AC into equidistant positions to form a relay network for the 6 agents doing the exploration. When an exploring agent reaches a relay agent, the relay agent starts to move to its final position on the interior dashed triangle. In this way the relay agents can perform the relay function for the exploring agents, and are also able to reach the exit when it is found within the bound $1 + 2y$.   ∎

References

1. Agmon, N., Peleg, D.: Fault-tolerant gathering algorithms for autonomous mobile robots. SIAM J. Comput. **36**(1), 56–82 (2006)
2. BaezaYates, R.A., Culberson, J.C., Rawlins, G.: Searching in the plane. Inf. Comput. **106**(2), 234–252 (1993)
3. Bagheri, I.: Evacuation of equilateral triangles by mobile agents of limited communication range. Master's thesis, Concordia University, Canada (2019)
4. Beck, A.: On the linear search problem. Israel J. Math. **2**(4), 221–228 (1964)
5. Beck, A., Newman, D.: Yet more on the linear search problem. Israel J. Math. **8**(4), 419–429 (1970)
6. Bonato, A., Nowakowski, R.: The Game of Cops and Robbers on Graphs. American Mathematical Society, Providence (2011)
7. Brandt, S., Laufenberg, F., Lv, Y., Stolz, D., Wattenhofer, R.: Collaboration without communication: evacuating two robots from a disk. In: Fotakis, D., Pagourtzis, A., Paschos, V.T. (eds.) CIAC 2017. LNCS, vol. 10236, pp. 104–115. Springer, Cham (2017). https://doi.org/10.1007/978-3-319-57586-5_10
8. Brandt, S., Uitto, J., Wattenhofer, R.: A tight bound for semi-synchronous collaborative grid exploration. In: 32nd International Symposium on Distributed Computing (DISC) (2018)
9. Chrobak, M., Gąsieniec, L., Gorry, T., Martin, R.: Group search on the line. In: Italiano, G.F., Margaria-Steffen, T., Pokorný, J., Quisquater, J.-J., Wattenhofer, R. (eds.) SOFSEM 2015. LNCS, vol. 8939, pp. 164–176. Springer, Heidelberg (2015). https://doi.org/10.1007/978-3-662-46078-8_14
10. Chuangpishit, H., Mehrabi, S., Narayanan, L., Opatrny, J.: Evacuating an equilateral triangle in the face-to-face model. In: Proceedings of OPODIS 2017, pp. 11:1–11:16 (2017)
11. Czyzowicz, J., Dobrev, S., Georgiou, K., Kranakis, E., MacQuarrie, F.: Evacuating two robots from multiple unknown exits in a circle. Theor. Comput. Sci. **709**, 20–30 (2018)
12. Czyzowicz, J., Gąsieniec, L., Gorry, T., Kranakis, E., Martin, R., Pajak, D.: Evacuating robots via unknown exit in a disk. In: Kuhn, F. (ed.) DISC 2014. LNCS, vol. 8784, pp. 122–136. Springer, Heidelberg (2014). https://doi.org/10.1007/978-3-662-45174-8_9
13. Czyzowicz, J., Georgiou, K., Kranakis, E., Narayanan, L., Opatrny, J., Vogtenhuber, B.: Evacuating robots from a disk using face-to-face communication (extended abstract). In: Paschos, V.T., Widmayer, P. (eds.) CIAC 2015. LNCS, vol. 9079, pp. 140–152. Springer, Cham (2015). https://doi.org/10.1007/978-3-319-18173-8_10
14. Czyzowicz, J., Kranakis, E., Krizanc, D., Narayanan, L., Opatrny, J.: Search on a line with faulty robots. In: Proceedings of PODC, pp. 405–413. ACM (2016)
15. Czyzowicz, J., Kranakis, E., Krizanc, D., Narayanan, L., Opatrny, J., Shende, S.: Wireless autonomous robot evacuation from equilateral triangles and squares, extended version, in preparation
16. Czyzowicz, J., Kranakis, E., Krizanc, D., Narayanan, L., Opatrny, J., Shende, S.: Wireless autonomous robot evacuation from equilateral triangles and squares. In: Papavassiliou, S., Ruehrup, S. (eds.) ADHOC-NOW 2015. LNCS, vol. 9143, pp. 181–194. Springer, Cham (2015). https://doi.org/10.1007/978-3-319-19662-6_13
17. Demaine, E.D., Fekete, S.P., Gal, S.: Online searching with turn cost. Theoret. Comput. Sci. **361**(2), 342–355 (2006)

18. Dieudonné, Y., Pelc, A., Peleg, D.: Gathering despite mischief. ACM Trans. Algorithms (TALG) **11**(1), 1 (2014)
19. Emek, Y., Langner, T., Stolz, D., Uitto, J., Wattenhofer, R.: How many ants does it take to find the food? Theor. Comput. Sci. **608**, 255–267 (2015)
20. Fekete, S., Gray, C., Kröller, A.: Evacuation of rectilinear polygons. In: Wu, W., Daescu, O. (eds.) COCOA 2010. LNCS, vol. 6508, pp. 21–30. Springer, Heidelberg (2010). https://doi.org/10.1007/978-3-642-17458-2_3
21. Flocchini, P., Prencipe, G., Santoro, N.: Distributed Computing by Oblivious Mobile Robots (Synthesis Lectures on Distributed Computing Theory). Morgan & Claypool Publishers, San Rafael (2016)
22. Flocchini, P., Prencipe, G., Santoro, N., Widmayer, P.: Arbitrary pattern formation by asynchronous, anonymous, oblivious robots. Theoret. Comput. Sci. **407**(1–3), 412–447 (2008)
23. Fraigniaud, P., Ilcinkas, D., Peer, G., Pelc, A., Peleg, D.: Graph exploration by a finite automaton. Theoret. Comput. Sci. **345**(2–3), 331–344 (2005)
24. Kao, M.-Y., Reif, J.H., Tate, S.R.: Searching in an unknown environment: An optimal randomized algorithm for the cow-path problem. Inf. Comput. **131**(1), 63–79 (1996)
25. Koutsoupias, E., Papadimitriou, C., Yannakakis, M.: Searching a fixed graph. In: Meyer, F., Monien, B. (eds.) ICALP 1996. LNCS, vol. 1099, pp. 280–289. Springer, Heidelberg (1996). https://doi.org/10.1007/3-540-61440-0_135
26. Pattanayak, D., Ramesh, H., Mandal, P.S., Schmid, S.: Evacuating two robots from two unknown exits on the perimeter of a disk with wireless communication. In: Proceedings of ICDCN 2018, pp. 20:1–20:4 (2018)

Fast Dispersion of Mobile Robots on Arbitrary Graphs

Ajay D. Kshemkalyani[1], Anisur Rahaman Molla[2], and Gokarna Sharma[3($\boxtimes$)]

[1] University of Illinois at Chicago, Chicago, USA
ajay@uic.edu
[2] Indian Statistical Institute, Kolkata, India
molla@isical.ac.in
[3] Kent State University, Kent, USA
sharma@cs.kent.edu

Abstract. The dispersion problem on graphs asks $k \leq n$ robots placed initially arbitrarily on the nodes of an n-node anonymous graph to reposition autonomously to reach a configuration in which each robot is on a distinct node of the graph. This problem is of significant interest due to its relationship to other fundamental robot coordination problems, such as exploration, scattering, load balancing, and relocation of self-driven electric cars (robots) to recharge stations (nodes). In this paper, we provide a novel deterministic algorithm for dispersion in arbitrary graphs in a synchronous setting where all robots perform their actions in every time step. Our algorithm has $O(\min(m, k\Delta) \cdot \log k)$ steps runtime using $O(\log n)$ bits of memory at each robot, where m is the number of edges and Δ is the maximum degree of the graph. This is a significant improvement over the $O(mk)$ steps best previously known algorithm that uses logarithmic memory at each robot. In particular, the runtime of our algorithm is optimal (up to a $O(\log k)$ factor) in constant-degree arbitrary graphs.

1 Introduction

The dispersion of autonomous mobile robots to spread them out evenly in a region is a problem of significant interest in distributed robotics, e.g., see [14,15]. Recently, this problem has been formulated by Augustine and Moses Jr. [1] in the context of graphs. They defined the problem as follows: Given any arbitrary initial configuration of $k \leq n$ robots positioned on the nodes of an n-node graph, the robots reposition autonomously to reach a configuration where each robot is positioned on a distinct node of the graph (which we call the DISPERSION problem). This problem has many practical applications, for example, in relocating self-driven electric cars (robots) to recharge stations (nodes), assuming that the cars have smart devices to communicate with each other to find a free/empty charging station [1,16]. This problem is also important due to its relationship to many other well-studied autonomous robot coordination problems, such as exploration, scattering, load balancing, covering, and self-deployment [1,16]. One

A. R. Molla was supported in part by DST Inspire Faculty research grant DST/INSPIRE/04/2015/002801.

of the key aspects of mobile-robot research is to understand how to use the resource-limited robots to accomplish some large task in a distributed manner [10,11]. In this paper, we study trade-off between memory requirement and time to solve DISPERSION.

Augustine and Moses Jr. [1] studied DISPERSION assuming $k = n$. They proved a memory lower bound of $\Omega(\log n)$ bits at each robot and a time lower bound of $\Omega(D)$ ($\Omega(n)$ in arbitrary graphs) for any deterministic algorithm in any graph, where D is the diameter of the graph. They then provided deterministic algorithms using $O(\log n)$ bits at each robot to solve DISPERSION on lines, rings, and trees in $O(n)$ time. For arbitrary graphs, they provided two algorithms, one using $O(\log n)$ bits at each robot with $O(mn)$ time and another using $O(n \log n)$ bits at each robot with $O(m)$ time, where m is the number of edges in the graph. Recently, Kshemkalyani and Ali [16] provided an $\Omega(k)$ time lower bound for arbitrary graphs for $k \leq n$. They then provided three deterministic algorithms for DISPERSION in arbitrary graphs: (i) The first algorithm using $O(k \log \Delta)$ bits at each robot with $O(m)$ time, (ii) The second algorithm using $O(D \log \Delta)$ bits at each robot with $O(\Delta^D)$ time, and (iii) The third algorithm using $O(\log(\max(k, \Delta)))$ bits at each robot with $O(mk)$ time, where Δ is the maximum degree of the graph. Randomized algorithms are presented in [18] to solve DISPERSION where the random bits are mainly used to reduce the memory requirement at each robot.

In this paper, we provide a new deterministic algorithm for solving DISPERSION in arbitrary graphs. Our algorithm improves significantly on the runtime of the best previously known algorithm with logarithmic memory at each robot; see Table 1.

Overview of the Model and Results. We consider the same model as in Augustine and Moses Jr. [1] and Kshemkalyani and Ali [16] where a system of $k \leq n$ robots are operating on an n-node anonymous graph G. The robots are *distinguishable*, i.e., they have unique IDs in the range $[1, k]$. The robots have no visibility; but they can communicate with each other only when they are at the same node of G. The graph G is assumed to be connected and undirected. The nodes of G are indistinguishable (G is anonymous) but the ports (leading to incident edges) at each node have unique labels from $[1, \delta]$, where δ is the degree of that node. It is assumed that the robots know m, n, Δ, k^1. Similar assumptions are made in the previous work in DISPERSION [1]. The nodes of G do not have memory and the robots have memory. *Synchronous* setting is considered as in [1] where all robots are activated in a round and they perform their operations simultaneously in synchronized rounds. Runtime is measured in rounds (or steps). We establish the following theorem in an arbitrary graph.

Theorem 1. *Given any initial configuration of $k \leq n$ mobile robots in an arbitrary, anonymous n-node graph G having m edges and maximum degree Δ, DISPERSION can be solved in $O(\min(m, k\Delta) \cdot \log k)$ time with $O(\log n)$ bits at each robot.*

Theorem 1 improves significantly over the $O(mk)$ time algorithm of [16] with logarithmic memory (Table 1). Notice that, when $\Delta \leq k$, the runtime depends only on k,

---

[1] In fact, it is enough to know only m, Δ and k to accomplish the results. Without robots knowing m, Theorem 1 achieves DISPERSION in $O(k\Delta \cdot \log k)$ time with $O(\log(\max(k, \Delta)))$ bits memory at each robot, which is better in terms of memory of $O(\log n)$ bits in Theorem 1 but not the time $O(\min(m, k\Delta) \cdot \log k)$ when $m < k\Delta$.

i.e., $O(k^2 \log k)$. For constant-degree arbitrary graphs (i.e., when $\Delta = O(1)$), the time becomes near-optimal – only a $O(\log k)$ factor away from the time lower bound $\Omega(k)$.

Table 1. The results on DISPERSION for $k \leq n$ robots on n-node arbitrary graphs with m edges, D diameter, and Δ maximum degree.

Algorithm	Memory per robot (in bits)	Time (in rounds)
Lower bound	$\Omega(\log(\max(k, \Delta)))$	$\Omega(k)$
First algorithm of [1][a]	$O(\log n)$	$O(mn)$
Second algorithm of [1]	$O(n \log n)$	$O(m)$
First algorithm of [16]	$O(k \log \Delta)$	$O(m)$
Second algorithm of [16]	$O(D \log \Delta)$	$O(\Delta^D)$
Third algorithm of [16]	$O(\log(\max(k, \Delta)))$	$O(mk)$
Theorem 1	$O(\log n)$	$O(\min(m, k\Delta) \cdot \log k)$

[a]The results in [1] are only for $k = n$.

Challenges and Techniques. The well-known *Depth First Search* (DFS) traversal approach [5] was used in the previous papers to solve DISPERSION [1,16]. If all k robots are positioned initially on a single node of G, then the DFS traversal finishes in $\min(4m - 2n + 2, k\Delta)$ rounds solving DISPERSION. If k robots are initially on k different nodes of G, then DISPERSION is solved by doing nothing. However, if not all of them are on a single node initially, then the robots on nodes with multiple robots need to reposition (except one) to reach to free nodes and settle. The natural approach is to run DFS traversals in parallel to minimize time.

The challenge arises when two or more DFS traversals meet before all robots settle. When this happens, the robots that have not settled yet need to find free nodes. For this, they may need to re-traverse the already traversed part of the graph by the DFS traversal. Care is needed here otherwise they may re-traverse sequentially and the total time for the DFS traversal increases by a factor of k to $\min(4m - 2n + 2, k\Delta) \cdot k$ rounds, in the worst-case. This is in fact the case in the previous algorithms of [1,16]. We design a smarter way to synchronize the parallel DFS traversals so that the total time increases only by a factor of $\log k$ to $\min(4m - 2n + 2, k\Delta) \cdot \log k$ rounds, in the worst-case. This approach is a non-trivial extension and requires overcoming many challenges on synchronizing the parallel DFS traversals efficiently.

Related Work. One problem closely related to DISPERSION is the graph exploration. The exploration problem has been heavily studied in the literature for specific as well as arbitrary graphs, e.g., [2,4,8,13,17]. It was shown that a robot can explore an anonymous graph using $\Theta(D \log \Delta)$-bits memory; the runtime of the algorithm is $O(\Delta^{D+1})$ [13]. In the model where graph nodes also have memory, Cohen *et al.* [4] gave two algorithms: The first algorithm uses $O(1)$-bits at the robot and 2 bits at each node, and the second algorithm uses $O(\log \Delta)$ bits at the robot and 1 bit at each node. The runtime of both algorithms is $O(m)$ with preprocessing time of $O(mD)$. The trade-off between exploration time and number of robots is studied in [17]. The collective exploration by a team of robots is studied in [12] for trees. Another problem related to DISPERSION is the scattering of k robots in graphs. This problem has been studied for rings [9,20] and grids [3]. Recently, Poudel and Sharma [19] provided a $\Theta(\sqrt{n})$-time algorithm for uniform scattering in a grid [7]. Furthermore, DISPERSION is related to the load balancing problem, where a given load at the nodes has to be (re-)distributed among several processors (nodes). This problem has been studied quite heavily in graphs, e.g., [6,21]. We refer readers to [10,11] for other recent developments in these topics.

Paper Organization. We discuss details of the model and some preliminaries in Sect. 2. We discuss the DFS traversal of a graph in Sect. 3. We present an algorithm for arbitrary graphs in Sect. 4. Finally, we conclude in Sect. 5 with a short discussion.

2   Model Details and Preliminaries

Graph. We consider the same graph model as in [1,16]. Let $G = (V, E)$ be an n-node m-edge graph, i.e., $|V| = n$ and $|E| = m$. G is assumed to be connected, unweighted, and undirected. G is *anonymous*, i.e., nodes do not have identifiers but, at any node, its incident edges are uniquely identified by a *label* (aka port number) in the range $[1, \delta]$, where δ is the *degree* of that node. The *maximum degree* of G is Δ, which is the maximum among the degree δ of the nodes in G. We assume that there is no correlation between two port numbers of an edge. Any number of robots are allowed to move along an edge at any time. The graph nodes do not have memory.

Robots. We also consider the same robot model as in [1,16]. Let $\mathcal{R} = \{r_1, r_2, \ldots, r_k\}$ be a set of $k \leq n$ robots residing on the nodes of G. For simplicity, we sometime use i to denote robot r_i. No robot can reside on the edges of G, but one or more robots can occupy the same node of G. Each robot has a unique $\lceil \log k \rceil$-bit ID taken from $[1, k]$. Robot has no visibility and hence a robot can only communicate with other robots present on the same node. Following [1,16], it is assumed that when a robot moves from node u to node v in G, it is aware of the port of u it used to leave u and the port of v it used to enter v. Furthermore, it is assumed that each robot is equipped with memory to store information, which may also be read and modified by other robots on the same node. Each robot is assumed to know parameters m, n, Δ, k. Such assumptions are also made in the previous work on DISPERSION [1].

Time Cycle. At any time a robot $r_i \in \mathcal{R}$ could be active or inactive. When a robot r_i becomes active, it performs the "Communicate-Compute-Move" (CCM) cycle as follows: (i) *Communicate:* For each robot $r_j \in \mathcal{R}$ that is at node v_i where r_i is, r_i can observe the memory of r_j. Robot r_i can also observe its own memory; (ii) *Compute:* r_i may perform an arbitrary computation using the information observed during the "communicate" portion of that cycle. This includes determination of a (possibly) port to use to exit v_i and the information to store in the robot r_j that is at v_i; and (iii) *Move:* At the end of the cycle, r_i writes new information (if any) in the memory of r_j at v_i, and exits v_i using the computed port to reach to a neighbor of v_i.

Time and Memory Complexity. We consider the synchronous setting where every robot is active in every CCM cycle and they perform the cycle in synchrony. Therefore, time is measured in *rounds* or *steps* (a cycle is a round or step). Another important parameter is memory. Memory comes from the number of bits stored at each robot.

Mobile Robot Dispersion. The DISPERSION problem can be defined as follows.

Definition 1 (DISPERSION). *Given any n-node anonymous graph $G = (V, E)$ having $k \leq n$ robots positioned initially arbitrarily on the nodes of G, the robots reposition autonomously to reach a configuration where each robot is on a distinct node of G.*

The goal is to solve DISPERSION optimizing two performance metrics: (i) **Time** – the number of rounds, and (ii) **Memory** – the number of bits stored at each robot.

Table 2. Description of the variables used in Sects. 3 and 4. These variables are maintained by each robot and may be read/updated by other robots (at the same node).

Symbol	Description
round	The counter that indicates the current round. Initially, $round \leftarrow 0$
pass	The counter that indicates the current pass. Initially, $pass \leftarrow 0$
parent	The port from which robot entered a node in forward phase. Initially, $parent \leftarrow 0$
child	The smallest port (except *parent* port) that was not taken yet. Initially, $child \leftarrow 0$
treelabel	The label of a DFS tree. Initially, $treelabel \leftarrow \top$
settled	A boolean flag that stores either 0 (false) or 1 (true). Initially, $settled \leftarrow 0$
mult	The number of robots at a node at the start of Stage 2. Initially, $mult \leftarrow 1$
home	The lowest ID unsettled robot at a node at the start of Stage 2 sets this to the ID of the settled robot at that node. Initially, $home \leftarrow \top$

3   DFS Traversal of a Graph

Consider an n-node arbitrary anonymous graph G. Let C_{init} be the initial configuration of $k \leq n$ robots positioned on a single node, say v, of G. Let the robots on v be represented as $N(v) = \{r_1, \ldots, r_k\}$, where r_i is the robot with ID i. We describe here a DFS traversal algorithm, $DFS(k)$, that disperses the robots in $N(v)$ to the k nodes of G guaranteeing exactly one robot per node. $DFS(k)$ will be used in Sect. 4.

Each robot r_i stores in its memory four variables $r_i.parent$ (initially assigned 0), $r_i.child$ (initially assigned 0), $r_i.treelabel$ (initially assigned $\top$), and $r_i.settled$ (initially assigned 0). $DFS(k)$ executes in two phases, $forward$ and $backtrack$ [5]. Variable $r_i.treelabel$ stores the ID of the smallest ID robot. Variable $r_i.parent$ stores the port from which r_i entered the node where it is currently positioned in the forward phase. Variable $r_i.child$ stores the smallest port of the node it is currently positioned at that has not been taken yet (while entering/exiting the node). Let $P(x)$ be the set of ports at any node $x \in G$.

We are now ready to describe $DFS(k)$. In round 1, the maximum ID robot r_k writes $r_k.treelabel \leftarrow 1$ (the ID of the smallest robot in $N(v)$, which is 1), $r_k.child \leftarrow 1$ (the smallest port at v among $P(v)$), and $r_k.settled \leftarrow 1$. The robots $N(v) \backslash \{r_k\}$ exit v

following port $r_k.child$; r_k stays (settles) at v. In the beginning of round 2, the robots $N(w) = N(v)\backslash\{r_k\}$ reach a neighbor node w of v. Suppose the robots entered w using port $p_w \in P(w)$. As w is free, robot $r_{k-1} \in N(w)$ writes $r_{k-1}.parent \leftarrow p_w$, $r_{k-1}.treelabel \leftarrow 1$ (the ID of the smallest robot in $N(w)$), and $r_{k-1}.settled \leftarrow 1$. If $r_{k-1}.child \leq \delta_w$, r_{k-1} writes $r_{k-1}.child \leftarrow r_{k-1}.child + 1$ if port $r_{k-1}.child + 1 \neq p_w$ and $r_{k-1}.child + 1 \leq \delta_w$, otherwise $r_{k-1}.child \leftarrow r_{k-1}.child + 2$. The robots $N(w)\backslash\{r_{k-1}\}$ decide to continue DFS in forward/backtrack phase as described below.

- **(forward phase)** if ($p_w = r_{k-1}.parent$ or $p_w =$ old value of $r_{k-1}.child$) and (there is (at least) a port at w that has not been taken yet). The robots $N(w)\backslash\{r_{k-1}\}$ exit w through port $r_{k-1}.child$.
- **(backtrack phase)** if ($p_w = r_{k-1}.parent$ or $p_w =$ old value of $r_{k-1}.child$) and (all the ports of w have been taken already). The robots $N(w)\backslash\{r_{k-1}\}$ exit w through port $r_{k-1}.parent$.

Assume that in round 2, the robots decide to proceed in forward phase. In the beginning of round 3, $N(u) = N(w)\backslash\{r_{k-1}\}$ robots reach some other node u (neighbor of w) of G. The robot r_{k-2} stays at u writing necessary information in its variables. In the forward phase in round 3, the robots $N(u)\backslash\{r_{k-2}\}$ exit u through port $r_{k-2}.child$. However, in the backtrack phase in round 3, r_{k-2} stays at u and robots $N(u)\backslash\{r_{k-2}\}$ exit u through port $r_{k-2}.parent$. This takes robots $N(u)\backslash\{r_{k-2}\}$ back to node w along $r_{k-1}.child$. Since r_{k-1} is already at w, r_{k-1} updates $r_{k-1}.child$ with the next port to take. Depending on whether $r_i.child \leq \delta_w$ or not, the robots $\{r_1, \ldots, r_{k-3}\}$ exit w using either $r_{k-1}.child$ (forward phase) or $r_{k-1}.parent$ (backtrack phase).

There is another condition, denoting the onset of a cycle, under which choosing backtrack phase is in order. When robots enter x through p_x and robot r is settled at x,

- **(backtrack phase)** if ($p_x \neq r.parent$ and $p_x \neq$ old value of $r.child$). The robots exit x through port p_x and no variables of r are altered.

This process then continues for $DFS(k)$ until at some node $y \in G$, $N(y) = \{r_1\}$. The robot r_1 then stays at y and $DFS(k)$ finishes.

Lemma 1. *Algorithm $DFS(k)$ correctly solves* DISPERSION *for $k \leq n$ robots initially positioned on a single node of a n-node arbitrary graph G in $\min(4m - 2n + 2, k\Delta)$ rounds using $O(\log(\max(k, \Delta)))$ bits at each robot.*

Proof. We first show that DISPERSION is achieved by $DFS(k)$. Because every robot starts at the same node and follows the same path as other not-yet-settled robots until it is assigned to a node, $DFS(k)$ resembles the DFS traversal of an anonymous port-numbered graph [1] with all robots starting from the same node. Therefore, $DFS(k)$ visits k different nodes where each robot is settled.

We now prove time and memory bounds. In $k\Delta$ rounds, $DFS(k)$ visits at least k different nodes of G. If $4m - 2n + 2 < k\Delta$, $DFS(k)$ visits all n nodes of G. Therefore, it is clear that the runtime of $DFS(k)$ is $\min(4m - 2n + 2, k\Delta)$ rounds. Regarding memory, variable *treelabel* takes $O(\log k)$ bits, *settled* takes $O(1)$ bits, and *parent* and *child* take $O(\log \Delta)$ bits. The k robots can be distinguished through $O(\log k)$ bits since their IDs are in the range $[1, k]$. Thus, each robot requires $O(\log(\max(k, \Delta)))$ bits. □

4   Algorithm

We present and analyze an algorithm, *Graph_Disperse(k)*, that solves DISPERSION of $k \leq n$ robots on an arbitrary n-node graph in $O(\min(m, k\Delta) \cdot \log k)$ time with $O(\log n)$ bits of memory at each robot. This algorithm significantly improves the $O(mk)$ time of the best previously known algorithm [16] for arbitrary graphs (Table 1).

4.1   High Level Overview of the Algorithm

Algorithm *Graph_Disperse(k)* runs in passes and each pass is divided into two stages. Each pass runs for $O(\min(m, k\Delta))$ rounds and there will be total $O(\log k)$ passes until DISPERSION is solved. The algorithm uses $O(\log n)$ bits memory at each robot. To be able to run passes and stages in the algorithm, we assume following [1] that robots know n, m, k, and Δ. At their core, each of the two stages uses a modified version of the DFS traversal by robots (Algorithm $DFS(k)$) described in Sect. 3.

At the start of stage 1, there may be multiple nodes, each with more than one robot (top left of Fig. 1). The (unsettled) robots at each such node begin a DFS in parallel, each such DFS instance akin to $DFS(k)$ described in Sect. 3. Each such concurrently initiated DFS induces a DFS tree where the *treelabel* of the robots that settle is common, and the same as the ID of the robot with the smallest ID in the group.

Unlike $DFS(k)$, here a DFS traversal may reach a node where there is a settled robot belonging to another (concurrently initiated) DFS instance. As the settled robot cannot track variables (*treelabel, parent, child*) for the multiple DFS trees owing to its limited memory, it tracks only one DFS tree instance and the other DFS instance(s) is/are stopped. Thus, some DFS instances may not run to completion and some of their robots may not be settled by the end of stage 1. Thus, groups of stopped robots exist at different nodes at the end of stage 1 (top right of Fig. 1).

In stage 2, all the groups of stopped robots at different nodes in the same connected component of nodes with settled robots are gathered together into one group at a single node in that connected component (bottom left of Fig. 1). Since stopped robots in a group do not know whether there are other groups of stopped robots, and if so, how many and where, one robot from each such group initiates a DFS traversal of its connected component of nodes with settled robots, to gather all the stopped robots at its starting node. The challenge is that due to such parallel initiations of DFS traversals, robots may be in the process of movement and gathering in different parts of the connected component of settled nodes. The algorithm ensures that despite the unknown number of concurrent initiations of the DFS traversals for gathering, all stopped robots in a connected component of settled robots get collected at a single node in that component at the end of stage 2. Our algorithm has the property that the number of nodes with such gathered (unsettled) robots in the entire graph at the end of stage 2 is at most half the number of nodes with more than one robot at the start of stage 1 (of the same pass). This implies the sufficiency of $\log k$ passes, each comprised of these two stages, to collect all graph-wide unsettled robots at one node. In the first stage of the last pass, DISPERSION is achieved (bottom right of Fig. 1).

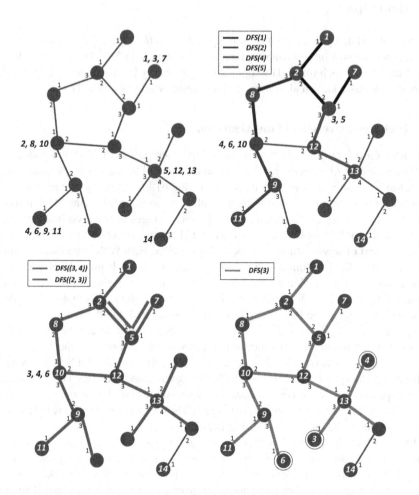

Fig. 1. An illustration of the two stages in a pass of Algorithm 1 for $k = 14$ robots in an 15-node graph G. (**top left**) shows C_{init} with one or more robots at 5 nodes of G; the rest of the nodes of G are empty. (**top right**) shows the configuration after Stage 1 finishes for $DFS(.)$ started by 4 nodes with multiple robots on them; the respective DFS trees formed are shown through colored edges (the same colored edges belong to the same DFS tree). A single robot (14) at a node settles there. (**bottom left**) shows the configuration after Stage 2 finishes for $DFS((.,.))$ started by two nodes with more than one robot (see top right) on them when Stage 1 finishes. The robots 3,4,6 are collected at the node of G where robot 10 is settled since $DFS((3,4))$ started from there has higher lexico-priority than $DFS((2,3))$ started from the node of G where 5 is settled. (**bottom right**) shows the configuration after Stage 1 of the next pass in which all k robot settle on k different nodes of G. There is only one DFS tree $DFS(3)$ started from the node of G (where 10 is settled and all robots are collected in Stage 2) that traverses G until all 3, 4, 6 are settled reaching the empty nodes of G. The nodes where they are settled are shown inside a circle. (Color figure online)

4.2 Detailed Description of the Algorithm

The pseudocode of the algorithm is given in Algorithm 1. The variables used by each robot are described in Table 2. We now describe the two stages of the algorithm; Fig. 1 illustrates the working principle of the stages.

Stage 1. We first introduce some terminology. A settled/unsettled robot i is one for which $i.settled = 1/0$. For brevity, we say a node is settled if it has a settled robot. At the start of stage 1, there may be multiple (≥ 1) unsettled robots at some of the nodes. Let $U^{s1}/U^{e1}/U^{e2}$ be the set of unsettled robots at a node at the start of stage 1/end of stage 1/end of stage 2. In general, we define a U-set to be the (non-empty) set of unsettled robots at a node. Let the lowest robot ID among U^{s1} at a node be U^{s1}_{min}. We use r to denote a settled robot.

In stage 1, the unsettled robots at a node begin $DFS(|U^{s1}|)$, following the lowest ID ($= U^{s1}_{min}$) robot among them. Each instance of the DFS algorithm, begun concurrently by different U^{s1}-sets from different nodes, induces a DFS tree in which the settled nodes have robots with the same $treelabel$, which is equal to the corresponding U^{s1}_{min}. During this DFS traversal, the robots visit nodes, at each of which there are four possibilities.

The node may be free, or may have a settled robot r, where $r.treelabel$ is less than, equals, or is greater than $x.ID$, where x is the visiting robot with the lowest ID. The second and fourth possibilities indicate that two DFS trees, corresponding to different $treelabels$ meet. As each robot is allowed only $O(\log n)$ bits memory, it can track the variables for only one DFS tree. We deal with these possibilities as described below.

1. If the node is free (line 6), the logic of $DFS(k)$ described in Sect. 3 is followed. Specifically, the highest ID robot from the visiting robots (call it r) settles, and sets $r.settled$ to 1 and $r.treelabel$ to $x.ID$. Robot x continues its DFS, after setting $r.parent$, $r.child$ and $r.phase$ for its own DFS as per the logic of $DFS(k)$ described in Sect. 3; and other visiting robots follow x.
2. If $r.treelabel < x.ID$ (line 11), all visiting robots stop at this node and discontinue growing their DFS tree.
3. If $r.treelabel = x.ID$ (line 13), robot x's traversal is part of the same DFS tree as that of robot r. Robot x continues its DFS traversal and takes along with it all unsettled (including stopped) robots from this node, after updating $r.child$ if needed as per the logic of $DFS(k)$ described in Sect. 3.
4. If $r.treelabel > x.ID$ (line 16), robot x continues growing its DFS tree and takes along all unsettled robots from this node with it. To continue growing its DFS tree, x overwrites robot r's variables set for r's old DFS tree by including this node and r in its own DFS tree. Specifically, $r.treelabel \leftarrow x.ID$, $r.parent$ is set to the port from which x entered this node, and $r.child$ is set as per the logic described for $DFS(k)$ in Sect. 3.

Note that if the robots stop at a node where $r.treelabel < x.ID$, they will start moving again if a robot x' arrives such that $x'.ID \leq r.treelabel$. At the end of stage 1, either all the robots from any U^{s1} are settled or some subset of them are stopped at some node where $r.treelabel < U^{s1}_{min}$.

Algorithm 1: Algorithm $Graph\_Disperse(k)$ to solve DISPERSION.

---

1 **if** i *is alone at node* **then**
2 | $i.settled \leftarrow 1$; do not set $i.treelabel$

3 **for** $pass = 1, \log k$ **do**
4 | Stage 1 (Graph_DFS: for group dispersion of unsettled robots)
5 | **for** $round = 0, \min(4m - 2n + 2, k\Delta)$ **do**
6 | | **if** *visited node is free* **then**
7 | | | highest ID robot r settles; $r.treelabel \leftarrow x$.ID, where x is robot with lowest ID
8 | | | x continues its DFS after r sets its $parent, child$ for DFS of x
9 | | | other visitors follow x
10 | | **else if** *visited node has a settled robot r* **then**
11 | | | **if** $r.treelabel < x.ID$ *for visitors x* **then**
12 | | | | all visiting robots: stop until ordered to move
13 | | | **else if** $r.treelabel \leq y.ID$ *for visitors y and $r.treelabel = x.ID$ for some visitor x* **then**
14 | | | | x continues its DFS after r updates $child$ if needed
15 | | | | all other unsettled robots follow x
16 | | | **else if** *visitor $x(x \neq r)$ has lowest ID and lower than $r.treelabel$* **then**
17 | | | | $r.treelabel \leftarrow x.ID$
18 | | | | x continues its DFS after r sets its $parent, child$ for DFS of x
19 | | | | all other unsettled robots follow x

20 | All settled robots: reset $parent, child$
21 | Stage 2 (Connected_Component_DFS_Traversal: for gathering unsettled robots)
22 | All robots: $mult \leftarrow$ count of local robots
23 | **if** i *has the lowest ID among unsettled robots at its node* **then**
24 | | $i.home \leftarrow r.ID$, $r.treelabel \leftarrow i.ID$, where r is the settled robot at that node
25 | | i initiates DFS traversal of connected component of nodes with settled robots
26 | **for** $round = 0, \min(4m - 2n + 2, 2k\Delta)$ **do**
27 | | **if** *visited node is free* **then**
28 | | | ignore the node; all visitors backtrack, i.e., retrace their step
29 | | **else if** *visited node has a settled robot r* **then**
30 | | | **if** *lexico-priority of r is highest and greater than that of all visitors* **then**
31 | | | | all visiting robots: stop until ordered to move
32 | | | **else if** *lexico-priority of r is highest but equal to that of some visitor x* **then**
33 | | | | x continues its DFS traversal after r updates $child$ if needed (until $x.home = r.ID$ and all ports at the node where r is settled are explored)
34 | | | | all other unsettled robots: follow x if $x.home \neq r.ID$
35 | | | **else if** *visitor $x(x \neq r)$ has highest lexico-priority and higher than that of r* **then**
36 | | | | $r.treelabel \leftarrow x.ID$, $r.mult \leftarrow x.mult$
37 | | | | x continues its DFS traversal after r sets $parent, child$ for DFS of x
38 | | | | all other unsettled robots follow x

39 | reset $parent, child, treelabel, mult, home$

Lemma 2. *For any U^{s1}-set, at the end of stage 1, either (i) all the robots in U^{s1} are settled or (ii) the unsettled robots among U^{s1} are present all together along with robot with ID U^{s1}_{min} (and possibly along with other robots outside of U^{s1}) at a single node with a settled robot r having $r.treelabel < U^{s1}_{min}$.*

Proof. The DFS traversal of the graph can complete in $4m - 2n + 2$ steps as each tree edge gets traversed twice, and each back edge, i.e., non-tree edge of the DFS tree, gets traversed 4 times (twice in the forward direction and twice in the backward direction) if the conditions in lines (6), (13), or (16) hold. The DFS traversal of the graph required to settle k robots and hence discover k new nodes, can also complete in $k\Delta$ steps as a node may be visited multiple times (at most its degree which is at most Δ times). As $k \geq |U^{s1}|$, possibility (i) is evident.

In the DFS traversal, if condition in line (11) holds, the unsettled robots remaining in U^{s1}, including that with ID U^{s1}_{min}, stop together at a node with a settled robot r' such that $r'.treelabel < U^{s1}_{min}$. They may move again together (lines (15) or (19)) if visited by a robot with ID U'_{min} equal to or lower than $r'.treelabel$ (lines (13) or (16)), and may either get settled (possibility (i)), or stop (the unsettled ones together) at another node with a settled robot r'' such that $r''.treelabel < U'_{min}$. This may happen up to $k - 1$ times. However, the remaining unsettled robots from U^{s1} never get separated from each other. If the robot with ID U^{s1}_{min} is settled at the end of stage 1, so are all the others in U^{s1}. If U^{s1}_{min} robot is not settled at the end of stage 1, the remaining unsettled robots from U^{s1} have always moved and stopped along with U^{s1}_{min} robot. This is because, if the robot with ID U^{s1}_{min} stops at a node with settled robot r''' (line 12), $r'''.treelabel < U^{s1}_{min}$ and hence $r'''.treelabel$ is also less than the IDs of the remaining unsettled robots from U^{s1}. If the stopped robot with ID U^{s1}_{min} begins to move (line 15 or 19), so do the other stopped (unsettled) robots from U^{s1} because they are at the same node as the robot with ID U^{s1}_{min}. Hence, (ii) follows. $\qquad\square$

Let us introduce some more terminology. Let $\mathcal{U}^{s1}$ be the set of all U^{s1}. Let $\mathcal{U}^{s1}_{min}$ be $\min_{U^{s1} \in \mathcal{U}^{s1}}(U^{s1}_{min})$. The set of robots in that U^{s1} having $U^{s1}_{min} = \mathcal{U}^{s1}_{min}$ are dispersed at the end of stage 1 because the DFS traversal of the robots in that U^{s1} is not stopped at any node by a settled robot having a lower $treelabel$ than that U^{s1}_{min}. Let u^{s1}_p, $u^{e1}_p = u^{s2}_p$, and u^{e2}_p denote the number of nodes with unsettled robots at the start of stage 1, at the end of stage 1(or at the start of stage 2), and at the end of stage 2 respectively, all for a pass p of the algorithm. Thus, u^{s1}_p ($= |\mathcal{U}^{s1}_p|$) is the number of U-sets at the start of stage 1 of pass p. Analogously, for $u^{e1}_p = u^{s2}_p$, and u^{e2}_p.

We now have the following corollary to Lemma 2.

Corollary 1. $u^{e1}_p \leq u^{s1}_p - 1$.

In stage 1, each set of unsettled robots U^{s1} induces a partial DFS tree, where the $treelabel$ of settled robots is U^{s1}_{min}. This identifies a sub-component $SC_{U^{s1}_{min}}$. Note that some subset of U^{s1} may be stopped at a node outside $SC_{U^{s1}_{min}}$, where the $treelabel < U^{s1}_{min}$.

Definition 2. *A sub-component SC_α is the set of all settled nodes having $treelabel = \alpha$. SC is used to denote the set of all SCs at the end of stage 1.*

Theorem 2. *There is a one-to-one mapping from the set of sub-components SC to the set of unsettled robots U^{s1}. The mapping is given by: $SC_\alpha \mapsto U^{s1}$, where $\alpha = U^{s1}_{min}$.*

Proof. From Definition 2, each SC_α corresponds to a $treelabel = \alpha$. The $treelabel$ is set to the lowest ID among visiting robots, and this corresponds to a unique set of unsettled robots U^{s1} whose minimum ID robot has ID α, i.e., $U^{s1}_{min} = \alpha$.   □

Lemma 3. *Sub-component SC_α is a connected sub-component of settled nodes, i.e., for any $a, b \in SC_\alpha$, there exists a path (a, b) in G such that each node on the path has a settled robot.*

Proof. For any nodes a and b in SC_α, the robot with ID U_{min} ($= \alpha$) has visited a and b. Thus there is some path from a to b in G that it has traversed. On that path, if there was a free node, a remaining unsettled robot from U (there is at least the robot with ID U_{min} that is unsettled) would have settled there. Thus there cannot exist a free node on that path and the lemma follows.   □

Within a sub-component, there may be stopped robots belonging to one or more different sets U^{s1} (having a higher U^{s1}_{min} than the $treelabel$ at the node where they stop). There may be multiple sub-components that are adjacent in the sense that they are separated by a common edge. Together, these sub-components form a connected component of settled nodes.

Definition 3. *A connected component of settled nodes (CCSN) is a set of settled nodes such that for any $a, b \in CCSN$, there exists a path (a, b) in G with each node on the path having a settled robot.*

Lemma 4. *If not all the robots of U^{s1} are settled by the end of stage 1, then $SC_{U^{s1}_{min}}$ is part of a CCSN containing nodes from at least two sub-components.*

Proof. Let the unsettled robots in U^{s1} begin from node a. The unsettled robots of U^{s1} stopped (line 12), and possibly moved again (line 15 or 19) only to be stopped again (line 12), c times, where $|U^{s1}| > c \geq 1$.

Consider the first time the robots arriving along edge (u, v) were stopped at some node v. $U^{s1}_{min} > r.treelabel$, where robot r is settled at v. Henceforth till the end of stage 1, $r.treelabel$ is monotonically non-increasing, i.e., it may only decrease if a visitor arrives with a lower ID (line 16). The path traced from a to u must have all settled nodes, each belonging to possibly more than one sub-component, i.e., possibly in addition to $SC_{U^{s1}_{min}}$, at the end of stage 1, which together form one or more adjacent sub-components. In any case, these sub-components are necessarily adjacent to the sub-component SC_α, where $\alpha = r.treelabel$. Thus, at least two sub-components including $SC_{U^{s1}_{min}}$ and SC_α are (possibly transitively) adjacent and form part of a CCSN.

Extending this reasoning to each of the c times the robots stopped, it follows that there are at least $c + 1$ sub-components in the resulting CCSN.(Additionally, (1) unsettled robots from the sub-component that stopped the unsettled robots of U^{s1} for the c-th time may be (transitively) stopped by robots in yet other sub-components, (2) other groups of unsettled robots may (transitively or independently) be stopped at nodes in the above identified sub-components, (3) other sub-components corresponding to even lower *treelabel*s may join the already identified sub-components, (4) other sub-components may have a node which is adjacent to one of the nodes in an above-identified sub-component. This only results in more sub-components, each having distinct *treelabel*s (Definition 2) and corresponding to as many distinct U-sets (Theorem 2), being adjacent in the resulting CCSN.)   □

Theorem 3. *For any U^{s1} at a, its unsettled robots (if any) belong to a single U^{e1} at b, where a and b belong to the same connected component of settled nodes (CCSN).*

Proof. From Lemma 2, it follows that the unsettled robots from U^{s1} (at a) end up at a single node b in the set U^{e1}. It follows that there must exist a path from a to b that these unsettled robots traversed. On this path, if there was a free node, a robot that belongs to U^{s1} and U^{e1} would have settled. Thus, there cannot exist such a free node. It follows that a and b belong to the same CCSN.   □

Using the reasoning of Lemma 2 and Corollary 1, if there are s sub-components within a CCSN, there may be stopped (unsettled) robots at at most $s-1$ nodes. In stage 2, all such unsettled robots within a CCSN are collected at a single node within that component.

Stage 2. Stage 2 begins with each robot setting variable *mult* to the count of robots at its node. The lowest ID unsettled robot x at each node (having $mult > 1$) concurrently initiates a DFS traversal of the CCSN after setting $x.home$ to the ID of the settled robot r and setting the $r.treelabel$ of the settled robot to its ID, $x.ID$. The DFS traversal is initiated by a single unsettled robot at a node rather than all unsettled robots at a node.

In the DFS traversal of the CCSN, there are four possibilities, akin to those in stage 1. If a visited node is free (line 27), the robot ignores that node and backtracks. This is because neither the free node nor any paths via the free node need to be explored to complete a DFS traversal of the CCSN.

If a visited node has a settled robot, the visiting robots may need to stop for two reasons. (i) Only the highest "priority" unsettled robot should be allowed to complete its DFS traversal while collecting all other unsettled robots. Other concurrently initiated DFS traversals for gathering unsettled robots should be stopped so that only one traversal for gathering succeeds. (ii) With the limited memory of $O(\log n)$ at each robot, only one DFS traversal can be enabled at each settled robot r in its $r.treelabel$, $r.parent$, and $r.child$. That is, the settled robot can record in its data structures, only the details for one DFS tree that is induced by one DFS traversal. The decision to continue the DFS or stop is based, not by comparing *treelabel* of the settled robot with the visiting robot ID, but by using a lexico-priority, defined next.

Definition 4. *The lexico-priority is defined by a tuple, $(mult, treelabel/ID)$. A higher value of mult is a higher priority; if mult is the same, a lower value of treelabel or ID has the higher priority.*

The lexico-priority of a settled robot r that is visited, $(r.mult, r.treelabel)$, is compared with $(x.mult, x.ID)$ of the visiting robots x. The lexico-priority is a total order. There are three possibilities, as shown in lines (30), (32), and (35).

- (line 30): Lexico-priority of r > lexico-priority of all visitors: All visiting robots stop (until ordered later to move) because they have a lower lexico-priority than r. The DFS traversal of the unsettled robot x' corresponding to $x'.ID = r.treelabel$ kills the DFS traversal of the visitors.
- (line 32): The visiting robot x having the highest lexico-priority among the visiting robots, and having the same lexico-priority as r continues the DFS traversal because it is part of the same DFS tree as r. r updates $r.child$ if needed as per the logic of $DFS(k)$ described in Sect. 3. This DFS search of x continues unless x is back at its home node from where it began its search and all ports at the home node have been explored. As x continues its DFS traversal, it takes along with it all unsettled robots at r.
- (line 35): The visiting robot x having the highest lexico-priority that is also higher than that of r overrides the $treelabel$ and $mult$ of r. It kills the DFS traversal and corresponding DFS tree that r is currently storing the data structures for. Robot x includes r in its own DFS traversal by setting $r.treelabel \leftarrow x.ID$, $r.mult \leftarrow x.mult$, and $r.parent$ to the port from which x entered this node; $r.child$ is set as per the logic of $DFS(k)$ described in Sect. 3. Robot x continues its DFS traversal and all other unsettled robots follow it.

The reason we use the lexico-priority defined on the tuple rather than on just the $treelabel/ID$ is that the sub-component with the lowest $treelabel$ may have no unsettled robots, but yet some node(s) in it are adjacent to those in other sub-components, thus being part of the same CCSN. The nodes in the sub-component with the lowest $treelabel$ would then stop other traversing robots originating from other sub-components, but no robot from that sub-component would initiate the DFS traversal.

Lemma 5. *Within a connected component of settled nodes (CCSN), let x be the unsettled robot with the highest lexico-priority at the start of Stage 2.*

1. *x returns to its home node from where it begins the DFS traversal of the component, at the end of Stage 2.*
2. *All settled nodes in the connected component have the same lexico-priority as x at the end of Stage 2.*

Proof. (Part 1): Robot x encounters case in line (35) for the first visit to each node in its CCSN and includes that node in its own DFS traversal, and on subsequent visits to that node, encounters the case in line (32) and continues its DFS traversal. Within $\min(4m - 2n + 2, 2k\Delta)$ steps, it can complete its DFS traversal of the CCSN and return to its home node. This is because it can visit all the nodes of the graph within $4m - 2n + 2$ steps. The robot can also visit the at most k settled nodes in $2k\Delta$ steps; $k\Delta$ steps may be required in the worst case to visit the k settled nodes in its CCSN and another at most $k\Delta$ steps to backtrack from adjacent visited nodes that are free.

(Part 2): When x visits a node with a settled robot r for the first time (line 35), the lexico-priority of r is changed to that of x (line 36). Henceforth, if other unsettled robots y visit r, r will not change its lexico-priority (line 30) because its lexico-priority is now highest. ◻

Analogous to stage 1, unsettled robots beginning from different nodes may move and then stop (on reaching a higher lexico-priority lp node), and then resume movement again (when visited by a robot with lexico-priority lp or higher). This may happen up to $s - 1$ times, where s is the number of sub-components in the CCSN. We show that, despite the concurrently initiated DFS traversals and these concurrent movements of unsettled robots, they all gather at the end of stage 2, at the home node of the unsettled robot having the highest lexico-priority (in the CCSN) at the start of stage 2.

Lemma 6. *Within a connected component of settled nodes (CCSN), let x be the unsettled robot with the highest lexico-priority at the start of Stage 2. All the unsettled robots in the component gather at the home node of x at the end of Stage 2.*

Proof. Let y be any unsettled robot at the start of the stage. At time step t, let y be at a node denoted by $v(t)$. Let τ be the earliest time step at which y is at a node with the highest lexico-priority that it encounters in Stage 2. We have the following cases.

1. lexico-priority(settled robot at $v(\tau)$) $<$ lexico-priority(x): We have a contradiction because at $t = \min(4m - 2n + 2, 2k\Delta)$, settled robots at all nodes have lexico-priority that of x, which is highest.
2. lexico-priority(settled robot at $v(\tau)$) $>$ lexico-priority(x): This contradicts the definition of x.
3. lexico-priority(settled robot at $v(\tau)$) $=$ lexico-priority(x).
    (a) $v(\tau) = x.home$: Robot y will not move from $x.home$ (line 32) and the lemma stands proved.
    (b) $v(\tau) \neq x.home$: y ends up at another node with lexico-priority that of x at time step τ. It will not move from node $v(\tau)$ unless robot x visits $v(\tau)$ at or after τ, in which case y will accompany x to $x.home$ and the lemma stands proved.

        We need to analyze the possibility that x does not visit $v(\tau)$ at or after τ. That is, the last visit by x to $v(\tau)$ was before τ. By definition of τ, lexico-priority(settled robot at $v(\tau - 1)$) $<$ lexico-priority(settled robot at $v(\tau)$) ($=$ lexico-priority of x in this case). By Lemma 5, x is yet to visit $v(\tau - 1)$, so the first visit of x to $v(\tau - 1)$ is after $\tau - 1$. As $v(\tau - 1)$ and $v(\tau)$ are neighbors and x is doing a DFS, x will visit $v(\tau)$ at or after $\tau + 1$. This contradicts that the last visit by x to $v(\tau)$ was before τ and therefore rules out the possibility that x does not visit $v(\tau)$ at or after τ.

$\square$

4.3   Correctness of the Algorithm

Having proved the properties of stage 1 and stage 2, we now prove the correctness of the algorithm.

Lemma 7. $u_p^{e2} = u_{p+1}^{s1} \leq \frac{1}{2} \cdot u_p^{s1}$

Proof. From Lemma 2, for any U^{s1} at the end of stage 1, (i) a set of unsettled robots U^{s1} is fully dispersed, or (ii) a subset of U^{s1} of unsettled robots is stopped and present together at at most one node with a settled robot r such that $r.treelabel < U_{min}^{s1}$.

In case (i), there are two possibilities. (i.a) There is no group of unsettled robots stopped at nodes in the CCSN where the robots of U have settled. In this case, this U^{s1}-set does not have its robots in any U^{e1}-set. (i.b) $z(\geq 1)$ groups of unsettled robots are stopped at nodes in the CCSN where the robots of U have settled. These groups correspond to at least $z+1$ unique U-sets and at least $z+1$ sub-components that form a CCSN (by using reasoning similar to that in the proof of Lemma 4). In case (ii), at least two sub-components, each having distinct *treelabels* and corresponding to as many distinct U-sets (Theorem 2), are adjacent in the CCSN (Lemma 4).

From Lemma 2, we also have that any U^{s1}-set cannot have unsettled robots in more than one U^{e1}. Each robot in each U^{s1}-set in the CCSN, that remains unsettled at the end of stage 1, belongs to some U^{e1}-set that also belongs to the *same* CCSN (Theorem 3). From Lemma 6 for stage 2, all the unsettled robots in these U^{e1}-sets in the CCSN, are gathered at one node in that CCSN. Thus, each unsettled robot from each U^{s1}-set in the same CCSN is collected at a single node as a U^{e2}-set in the same CCSN. Thus, in cases (i-b) and (ii) above, *two or more* sub-components, each corresponding to a distinct *treelabel* and a distinct U^{s1}-set (Theorem 2), combine into a single CCSN (Lemma 4) and in stage 2, there is a single node with unsettled robots from all the U^{s1}-sets belonging to the same CCSN, i.e., a single U^{e2}-set, or a single U^{s1}-set for the next round. Note that each sub-component SC_α is a connected sub-component (Lemma 3) and hence belongs to the same CCSN; thus when sub-components merge, i.e., their corresponding U^{s1}-sets merge, and we have a single U^{e2}-set in the CCSN, there is no double-counting of the same SC_α and of its corresponding U^{s1}-set in different CCSNs. Thus, u_p^{e2} $(= u_{p+1}^{s1})$, the number of U-sets after stage 2, is $\leq \frac{1}{2} \cdot u_p^{s1}$, where u_p^{s1} is the number of U-sets before stage 1.   □

Theorem 4. DISPERSION *is solved in* $\log k$ *passes in Algorithm 1.*

Proof. $u_1^{s1} \leq k/2$. From Lemma 7, it will take at most $\log k - 1$ passes for there to be a single U-set. In the first stage of the $\log k$-th pass, there will be a single U-set. By Lemma 2, case (i) holds and all robots in the U-set get settled. (Case (ii) will not hold because there is no node with a *treelabel* $< U_{min}$ as all *treelabels* of settled nodes are reset to $\top$ (the highest value) at the end of stage 2 of the previous pass and all singleton robots before the first pass settle with *treelabel* $= \top$ (line 2)). Thus, DISPERSION will be achieved by the end of stage 1 of pass $\log k$.   □

Note that the DFS traversal of stage 2 is independent of the DFS traversal of stage 1 within a pass (but the *treelabels* are not erased), and the DFS traversal of stage 1 of the next pass is independent of the DFS traversal of stage 2 of the current pass.

Proof of Theorem 1 : Theorem 4 proved that DISPERSION is achieved by Algorithm 1. The time complexity is evident due to the two loops of $O(\min(4m - 2n + 2, 2\Delta k))$ for the two stages nested within the outer loop of $O(\log k)$ passes. The space complexity is evident from the size of the variables: *treelabel* ($\log k$ bits), *parent* ($\log \Delta$ bits), *child* ($\log \Delta$ bits), *settled* (1 bit), *mult* ($\log k$ bits), *home* ($\log k$ bits), *pass* ($\log \log k$ bits), *round* ($O(\log n)$ bits to maintain the value $O(\min(m, k\Delta)$ for each pass).   □

We have the following corollary to Theorem 1 when $\Delta \leq k$.

Corollary 2. *Given $k \leq n$ robots in an n-node arbitrary graph G with maximum degree $\Delta \leq k$, Algorithm $Graph\_Disperse(k)$ solves* DISPERSION *in $O(\min(m, k^2) \cdot \log k)$ rounds with $O(\log n)$ bits at each robot.*

We also have the following corollary to Theorem 1 when $\Delta = O(1)$.

Corollary 3. *Given $k \leq n$ robots in an n-node arbitrary graph G with maximum degree $\Delta = O(1)$, algorithm $Graph\_Disperse(k)$ solves* DISPERSION *in $O(\min(m, k) \cdot \log k)$ rounds with $O(\log n)$ bits at each robot.*

5   Concluding Remarks

We have presented a deterministic algorithm for solving DISPERSION of $k \leq n$ robots on n-node arbitrary graphs. Our result significantly improves the $O(mk)$ runtime of the best previously known algorithm with logarithmic memory at each robot [16] to $O(\min(m, k\Delta) \cdot \log k)$ with logarithmic memory at each robot. For future work, it will be interesting to solve DISPERSION on arbitrary graphs with time $O(k)$ or improve the existing time lower bound of $\Omega(k)$ to $\Omega(\min(m, k\Delta))$. Another interesting direction is to remove the $\log k$ factor from the time bound in Theorem 1. Furthermore, it will be interesting to achieve Theorem 1 without each robot knowing parameters m, Δ, and k. Finally, another interesting direction will be to extend our algorithms to solve DISPERSION in semi-synchronous and asynchronous settings.

References

1. Augustine, J., Moses Jr., W.K.: Dispersion of mobile robots: a study of memory-time trade-offs. CoRR, abs/1707.05629, [v4] (2018). (A preliminary version in ICDCN 2018)
2. Bampas, E., Gąsieniec, L., Hanusse, N., Ilcinkas, D., Klasing, R., Kosowski, A.: Euler tour lock-in problem in the rotor-router model. In: Keidar, I. (ed.) DISC 2009. LNCS, vol. 5805, pp. 423–435. Springer, Heidelberg (2009). https://doi.org/10.1007/978-3-642-04355-0_44
3. Barriere, L., Flocchini, P., Mesa-Barrameda, E., Santoro, N.: Uniform scattering of autonomous mobile robots in a grid. In: IPDPS, pp. 1–8 (2009)
4. Cohen, R., Fraigniaud, P., Ilcinkas, D., Korman, A., Peleg, D.: Label-guided graph exploration by a finite automaton. ACM Trans. Algorithms 4(4), 42:1–42:18 (2008)
5. Cormen, T.H., Leiserson, C.E., Rivest, R.L., Stein, C.: Introduction to Algorithms, 3rd edn. The MIT Press, Cambridge (2009)
6. Cybenko, G.: Dynamic load balancing for distributed memory multiprocessors. J. Parallel Distrib. Comput. 7(2), 279–301 (1989)
7. Das, S., Flocchini, P., Prencipe, G., Santoro, N., Yamashita, M.: Autonomous mobile robots with lights. Theor. Comput. Sci. 609, 171–184 (2016)
8. Dereniowski, D., Disser, Y., Kosowski, A., Pajak, D., Uznański, P.: Fast collaborative graph exploration. Inf. Comput. 243(C), 37–49 (2015)
9. Elor, Y., Bruckstein, A.M.: Uniform multi-agent deployment on a ring. Theor. Comput. Sci. 412(8–10), 783–795 (2011)
10. Flocchini, P., Prencipe, G., Santoro, N.: Distributed computing by oblivious mobile robots. Synth. Lect. Distrib. Comput. Theory 3(2), 1–185 (2012)

11. Flocchini, P., Prencipe, G., Santoro, N.: Distributed Computing by Mobile Entities. Theoretical Computer Science and General Issues, vol. 1. Springer, Cham (2019). https://doi.org/10.1007/978-3-030-11072-7

12. Fraigniaud, P., Gasieniec, L., Kowalski, D.R., Pelc, A.: Collective tree exploration. Networks **48**(3), 166–177 (2006)

13. Fraigniaud, P., Ilcinkas, D., Peer, G., Pelc, A., Peleg, D.: Graph exploration by a finite automaton. Theor. Comput. Sci. **345**(2–3), 331–344 (2005)

14. Hsiang, T.-R., Arkin, E.M., Bender, M.A., Fekete, S., Mitchell, J.S.B.: Online dispersion algorithms for swarms of robots. In: SoCG, pp. 382–383 (2003)

15. Hsiang, T.-R., Arkin, E.M., Bender, M.A., Fekete, S.P., Mitchell, J.S.B.: Algorithms for rapidly dispersing robot swarms in unknown environments. In: Boissonnat, J.-D., Burdick, J., Goldberg, K., Hutchinson, S. (eds.) Algorithmic Foundations of Robotics V. STAR, vol. 7, pp. 77–93. Springer, Heidelberg (2004). https://doi.org/10.1007/978-3-540-45058-0_6

16. Kshemkalyani, A.D., Ali, F.: Efficient dispersion of mobile robots on graphs. In: ICDCN, pp., 218–227 (2019)

17. Menc, A., Pajak, D., Uznanski, P.: Time and space optimality of rotor-router graph exploration. Inf. Process. Lett. **127**, 17–20 (2017)

18. Molla, A.R., Moses, W.K.: Dispersion of mobile robots: the power of randomness. In: Gopal, T.V., Watada, J. (eds.) TAMC 2019. LNCS, vol. 11436, pp. 481–500. Springer, Cham (2019). https://doi.org/10.1007/978-3-030-14812-6_30

19. Poudel, P., Sharma, G.: Time-optimal uniform scattering in a grid. In: ICDCN, pp. 228–237 (2019)

20. Shibata, M., Mega, T., Ooshita, F., Kakugawa, H., Masuzawa, T.: Uniform deployment of mobile agents in asynchronous rings. In: PODC, pp. 415–424 (2016)

21. Subramanian, R., Scherson, I.D.: An analysis of diffusive load-balancing. In: SPAA, pp. 220–225 (1994)

Pushing Lines Helps: Efficient Universal Centralised Transformations for Programmable Matter

Abdullah Almethen[✉], Othon Michail, and Igor Potapov

Department of Computer Science, University of Liverpool, Liverpool, UK
{A.Almethen,Othon.Michail,Potapov}@liverpool.ac.uk

Abstract. In this paper, we study a discrete system of entities residing on a two-dimensional square grid. Each entity is modelled as a node occupying a distinct cell of the grid. The set of all n nodes forms initially a connected shape A. Entities are equipped with a linear-strength pushing mechanism that can push a whole line of entities, from 1 to n, in parallel in a single time-step. A target connected shape B is also provided and the goal is to *transform* A into B via a sequence of line movements. Existing models based on local movement of individual nodes, such as rotating or sliding a single node, can be shown to be special cases of the present model, therefore their (inefficient, $\Theta(n^2)$) *universal transformations* carry over. Our main goal is to investigate whether the parallelism inherent in this new type of movement can be exploited for efficient, i.e., sub-quadratic worst-case, transformations. As a first step towards this, we restrict attention solely to centralised transformations and leave the distributed case as a direction for future research. Our results are positive. By focusing on the apparently hard instance of transforming a diagonal A into a straight line B, we first obtain transformations of time $O(n\sqrt{n})$ without and with preserving the connectivity of the shape throughout the transformation. Then, we further improve by providing two $O(n \log n)$-time transformations for this problem. By building upon these ideas, we first manage to develop an $O(n\sqrt{n})$-time universal transformation. Our main result is then an $O(n \log n)$-time universal transformation. We leave as an interesting open problem a suspected $\Omega(n \log n)$-time lower bound.

1 Introduction

As a result of recent advances in components such as micro-sensors, electromechanical actuators, and micro-controllers, a number of interesting systems are now within reach. A prominent type of such systems concerns collections of small robotic entities. Each individual robot is equipped with a number of actuation/sensing/communication/computation components that provide it

---

The full version of the paper with all omitted details is available on arXiv at: https://arxiv.org/abs/1904.12777.

© Springer Nature Switzerland AG 2019
F. Dressler and C. Scheideler (Eds.): ALGOSENSORS 2019, LNCS 11931, pp. 41–59, 2019.
https://doi.org/10.1007/978-3-030-34405-4_3

with some autonomy; for instance, the ability to move locally and to communicate with neighbouring robots. Still, individual local dynamics are uninteresting, and individual computations are restricted due to limited computational power, resources, and knowledge. What makes these systems interesting is the collective complexity of the population of devices. A number of fascinating recent developments in this direction have demonstrated the feasibility and potential of such collective robotic systems, where the scale can range from milli/micro [BG15, GKR10, KCL+12, RCN14, YSS+07] down to nano [DDL+09, Rot06].

This progress has motivated the parallel development of a theory of such systems. It has been already highlighted [MS18] that a formal theory (including modelling, algorithms, and computability/complexity) is necessary for further progress in systems. This is because theory can accurately predict the most promising designs, suggest new ways to optimise them, by identifying the crucial parameters and the interplay between them, and provide with those (centralised or distributed) algorithmic solutions that are best suited for each given design and task, coupled with provable guarantees on their performance. As a result, a number of sub-areas of theoretical computer science have emerged such as mobile and reconfigurable robotics [ABD+13, BKRT04, CFPS12, CKLWL09, DFSY15, DDG+18, DGMRP06, DDG+14, DGR+15, DGR+16, DLFS+19, DLFP+18, FPS12, KKM10, MSS19, SMO+18, YS10, YUY16, YSS+07], passively-mobile systems [AAD+06, AAER07, MS16, MS18] including the theory of DNA self-assembly [Dot12, RW00, Win98, WCG+13], and metamorphic systems [DP04, DSY04a, DSY04b, NGY00, WWA04]; connections are even evident with the theory of puzzles [BDF+19, Dem01, HD05]. A latest ongoing effort is to join these theoretical forces and developments within the emerging area of "Algorithmic Foundations of Programmable Matter" [FRRS16]. *Programmable matter* refers to any type of matter that can *algorithmically* change its physical properties. "Algorithmically" means that the change (or *transformation*) is the result of executing an *underlying program*.

In this paper, we embark from the model studied in [DP04, DSY04a, DSY04b, MSS19], in which a number of spherical devices are given in the form of a (typically connected) shape A lying on a two-dimensional square grid, and the goal is to transform A into a desired target shape B via a sequence of valid movements of individual devices. In those papers, the considered mechanisms were the ability to rotate and slide a device over neighbouring devices (always through empty space). We here consider an alternative (linear-strength) mechanism, by which a line of one or more devices can translate by one position in a single time-step.

As our main goal is to determine whether the new movement under consideration can *in principle* be exploited for sub-quadratic worst-case transformations, we naturally restrict our attention to centralised transformations. We generally allow the transformations to break connectivity, even though we also develop some connectivity-preserving transformations on the way. Our main result is a universal transformation of $O(n \log n)$ worst-case running time that is permitted to break connectivity. Distributed transformations and connectivity-preserving universal transformations are left as interesting future research directions.

1.1 Our Approach

In [MSS19], it was proved that if the devices (called *nodes* from now on) are equipped only with a rotation mechanism, then the decision problem of transforming a connected shape A into a connected shape B is in **P**, and a constructive characterisation of the (rich) class of pairs of shapes that are transformable to each other was given. In the case of combined availability of rotation and sliding, universality has been shown [DP04, MSS19], that is, any pair of connected shapes are transformable into each other. Still, in these and related models, where in any time step at most one node can move a single position in its local neighbourhood, it can be proved (see, for instance, [MSS19]) that there will be pairs of shapes that require $\Omega(n^2)$ steps to be transformed into each other. This follows directly from the inherent "distance" between the two shapes and the fact that this distance can be reduced by only a constant in every time step. An immediate question is then *"How can we come up with more efficient transformations?"*

Two main alternatives have been explored in the literature in an attempt to answer this question. One is to consider parallel time, meaning that the transformation algorithm can move more than one node (up to a linear number of nodes if possible) in a single time step, such as transformations based on pipelining [DSY04b, MSS19, RCN14]. The other approach is to consider more powerful actuation mechanisms, that have the potential to reduce the inherent distance faster than a constant per sequential time-step. Prominent examples in the literature are the linear-strength models of Aloupis *et al.* [ABD+13, ACD+08], in which nodes are equipped with extend/contract arms and of Woods *et al.* [WCG+13], in which a whole line of nodes can rotate around a single node (acting as a linear-strength rotating arm). The present paper follows this approach, by introducing and investigating a linear-strength model in which a node can push a line of consecutive nodes one position (towards an empty cell) in a single time-step.

In terms of transformability, our model can easily simulate the combined rotation and sliding mechanisms of [DP04, MSS19] by restricting movements to lines of length 1 (i.e., individual nodes). It follows that this model is also capable of universal transformations, with a time complexity at most twice the worst-case of those models, i.e., again $O(n^2)$. Naturally, our focus is set on exploring ways to exploit the parallelism inherent in moving lines of larger length in order to speed-up transformations and, if possible, to come up with a more efficient in the worst case universal transformation. Further, as reversibility of movements is still valid for any line movement in our model, we adopt the approach of transforming any given shape A into a spanning line L (vertical or horizontal). This is convenient, because if one shows that any shape A can transform fast into a line L, then any pair of shapes A and B can then be transformed fast to each other by first transforming fast A into L and then L into B by reversing the fast transformation of B into L.

We start this investigation by identifying the diagonal shape D (which is considered connected in our model and is very similar to the staircase worst-case shape of [MSS19]) as a potential worst-case initial shape to be transformed into a line L. This intuition is supported by the $O(n^2)$ individual node distance between the two shapes and by the initial unavailability of long line movements: the transformation may move long lines whenever available, but has to pay first a number of movements of small lines in order to construct longer lines. In this benchmark (special) case, the trivial lower and upper bounds $\Omega(n)$ and $O(n^2)$, respectively, hold.

First, we prove that by partitioning the diagonal into $\sqrt{n}$ diagonal segments of length $\sqrt{n}$ each, we can first transform each segment in time quadratic in its length into a straight line segment, then push all segments down to a "collection row" y_0 in time $O(n\sqrt{n})$ and finally re-orient all line segments to form a horizontal line in y_0, paying a linear additive factor. Thus, this transformation takes total time $O(n\sqrt{n})$, which constitutes our first improvement compared to the $\Omega(n^2)$ lower bound of [MSS19]. We then take this algorithmic idea one step further, by developing two transformations building upon it, that can achieve the same time-bound while *preserving connectivity* throughout their course: one is based on *folding* segments and the other on *extending* them.

As the $O(\sqrt{n})$ length of uniform partitioning into segments is optimal for the above type of transformation, we turn our attention into different approaches, aiming at further reducing the running time of transformations. Allowing once more to break connectivity, we develop an alternative transformation based on *successive doubling*. The partitioning is again uniform for individual "phases", but different phases have different partitioning length. The transformation starts from a minimal partitioning into $n/2$ lines of length 2, then matches them to the closest neighbours via shortest paths to obtain a partitioning into $n/4$ lines of length 4, and, continuing in the same way for $\log n$ phases, it maintains the invariant of having $n/2^i$ individual lines in each phase i, for $1 \leq i \leq \log n$. By proving that the cost of pairwise merging through shortest paths in each phase is linear in n, we obtain that this approach transforms the diagonal into a line in time $O(n \log n)$, thus yielding a substantial improvement. Observe that the problem of transforming the diagonal into a line seems to involve solving the same problem into smaller diagonal segments (in order to transform those into corresponding line segments). Then, one may naturally wonder whether a recursive approach could be applied in order to further reduce the running time. We provide a negative answer to this, for the special case of uniform recursion and at the same time obtain an alternative $O(n \log n)$ transformation for the diagonal-to-line problem.

Our final aim is to generalise the ideas developed for the above benchmark case in order to come up with *equally efficient universal transformations*. We successfully generalise both the $O(n\sqrt{n})$ and the $O(n \log n)$ approaches, obtaining universal transformations of worst-case running times $O(n\sqrt{n})$ and $O(n \log n)$, respectively. We achieve this by enclosing the initial shape into a square bounding box and then subdividing the box into square sub-boxes of appropriate dimension. For the $O(n\sqrt{n})$ bound, a single such partitioning into sub-boxes of dimension $\sqrt{n}$ turns out to be sufficient. For the $O(n \log n)$ bound we again employ a successive doubling approach through phases of an increasing dimension of the sub-boxes, that is, through a new partitioning in each phase. Therefore, our ultimate theorem (followed by a constructive proof, providing the claimed transformation) states that: *"In this model, when connectivity need not necessarily be preserved during the transformation, any pair of connected shapes A and B can be transformed to each other in sequential time $O(n \log n)$"*.

Table 1 summarises the running times of all the transformations developed in this paper.

Table 1. A summary of our transformations and their corresponding worst-case running times (the trivial lower bound is in all cases $\Omega(n)$). The Diagonal, Diagonal Connected, and Universal problems correspond to the DIAGONALTOLINE, DIAGONAL-TOLINECONNECTED, and UNIVERSALTRANSFORMATION problems, respectively (being formally defined in Sect. 2).

Transformation	Problem	Running time	Lower bound
DL-Partitioning	Diagonal	$O(n\sqrt{n})$	$\Omega(n)$
DL-Doubling	Diagonal	$O(n \log n)$	$\Omega(n)$
DL-Recursion	Diagonal	$O(n \log n)$	$\Omega(n)$
DLC-Folding	Diagonal Connected	$O(n\sqrt{n})$	$\Omega(n)$
DLC-Extending	Diagonal Connected	$O(n\sqrt{n})$	$\Omega(n)$
U-Box-Partitioning	Universal	$O(n\sqrt{n})$	$\Omega(n)$
U-Box-Doubling	Universal	$O(n \log n)$	$\Omega(n)$

Section 2 brings together all definitions and basic facts that are used throughout the paper. In Sect. 3, we study the problem of transforming a diagonal shape into a line, without and with connectivity preservation. Section 4 presents our universal transformations. In Sect. 5 we conclude and discuss further research directions that are opened by our work.

2   Preliminaries and Definitions

The transformations considered here run on a two-dimensional square grid. Each cell of the grid possesses a unique location addressed by non-negative coordinates (x, y), where x denotes columns and y indicates rows. A *shape* S is a set of n *nodes* on the grid, where each individual node $u \in S$ occupies a single cell $cell(u) = (x_u, y_u)$, therefore we may also refer to a node by the coordinates of the cell that it occupies at a given time. Two distinct nodes (x_1, y_1), (x_2, y_2) are *neighbours* (or *adjacent*) iff $x_2 - 1 \le x_1 \le x_2 + 1$ and $y_2 - 1 \le y_1 \le y_2 + 1$ (i.e., their cells are adjacent vertically, horizontally or diagonally). A shape S is *connected* iff the graph defined by S and the above neighbouring relation on S is connected. Throughout, n denotes the number of nodes in a shape under consideration.

A line, $L \subseteq S$, is defined by one or more consecutive nodes in a column or row. That is, $L = (x_0, y_0), (x_1, y_1), \dots, (x_k, y_k)$, for $0 \le k \le n$, $k \in \mathbb{Z}$, is a line iff

$x_0 = x_1 = \cdots = x_k$ and $|y_k - y_0| = k$, or $y_0 = y_1 = \cdots = y_k$ and $|x_k - x_0| = k$. A *line move*, is an operation by which all nodes of a line L move together in a single step, towards an empty *cell* adjacent to one of L's endpoints. A line move may also be referred to as *step* (or *move* or *movement*) and time is discrete and measured in number of steps throughout. A move in this model is equivalent to choosing a node u and a direction $d \in \{up, down, left, right\}$ and moving u one position in direction d. This will additionally push by one position the whole line L of nodes in direction d, L (possibly empty) starting from a neighbour of u in d and ending at the first empty cell.

More formally and in slightly different terms: A line $L = (x_1, y)$, $(x_2, y), \ldots, (x_k, y)$ of length k, where $1 \leq k \leq n$, can push all k nodes rightwards in a single step to positions $(x_2, y), (x_3, y), \ldots, (x_{k+1}, y)$ iff there exists an empty cell to the right of L at (x_{k+1}, y). The "down", "left", and "up" movements are defined symmetrically, by rotating the whole system $90°$, $180°$, and $270°$ clockwise, respectively.

As already mentioned, we know that there are related settings in which any pair of connected shapes A and B of the same order ("order" of a shape S meaning the number of nodes of S throughout the paper) can be transformed to each other while preserving the connectivity throughout the course of the transformation.[1] This, for example, has been proved for the case in which the available movements to the nodes are rotation and sliding [DP04, MSS19]. It can be shown that the model of [DP04, MSS19] is a special case of our model, implying all transformations established there (with their running time at most doubled, including universal transformations, are also valid transformations in the present model).

Lemma 1. *The minimum number of line moves by which a line of length k, $1 \leq k \leq n$, can completely change its orientation[2], is $2k - 2$.*

A property that typically facilitates the development of universal transformations, is reversibility of movements. To this end, we next show that line movements are reversible.

Lemma 2 (Reversibility). *Let (S_I, S_F) be a pair of connected shapes of the same number of nodes n. If $S_I \rightarrow S_F$ ("$\rightarrow$" denoting "can be transformed to via a sequence of line movements") then $S_F \rightarrow S_I$.*

Definition 1 (Nice Shape). *A connected shape $S \in NICE$ if there exists a central line $L_C \subseteq S$, such that every node $u \in S \setminus L_C$ is connected to L_C via a line perpendicular to L_C.*

Proposition 1. *Let S_{Nice} be a nice shape and S_L a straight line, both of the same order n. Then $S_{Nice} \rightarrow S_L$ (and $S_L \rightarrow S_{Nice}$) in $O(n)$ steps.*

---

[1] In this paper, whenever transforming into a target shape B, we allow any placement of B on the grid, i.e., any shape B' obtained from B through a sequence of rotations and translations.

[2] From vertical to horizontal and vice versa.

We now formally define the problems to be considered in this paper.

DIAGONALTOLINE. Given an initial connected diagonal line S_D and a target vertical or horizontal connected spanning line S_L of the same order, transform S_D into S_L, without necessarily preserving the connectivity during the transformation.

DIAGONALTOLINECONNECTED. Restricted version of DIAGONALTOLINE in which connectivity must be preserved during the transformation.

UNIVERSALTRANSFORMATION. Give a general transformation, such that, for all pairs of shapes (S_I, S_F) of the same order, where S_I is the initial shape and S_F the target shape, it will transform S_I into S_F, without necessarily preserving connectivity during its course.

3 Transforming the Diagonal into a Line

We begin our study from the case in which the initial shape is a diagonal line S_D of order n. Our goal throughout the section is to transform S_D into a spanning line S_L, i.e., solve the DIAGONALTOLINE and/or DIAGONALTOLINECON-NECTED problems. We do this, because these problems seem to capture the worst-case complexity of transformations in this model.

3.1 An $O(n\sqrt{n})$-Time Transformation

We start from DIAGONALTOLINE (i.e., no requirement to preserve connectivity). Our strategy (called *DL-Partitioning*) is as follows. We partition the diagonal into equal segments, as in Fig. 1(a). Then in each segment, we perform a trivial (inefficient, but enough for our purposes) line formation by moving each node independently to the leftmost column in that segment (Fig. 1(b)), which transforms all segments into lines (Fig. 1(c)). Then, we transfer each line segment all the way down to the bottommost row of the diagonal S_D, see Fig. 1(d). Finally, we change the orientation of all line segments to form the target spanning line (Fig. 1(e)). More formally, let S_D be a diagonal, occupying $(x, y), (x + 1, y + 1), \ldots, (x + n - 1, y + n - 1)$, such that x and y are the leftmost column and the bottommost row of S_D, respectively. S_D is divided into $\lceil\sqrt{n}\rceil$ segments, $l_1, l_2, \ldots, l_{\lceil\sqrt{n}\rceil}$, each of length $\lfloor\sqrt{n}\rfloor$, apart possibly from a single smaller one. Figure 1(a) illustrates the case of integer $\sqrt{n}$ and in what follows, w.l.o.g., we present the case of integer $\sqrt{n}$ for simplicity. This strategy consists of three phases:

Phase 1: Transforms each diagonal segment $l_1, l_2, \ldots, l_{\sqrt{n}}$ into a line segment. Notice that segment l_k, $1 \leq k \leq \sqrt{n}$, contains $\sqrt{n}$ nodes occupying positions $(x + h_k, y + h_k), (x + h_k + 1, y + h_k + 1), \ldots, (x + h_k + \sqrt{n} - 1, y + h_k + \sqrt{n} - 1)$, for $h_k = n - k\sqrt{n}$; see Fig. 1(b). Each of these nodes moves independently to the leftmost column of l_k, namely column $x + h_k$, and the new positions of the nodes become $(x + h_k, y + h_k), (x + h_k, y + h_k + 1), \ldots, (x + h_k, y + h_k + \sqrt{n} - 1)$. Due to symmetry, any segment follows the same procedure of gathering at its

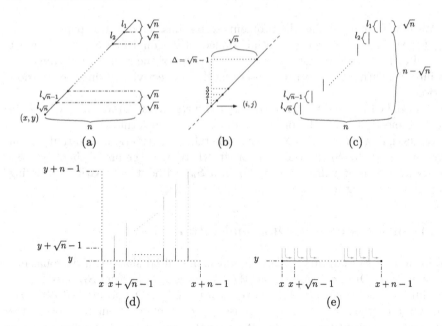

Fig. 1. (a) Dividing the diagonal into $\sqrt{n}$ segments of length $\sqrt{n}$ each (integer $\sqrt{n}$ case). (b) A closer view of a single segment, where $1, 2, 3, \ldots, \sqrt{n}-1$ are the required distances for the nodes to form a line segment at the leftmost column (of the segment). (c) Each line segment is transformed into a line and transferred towards the bottommost row of the shape, ending up as in (d). (e) All line segments are turned into the bottommost row to form the target spanning line.

bottommost row. By the end of Phase 1, $\sqrt{n}$ vertical line segments have been created (Fig. 1(c)).

Phase 2: Transfers all $\sqrt{n}$ line segments from Phase 1 down to the bottommost row y of the diagonal S_D. Observe that line segment l_k has to move distance h_k (see Fig. 1(d)).

Phase 3: Turns all $\sqrt{n}$ line segments into the bottommost row y (Fig. 1(e)). In particular, line l_k will be occupying positions $(x + h_k, y), (x + h_k + 1, y), \ldots, (x + h_k + \sqrt{n} - 1, y)$.

Theorem 1. *Given an initial diagonal of n nodes, DL-Partitioning solves the* DIAGONALTOLINE *problem in $O(n\sqrt{n})$ steps.*

Going one step further, we provide two $O(n\sqrt{n})$-time transformations, *DLC-Folding* and *DLC-Extending*, that additionally preserve connectivity of the shape throughout the transformation.[3]

Theorem 2. *Given an initial connected diagonal of n nodes, DLC-Folding and DLC-Extending solve the* DIAGONALTOLINECONNECTED *problem in $O(n\sqrt{n})$ steps.*

---

[3] Due to space restrictions, these can be found in the full version of the paper.

3.2   An $O(n \log n)$-Time Transformation

We now investigate another approach (called *DL-Doubling*) for DIAGONALTO-
LINE (i.e., without necessarily preserving connectivity). The main idea is as follows. The initial configuration can be viewed as n lines of length 1. We start (in
phases) to successively double the length of lines (while halving their number)
by matching them in pairs through shortest paths, until a single spanning line
remains. Let the lines existing in each phase be labelled $1, 2, 3, \ldots$ from top-right
to bottom-left. In each phase, we shall distinguish two types of lines, *free* and
stationary, which correspond to the odd $(1, 3, 5, \ldots)$ and even $(2, 4, 6, \ldots)$ lines
from top-right to bottom-left, respectively. In any phase, only the *free* lines move,
while the *stationary* stay still. In particular, in phase i, every free line j moves
via a shortest path to merge with the next (top-right to bottom-left) stationary
line $j + 1$. This operation merges two lines of length k into a new line of length
$2k$ residing at the column of the stationary line. In general, at the beginning of
every phase i, $1 \leq i \leq \log n$, there are $n/2^{i-1}$ lines of length 2^{i-1} each. These
are interchangeably free and stationary, starting from a free top-right one, and
at distance 2^{i-1} from each other. The minimum number of steps by which any
free line of length k_i, $1 \leq k_i \leq n/2$ can be merged with the stationary next to it
is roughly at most $4k_i = 4 \cdot 2^i$ (by two applications of turning of Lemma 1). By
the end of phase i (as well as the beginning of phase $i + 1$), there will be $n/2^i$
lines of length 2^i each, at distances 2^i from each other. The total cost for phase i
is obtained then by observing that each of $n/2^i$ free lines is paying at most $4 \cdot 2^i$
to merge with the next stationary. Thus, the transformation performs a linear
number of steps in each of the $\log n$ phases. See Fig. 2 for an illustration.

Lemma 3. *By the end of phase i, for all $1 \leq i \leq \log n$, DL-Doubling has created
$n/2^i$ lines, each of length 2^i, by performing $O(n)$ steps in that phase.*

Theorem 3. DL-Doubling *transforms any diagonal S_D of order n into a line
S_L in $O(n \log n)$ steps.*

An interesting observation for DIAGONALTOLINE (i.e., without necessarily
preserving connectivity), is that the problem is essentially self-reducible. This
means that any transformation for the problem can be applied to smaller parts of
the diagonal, resulting in small lines, and then trying to merge those lines into
a single spanning line. An immediate question is then whether such recursive
transformations can improve upon the $O(n \log n)$ best upper bound established
so far. The extreme application of this idea is to employ a full uniform recursion (call it *DL-Recursion*), where S_D is first partitioned into two diagonals of
length $n/2$ each, and each of them is being transformed into a line of length
$n/2$, by recursively applying to them the same halving procedure. Finally, the
top-right half has to pay a total of at most $4(n/2) = 2n$ to merge with the
bottom-left half and form a single spanning line (and the same is being recursively performed by smaller lines). By analysing the running time of such a
uniform recursion, we obtain that it is still $O(n \log n)$, partially suggesting that
recursive transformations might not be enough to improve upon $O(n \log n)$ (also

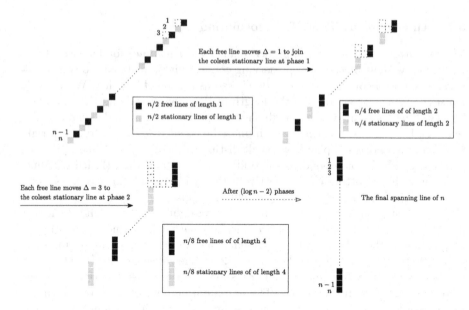

Fig. 2. The process of the $O(n \log n)$-time *DL-Doubling*. Nodes reside inside the black and grey cells.

possibly because of an $\Omega(n \log n)$ matching lower bound, which is left as an open question). If we denote by T_k the total time needed to split and merge lines of length k, then the recursion starts from 1 line incurring T_n and ends up with n lines incurring T_1. In particular, we analyse the recurrence relation:
$$T_n = 2T_{n/2} + 2n = 2(2T_{n/4} + n) + 2n = 4T_{n/4} + 4n = 4(2T_{n/8} + n/2) + 4n = 8T_{n/8} + 6n = \cdots = 2^i T_{n/2^i} + 2i \cdot n = \cdots = 2^{\log n} T_{n/2^{\log n}} + 2(\log n)n = n \cdot T_1 + 2n \log n = n + 2n \log n = O(n \log n), \text{ because } T_1 = 1.$$

Theorem 4. DL-Recursion *transforms any diagonal S_D of order n into a line S_L of the same order in $O(n \log n)$ steps.*

4   Universal Transformations

4.1   An $O(n\sqrt{n})$-Time Universal Transformation

In this section, we develop a universal transformation, called *U-Box-Partitioning*, which exploits line movements in order to transform *any* initial connected shape S_I into *any* target shape S_F of the same order n, in $O(n\sqrt{n})$ steps. Due to reversibility (Lemma 2), it is sufficient to show that any initial connected shape S_I can be transformed into a spanning line (implying then that any pair of shapes can be transformed to each other via the line and by reversing one of the two transformations). We maintain our focus on transformations that are allowed to break connectivity during their course. Observe that any initial connected shape

S_I of order n can be enclosed in an appropriately positioned $n \times n$ square (called a *box*). Our universal transformation is divided into three phases:

Phase A: Partition the $n \times n$ box into $\sqrt{n} \times \sqrt{n}$ sub-boxes (n in total in order to cover the whole $n \times n$ box). For each sub-box move all nodes in it down towards the bottommost row of that sub-box as follows. Start filling in the bottommost row from left to right, then if there is no more space continue to the next row from left to right and so on until all nodes in the sub-box have been exhausted (resulting in zero or more complete rows and at most one incomplete row). Moving down is done via shortest paths (where in the worst case a node has to move distance $2\sqrt{n}$); see Fig. 3.

Phase B: Choose one of the four length-n boundaries of the $n \times n$ box, say w.l.o.g. the left boundary. This is where the spanning line will be formed. Then, transfer every line via a shortest path to that boundary (incurring a maximum distance of $n - \sqrt{n}$ per line).

Phase C: Turn all lines (possibly consisting of more than one line on top of each other), by a procedure similar to that of Fig. 1(e), to end up with a spanning line of n nodes on the left boundary.

Fig. 3. An example of moving all nodes in a $\sqrt{n} \times \sqrt{n}$ sub-box to fill in the bottommost rows of the sub-box (Phase A).

Lemma 4. *A connected shape S_I of order n, occupies $O(\sqrt{n})$ sub-boxes.*

Proof. It follows directly from Corollary 1, which states that for a given connected shape S_I of n nodes enclosed by a square box of size $n \times n$ and any uniform partitioning of that box into sub-boxes of dimension d, then, it holds that S_I can occupy at most $O(\frac{n}{d})$ sub-boxes. Here, *U-Box-Partitioning* is dividing the $n \times n$ square box into $\sqrt{n} \times \sqrt{n}$ sub-boxes of dimension $d = \sqrt{n}$, therefore, S_I can occupy at most $\frac{n}{\sqrt{n}} = O(\sqrt{n})$ sub-boxes. $\square$

Lemma 5. *Starting from any connected shape S_I of order n, Phases A and B complete in $O(n\sqrt{n})$ steps each.*

Lemma 6. *Consider any length-n boundary and n nodes forming k lines, where $1 \le k \le n$, that are perpendicular to that boundary. Then, by line movements, the k lines require at most $O(n)$ steps to form a line of length n on that boundary. This implies that Phase C is completed in $O(n)$ steps.*

Proof. See Fig. 4. Observe that the k lines of n nodes are connected perpendicularly to the length-n boundary via k nodes, where $1 \leq k \leq n$. It means that there are $n - k$ nodes still waiting to be pushed into that boundary. According to Lemma 1, each of the $n - k$ nodes requires 2 steps to occupy the border, with a total of $2(n - k)$ steps for all $n - k$ nodes to completely fill up the boundary of length n. Following that, *U-Box-Partitioning* pushes all k lines in a total t of at most,

$$t = 2(n - k) = 2n - 2k$$
$$= O(n). \qquad \qquad \square$$

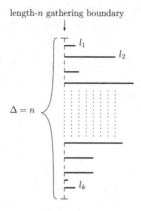

length-n gathering boundary

$\Delta = n$

l_1

l_2

l_k

Fig. 4. The dashed line is a length-n gathering boundary of the $n \times n$ box, which is connected perpendicularly to k lines of n nodes.

Lemma 7. U-Box-Partitioning *transforms any connected shape* S_I *into a straight line* S_L *of the same order* n, *in* $O(n\sqrt{n})$ *steps.*

Putting Lemma 7 and reversibility (Lemma 2) together gives:

Theorem 5. *For any pair of connected shapes* S_I *and* S_F *of the same order* n, U-Box-Partitioning *can be used to transform* S_I *into* S_F *(and* S_F *into* S_I*) in* $O(n\sqrt{n})$ *steps.*

4.2   An $O(n \log n)$-Time Universal Transformation

We now present an alternative universal transformation, called *U-Box-Doubling*, that transforms any pair of connected shapes, of the same order, to each other in $O(n \log n)$ steps. Given a connected shape S_I of order n, do the following. *Enclose* S_I *into an arbitrary* $n \times n$ *box as in* *U-Box-Partitioning* (Sect. 4.1). For simplicity, we assume that n is a power of 2, but this assumption can be dropped. Proceed in $\log n$ phases as follows: In every phase i, where $1 \leq i \leq \log n$, partition the $n \times n$ box into $2^i \times 2^i$ sub-boxes, disjoint and completely covering the $n \times n$ box. Assume that from any phase $i - 1$, any $2^{i-1} \times 2^{i-1}$ sub-box is either empty or has its k, where $0 \le k \le 2^{i-1}$, bottommost rows completely filled in with nodes, possibly followed by a single incomplete row on top of them containing l, where $1 \le l < 2^{i-1}$, consecutive nodes that are left aligned on that row. This case holds trivially for phase 1 and inductively for every phase. That is, in odd phases, we assume that nodes fill in the leftmost columns of boxes in a symmetric way. Every $2^i \times 2^i$ sub-box (of phase i) consists of four $2^{i-1} \times 2^{i-1}$ sub-boxes from phase $i - 1$, each of which is either empty or occupied as described above.

Consider the case where i is odd, thus, the nodes in the $2^{i-1} \times 2^{i-1}$ sub-boxes are bottom aligned. For every $2^i \times 2^i$ sub-box, move each line from the previous phase that resides in the sub-box to the left as many steps as required until that row contains a single line of consecutive nodes, starting from the left boundary of the sub-box, as shown in Fig. 5(a). With a linear procedure similar to that of Lemma 6 (and of *nice shapes*), start filling in the columns of the $2^i \times 2^i$ sub-box from the leftmost column and continuing to the right. If an incomplete column remains, push the nodes in it to the bottom of that column; see Fig. 5(b) for an example. The case of even i is symmetric, the only difference being that the arrangement guarantee from $i - 1$ is left alignment on the columns of the $2^{i-1} \times 2^{i-1}$ sub-boxes and the result will be bottom alignment on the rows of the $2^i \times 2^i$ sub-boxes of the current phase. This completes the description of the transformation. We first prove *correctness*:

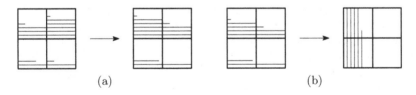

(a)   (b)

Fig. 5. (a) Pushing left in each $2^i \times 2^i$ sub-box. (b) Cleaning the orientation by aligning (filling) the leftmost columns.

Lemma 8. *Starting from any connected shape S_I of order n, U-Box-Doubling forms by the end of phase $\log n$ a line of length n.*

Proof. In phase $\log n$, the procedure partitions into a single box, which is the whole original $n \times n$ box. Independently of whether gathering will be on the leftmost column or on the bottommost row of the box, as all n nodes are contained in it, the outcome will be a single line of length n, vertical or horizontal, respectively.   □

Now, we shall analyse the running time of *U-Box-Doubling*. To facilitate exposition, we break this down into a number of lemmas.

Lemma 9. *In every phase i, the "super-shape" formed by the occupied $2^i \times 2^i$ sub-boxes is connected.*

Proof. By induction on the phase number i (starting from S_I connected) and the observation that a sub-box is occupied iff any of its own sub-boxes (of any size) had ever been occupied, because nodes are not transferred between $2^i \times 2^i$ sub-boxes before phase $i + 1$.   □

Lemma 10. *Given that* U-Box-Doubling *starts from a connected shape S_I of order n, the number of occupied sub-boxes in any phase i is $O(\frac{n}{2^i})$.*

Proof. First, observe that a $2^i \times 2^i$ sub-box of phase i is occupied in that phase iff S_I was originally going through that box. This follows from the fact that nodes are not transferred by this transformation between $2^i \times 2^i$ sub-boxes before phase $i + 1$. Therefore, the $2^i \times 2^i$ sub-boxes occupied in (any) phase i are exactly the $2^i \times 2^i$ sub-boxes that the original shape S_I would have occupied, thus, it is sufficient to upper bound the number of $2^i \times 2^i$ sub-boxes that a connected shape of order n can occupy. Or equivalently, we shall lower bound the number N_k of nodes needed to occupy k sub-boxes.

In order to simplify the argument, whenever S_I occupies another unoccupied sub-box, we will award it a constant number of additional occupations for free and only calculate the additional distance (in nodes) that the shape has to cover in order to reach another unoccupied sub-box. In particular, pick any node of S_I and consider as freely occupied that sub-box and the 8 sub-boxes surrounding it. Giving sub-boxes for free can only help the shape, therefore, any lower bound established including the free sub-boxes will also hold for shapes that do not have them (thus, for the original problem). Given that free boxes are surrounding the current node, in order for S_I to occupy another sub-box, at least one surrounding $2^i \times 2^i$ sub-box must be exited. This requires covering a distance of at least 2^i, through a connected path of nodes. Once this happens, S_I has just crossed the boundary between an occupied sub-box and an unoccupied sub-box. Then, by giving it for free at most 5 more unoccupied sub-boxes, S_I has to pay another 2^i nodes to occupy another unoccupied sub-box. We then continue applying this 5-for-free strategy until all n nodes have been used.

To sum up, the shape has been given 8 sub-boxes for free, and then for every sub-box covered it has to pay 2^i and gets 5 sub-boxes. Thus, to occupy $k = 8 + l \cdot 5$ sub-boxes, at least $l \cdot 2^i$ nodes are needed, that is, $N_k \geq l \cdot 2^i = \frac{k-8}{5} \cdot 2^i$. But shape S_I has order n, which means that the number of nodes available is upper bounded by n, i.e., $N_k \leq n$, which gives $\frac{k-8}{5} \cdot 2^i \leq N_k \leq n \Rightarrow \frac{k-8}{5} \cdot 2^i \leq n \Rightarrow \frac{k-8}{5} \leq \frac{n}{2^i} \Rightarrow k \leq 5(\frac{n}{2^i}) + 8$. We conclude that the number of $2^i \times 2^i$ sub-boxes that can be occupied by a connected shape S_I, and, thus, also the number of $2^i \times 2^i$ sub-boxes that are occupied by the transformation in phase i, is at most $5(\frac{n}{2^i}) + 8 = O(\frac{n}{2^i})$.   □

As a corollary of this, we obtain:

Corollary 1. *Given a uniform partitioning of $n \times n$ square box containing a connected shape S_I of order n into $d \times d$ sub-boxes, it holds that S_I can occupy at most $O(\frac{n}{d})$ sub-boxes.*

By using Lemma 10, we can then show that:

Lemma 11. *Starting from any connected shape of n nodes, U-Box-Doubling performs $O(n \log n)$ steps during its course.*

Proof. We prove this by showing that in every phase i, $1 \leq i \leq \log n$, the transformation performs at most a linear number of steps. We partition the occupied $2^i \times 2^i$ sub-boxes into two disjoint sets, B_1 and B_0, where sub-boxes in B_1 have at least 1 *complete line* (from the previous phase), i.e., a line of length 2^{i-1}, and sub-boxes in B_0 have 1 to 4 *incomplete lines*, i.e., lines of length between 1 and $2^{i-1} - 1$. For B_1, we have that $|B_1| \leq \frac{n}{2^{i-1}}$. Moreover, for every complete line, we pay at most 2^{i-1} to transfer it left or down, depending on the parity of i. As there are at most $\frac{n}{2^{i-1}}$ such complete lines in phase i, the total cost for this is at most $2^i \cdot \left(\frac{n}{2^{i-1}}\right) = n$.

Each sub-box in B_1 may also have at most 4 incomplete lines from the previous phase, where at most two of them may have to pay a maximum of 2^{i-1} to be transferred left or down, depending on the parity of i (as the other two are already aligned). As there are at most $\frac{n}{2^{i-1}}$ sub-boxes in B_1, the total cost for this is at most $2 \cdot 2^{i-1} \cdot \left(\frac{n}{2^{i-1}}\right) = 2n$.

Therefore, the total cost for pushing all lines towards the required border in B_1 sub-boxes is at most $n + 2n = 3n$. For B_0, we have (by Lemma 10) that the total number of occupied sub-boxes in phase i is at most $5\left(\frac{n}{2^{i-1}}\right) + 8$, then $|B_0| \leq 5\left(\frac{n}{2^{i-1}}\right) + 8$ (taking into account also the worst case where every occupied sub-box may be of type B_0). There is again a maximum of 2 incomplete lines per such sub-box that need to be transferred a distance of at most 2^{i-1}, therefore, the total cost for this to happen in every B_0 sub-box is at most $2 \cdot 2^{i-1}(5 \cdot \frac{n}{2^i} + 8) = 5n + 8 \cdot 2^i \leq 13n$. By paying the above costs, all occupied sub-boxes have their lines aligned horizontally to their left or vertically to their bottom border, and the final task of the transformation for this phase is to apply a linear procedure in order to fill in the left (bottom) border. This procedure costs at most $2k$ for every k nodes aligned as above (Lemma 1), therefore, in total at most $2n$. This completes the operation of the transformation for phase i. Putting everything together, we obtain that the total cost T_i, in steps, for phase i is $T_i \leq 3n + 13n + 2n = 18n$. As there is a total of $\log n$ phases, we conclude that the total cost T of the transformation is $T \leq 18n \cdot \log n = O(n \log n)$. □

Finally, Lemmas 8 and 11, and reversibility (Lemma 2) imply that:

Theorem 6. *For any pair of connected shapes S_I and S_F of the same order n, transformation U-Box-Doubling can be used to transform S_I into S_F (and S_F into S_I) in $O(n \log n)$ steps.*

5   Conclusions

In this work, we studied a new linear-strength model of line movements. The nodes can now move in parallel by translating a line of any length by one position in a single time-step. This model, having the model of [DP04, MSS19] as a special case, adopts all its transformability results (including universal transformations). Then, our focus naturally turned to investigating if pushing lines can help achieve a substantial gain in performance (compared to the $\Theta(n^2)$ of those models). Even though it can be immediately observed that there are instances in which this is the case (e.g., initial shapes in which there are many long lines, thus, much initial parallelism to be exploited), it was not obvious that this holds also for the worst case. By identifying the diagonal as a potentially worst-case shape (essentially, because in it any parallelism to be exploited does not come for free), we managed to first develop an $O(n\sqrt{n})$-time transformation for transforming the diagonal into a line, then to improve upon this by two transformations that achieve the same bound while preserving connectivity, and finally to provide an $O(n \log n)$-time transformation (that breaks connectivity). Going one step further, we developed two universal transformations that can transform any pair of connected shapes to each other in time $O(n\sqrt{n})$ and $O(n \log n)$, respectively.

There is a number of interesting problems that are opened by this work. The obvious first target (and apparently intriguing) is to answer whether there is an $o(n \log n)$-time transformation (e.g., linear) or whether there is an $\Omega(n \log n)$-time lower bound matching our best transformations. We suspect the latter, but do not have enough evidence to support or prove it. Moreover, we didn't consider parallel time in this paper. If more than one line can move in parallel in a time-step, then are there variants of our transformations (or alternative ones) that further reduce the running time? In other words, are there parallelisable transformations in this model? In particular, it would be interesting to investigate whether the present model permits an $O(\log n)$ parallel time (universal) transformation, i.e., matching the best transformation in the model of Aloupis et al. [ACD+08]. It would also be worth studying in more depth the case in which connectivity has to be preserved during the transformations. In the relevant literature, a number of alternative types of grids have been considered, like triangular (e.g., in [DDG+14]) and hexagonal (e.g., in [WWA04]), and it would be interesting to investigate how our results translate there. Finally, an immediate next goal is to attempt to develop distributed versions of the transformations provided here.

References

[AAD+06] Angluin, D., Aspnes, J., Diamadi, Z., Fischer, M.J., Peralta, R.: Computation in networks of passively mobile finite-state sensors. Distrib. Comput. **18**(4), 235–253 (2006)

[AAER07] Angluin, D., Aspnes, J., Eisenstat, D., Ruppert, E.: The computational power of population protocols. Distrib. Comput. **20**(4), 279–304 (2007)

[ABD+13] Aloupis, G., et al.: Efficient reconfiguration of lattice-based modular robots. Comput. Geom. **46**(8), 917–928 (2013)

[ACD+08] Aloupis, G., Collette, S., Demaine, E.D., Langerman, S., Sacristán, V., Wuhrer, S.: Reconfiguration of cube-style modular robots using $O(\log n)$ parallel moves. In: Hong, S.-H., Nagamochi, H., Fukunaga, T. (eds.) ISAAC 2008. LNCS, vol. 5369, pp. 342–353. Springer, Heidelberg (2008). https://doi.org/10.1007/978-3-540-92182-0_32

[BDF+19] Becker, A.T., Demaine, E.D., Fekete, S.P., Lonsford, J., Morris-Wright, R.: Particle computation: complexity, algorithms, and logic. Nat. Comput. **18**(1), 181–201 (2019)

[BG15] Bourgeois, J., Goldstein, S.C.: Distributed intelligent MEMS: progresses and perspective. IEEE Syst. J. **9**(3), 1057–1068 (2015)

[BKRT04] Butler, Z., Kotay, K., Rus, D., Tomita, K.: Generic decentralized control for lattice-based self-reconfigurable robots. Int. J. Rob. Res. **23**(9), 919–937 (2004)

[CFPS12] Cieliebak, M., Flocchini, P., Prencipe, G., Santoro, N.: Distributed computing by mobile robots: gathering. SIAM J. Comput. **41**(4), 829–879 (2012)

[CKLWL09] Cornejo, A., Kuhn, F., Ley-Wild, R., Lynch, N.: Keeping mobile robot swarms connected. In: Keidar, I. (ed.) DISC 2009. LNCS, vol. 5805, pp. 496–511. Springer, Heidelberg (2009). https://doi.org/10.1007/978-3-642-04355-0_50

[DDG+14] Derakhshandeh, Z., Dolev, S., Gmyr, R., Richa, A.W., Scheideler, C., Strothmann, T.: Brief announcement: Amoebot-a new model for programmable matter. In: Proceedings of the 26th ACM Symposium on Parallelism in Algorithms and Architectures (SPAA), pp. 220–222. ACM (2014)

[DDG+18] Daymude, J.J., et al.: On the runtime of universal coating for programmable matter. Nat. Comput. **17**(1), 81–96 (2018)

[DDL+09] Douglas, S.M., Dietz, H., Liedl, T., Högberg, B., Graf, F., Shih, W.M.: Self-assembly of DNA into nanoscale three-dimensional shapes. Nature **459**(7245), 414 (2009)

[Dem01] Demaine, E.D.: Playing games with algorithms: algorithmic combinatorial game theory. In: Sgall, J., Pultr, A., Kolman, P. (eds.) MFCS 2001. LNCS, vol. 2136, pp. 18–33. Springer, Heidelberg (2001). https://doi.org/10.1007/3-540-44683-4_3

[DFSY15] Das, S., Flocchini, P., Santoro, N., Yamashita, M.: Forming sequences of geometric patterns with oblivious mobile robots. Distrib. Comput. **28**(2), 131–145 (2015)

[DGMRP06] Défago, X., Gradinariu, M., Messika, S., Raipin-Parvédy, P.: Fault-tolerant and self-stabilizing mobile robots gathering. In: Dolev, S. (ed.) DISC 2006. LNCS, vol. 4167, pp. 46–60. Springer, Heidelberg (2006). https://doi.org/10.1007/11864219_4

[DGR+15] Derakhshandeh, Z., Gmyr, R., Richa, A.W., Scheideler, C., Strothmann, T.: An algorithmic framework for shape formation problems in self-organizing particle systems. In: Proceedings of the Second Annual International Conference on Nanoscale Computing and Communication, p. 21. ACM (2015)

[DGR+16] Derakhshandeh, Z., Gmyr, R., Richa, A.W., Scheideler, C., Strothmann, T.: Universal shape formation for programmable matter. In: Proceedings of the 28th ACM Symposium on Parallelism in Algorithms and Architectures, pp. 289–299. ACM (2016)

[DLFP+18] Di Luna, G.A., Flocchini, P., Prencipe, G., Santoro, N., Viglietta, G.: Line recovery by programmable particles. In: Proceedings of the 19th International Conference on Distributed Computing and Networking, ICDCN 2018, pp. 4:1–4:10. ACM, New York (2018)

[DLFS+19] Di Luna, G.A., Flocchini, P., Santoro, N., Viglietta, G., Yamauchi, Y.: Shape formation by programmable particles. Distrib. Comput. (2019). https://doi.org/10.1007/s00446-019-00350-6

[Dot12] Doty, D.: Theory of algorithmic self-assembly. Commun. ACM **55**, 78–88 (2012)

[DP04] Dumitrescu, A., Pach, J.: Pushing squares around. In: Proceedings of the Twentieth Annual Symposium on Computational Geometry, pp. 116–123. ACM (2004)

[DSY04a] Dumitrescu, A., Suzuki, I., Yamashita, M.: Formations for fast locomotion of metamorphic robotic systems. Int. J. Rob. Res. **23**(6), 583–593 (2004)

[DSY04b] Dumitrescu, A., Suzuki, I., Yamashita, M.: Motion planning for metamorphic systems: feasibility, decidability, and distributed reconfiguration. IEEE Trans. Rob. Autom. **20**(3), 409–418 (2004)

[FPS12] Flocchini, P., Prencipe, G., Santoro, N.: Distributed Computing by Oblivious Mobile Robots. Synthesis Lectures on Distributed Computing Theory, vol. 3(2), pp. 1–185. Morgan & Claypool Publishers, San Rafael (2012)

[FRRS16] Fekete, S., Richa, A.W., Römer, K., Scheideler, C.: Algorithmic foundations of programmable matter (Dagstuhl Seminar 16271). In: Dagstuhl Reports, vol. 6. Schloss Dagstuhl-Leibniz-Zentrum fuer Informatik, (2016). Also in ACM SIGACT News, vol. 48.2, pp. 87–94 (2017)

[GKR10] Gilpin, K., Knaian, A., Rus, D.: Robot pebbles: one centimeter modules for programmable matter through self-disassembly. In: IEEE International Conference on Robotics and Automation (ICRA), pp. 2485–2492. IEEE (2010)

[HD05] Hearn, R.A., Demaine, E.D.: PSPACE-completeness of sliding-block puzzles and other problems through the nondeterministic constraint logic model of computation. Theor. Comput. Sci. **343**(1–2), 72–96 (2005)

[KCL+12] Knaian, A.N., Cheung, K.C., Lobovsky, M.B., Oines, A.J., Schmidt-Neilsen, P., Gershenfeld, N.A.:. The milli-motein: a self-folding chain of programmable matter with a one centimeter module pitch. In: IEEE/RSJ International Conference on Intelligent Robots and Systems, pp. 1447–1453. IEEE (2012)

[KKM10] Kranakis, E., Krizanc, D., Markou, E.: The Mobile Agent Rendezvous Problem in the Ring. Synthesis Lectures on Distributed Computing Theory, vol. 1(1), pp. 1–122. Morgan & Claypool Publishers, San Rafael (2010)

[MS16] Michail, O., Spirakis, P.G.: Simple and efficient local codes for distributed stable network construction. Distrib. Comput. **29**(3), 207–237 (2016)

[MS18] Michail, O., Spirakis, P.G.: Elements of the theory of dynamic networks. Commun. ACM **61**(2), 72–81 (2018)

[MSS19] Michail, O., Skretas, G., Spirakis, P.G.: On the transformation capability of feasible mechanisms for programmable matter. J. Comput. Syst. Sci. **102**, 18–39 (2019)

[NGY00] Nguyen, A., Guibas, L.J., Yim, M.: Controlled module density helps reconfiguration planning. In: Proceedings of 4th International Workshop on Algorithmic Foundations of Robotics, pp. 23–36 (2000)

[RCN14] Rubenstein, M., Cornejo, A., Nagpal, R.: Programmable self-assembly in a thousand-robot swarm. Science **345**(6198), 795–799 (2014)

[Rot06]   Rothemund, P.W.: Folding DNA to create nanoscale shapes and patterns. Nature **440**(7082), 297–302 (2006)

[RW00]   Rothemund, P.W.K., Winfree, E.: The program-size complexity of self-assembled squares. In: Proceedings of the 32nd Annual ACM Symposium on Theory of Computing (STOC), pp. 459–468. ACM (2000)

[SMO+18]   Shibata, M., Mega, T., Ooshita, F., Kakugawa, H., Masuzawa, T.: Uniform deployment of mobile agents in asynchronous rings. J. Parallel Distrib. Comput. **119**, 92–106 (2018)

[WCG+13]   Woods, D., Chen, H.-L., Goodfriend, S., Dabby, N., Winfree, E., Yin, P.: Active self-assembly of algorithmic shapes and patterns in polylogarithmic time. In: Proceedings of the 4th Conference on Innovations in Theoretical Computer Science, pp. 353–354. ACM (2013)

[Win98]   Winfree, E.: Algorithmic self-assembly of DNA. Ph.D thesis, California Institute of Technology, June 1998

[WWA04]   Walter, J.E., Welch, J.L., Amato, N.M.: Distributed reconfiguration of metamorphic robot chains. Distrib. Comput. **17**(2), 171–189 (2004)

[YS10]   Yamashita, M., Suzuki, I.: Characterizing geometric patterns formable by oblivious anonymous mobile robots. Theor. Comput. Sci. **411**(26–28), 2433–2453 (2010)

[YSS+07]   Yim, M., et al.: Modular self-reconfigurable robot systems [grand challenges of robotics]. IEEE Rob. Autom. Mag. **14**(1), 43–52 (2007)

[YUY16]   Yamauchi, Y., Uehara, T., Yamashita, M.: Brief announcement: pattern formation problem for synchronous mobile robots in the three dimensional Euclidean space. In: Proceedings of the 2016 ACM Symposium on Principles of Distributed Computing, pp. 447–449. ACM (2016)

Foundations

Existence of Connected Intersection-Free Subgraphs in Graphs with Redundancy and Coexistence Property

Lucas Böltz[(✉)] and Hannes Frey

University of Koblenz-Landau, 56070 Koblenz, Germany
{boeltz,frey}@uni-koblenz.de

Abstract. Constructing connected intersection-free graphs is a relevant building block for local algorithmic solutions for data communication, task coordination and network maintenance in wireless sensor networks, sensor-actuator networks and distributed robotics. One way to construct such graph is to remove edges from the given network graph. Though an intersection-free graph can always be constructed that way, assuring connectivity at the same time is not possible for arbitrary graphs. It requires the underlying graph to have a supporting structure. In search of algorithms for constructing intersection-free subgraphs in wireless networks redundancy and coexistence have been identified as such properties. Practical evidence shows that these properties may hold with high probability in many practical wireless network graphs. In this work we study graphs obeying redundancy and coexistence. We demonstrate that so far existing solutions cannot guarantee connectivity of the constructed intersection-free subgraphs. Thus, one fundamental question stood open so far, if graphs obeying redundancy and coexistence property always contain a connected intersection-free subgraph at all. The contribution of this work is in answering this question in the positive.

Keywords: Redundancy property · Coexistence property · Connected subgraph · Intersection-free subgraph

1 Introduction

1.1 Connected and Intersection-Free Subgraphs

Constructing *intersection-free* and *connected* graphs based on a given connected network graph is a key building block for many local algorithmic solutions in the context of wireless networks including sensor networks, sensor-actuator networks, and autonomous robots. Here connected means that for each vertex at least one path has to exist in the constructed graph. Intersection-free means that the graph is given with its vertices embedded on the euclidean plane, it's edges represented

This work is funded in part by the DFG grant FR 2978/1-2.

F. Dressler and C. Scheideler (Eds.): ALGOSENSORS 2019, LNCS 11931, pp. 63–78, 2019.
https://doi.org/10.1007/978-3-030-34405-4_4

by a line drawing (typically a straight line) and none of it's edges are allowed to intersect with another one. Two edges are said to *intersect* if they have a point in common that is not an endpoint of both edges.

The network graph can be given directly with it's vertices representing the devices (typically the device positions) and devices being connected if they can communicate. Alternatively, we are given a virtual overlay graph drawing where none of the vertices and edges are direct physical network devices and connections. Such virtual overlay vertices and edges then have representatives/responsibilities among the physical devices. In all cases the task is to find connected intersection-free graph drawings.

The most prominent local algorithms resorting to intersection-free drawings are all sorts of local data communication[1] including geographic unicast routing (Karp and Kung (2000); Bose et al. (2001)), multicast (Sanchez et al. (2007); Frey et al. (2008)), geocast (Stojmenovic (2004)), anycast (Mitton et al. (2009)), mobicast (Huang et al. (2004)), and broadcast (Seddigh et al. (2001); Stojmenovic et al. (2002)). Other algorithmic solutions include void and boundary detection (Fang et al. (2004)), distributed data storage (Ratnasamy et al. (2003); Deng and Stojmenovic (2009)), tracking of mobile objects (Tsai et al. (2007)), localized address autoconfiguration (Li et al. (2010)), or coordination of mobile sensors (Tan (2008)).

Many approaches to construct connected intersection-free subgraphs in the context of wireless networks are known. The majority of the approaches require the network graph to be given as a *unit disk graph*. In such graph two vertices are connected iff their euclidean distance is less or equal than a prescribed unit disk radius. Well known representatives working on unit disk graphs include Gabriel graph (Bose et al. (2001)), relative neighborhood graph (Karp and Kung (2000)), Delaunay triangulation based approaches (Gao et al. (2001)); Li et al. (2002)) and approaches based on geographic clustering (Frey (2005)).

The search for solutions beyond the simplified unit disk graph model yielded the concept of *quasi unit disk graphs* defined by Barrière et al. (2003). In such graph two vertices are connected if their distance is less or equal than a minimum transmission radius r and they are not connected if their distance is more than a maximum transmission radius R. In between both radii vertices are allowed to be connected but need not to be. In the work of Barrière et al. (2003); Kuhn et al. (2003) a concept to add virtual links to such quasi unit disk graphs is described and analyzed. Based on that extended graph an intersection-free connected drawing can always be found, provided the relation between maximum and minimum radius is at most $\sqrt{2}$.

With the introduction of quasi unit disk graphs the gap between theoretical algorithmic research and its practical applicability in real wireless networks was significantly reduced. However, it still remains of particular importance to further narrow and finally close that gap, for example by getting rid of circle geometry in the graph requirements. The principle idea is to find structural properties

---

[1] Many more paper can be listed here and the following paragraph for most of the discussed problems and approaches. To avoid clutter we pick only one or two representative references for each specific algorithm class.

inherent or at least highly probable in realistic wireless networks which can be exploited algorithmically with provable guarantees.

1.2 Redundancy and Coexistence Property

Gao et al. (2001) observed and proved (Lemma 4.1 in that paper) for unit disk graphs that for any two intersecting edges at least one edge end point has to be connected to all other ones. We term this as *redundancy* property in the following. Frey and Görgen (2005) observed an proved (Theorem 1 in that paper) that this property is inherited when constructing an overlay graph F of a given graph G based on a hexagon tessellation of the plane. If the underlying graph G is unit disk then the redundancy property is as well satisfied for the so constructed overlay graph F. This was as well observed by Philip et al. (2006)[2] for the same principle applied on square tessellations (Lemma 2 and the discussion thereafter in that paper), and proved there by referring to the proof in the report by Philip (2005).

Philip et al. (2006) studied for the first time if a connected undirected graph satisfying redundancy property can be transformed into a connected intersection-free subgraph by just removing edges. For the algorithm defined there (Algorithms 1 and 2) the authors observed that the resulting graphs are always intersection-free but sometimes not connected. This is not a peculiarity of that algorithm as it was later theoretically substantiated by Frey and Simplot-Ryl (2007) showing with a simple example (Fig. 5(b) in that paper) that in general there are connected graphs which satisfy redundancy property but which can not be transformed into a connected intersection-free subgraph by just removing edges. Thus, the question remained open, which additional structural graph property besides redundancy assures that unit disk graphs can be transformed into such subgraphs.

The problem then seemed to be solved theoretically by Mathews and Frey (2012) introducing the LLRAP algorithm (see Theorem 1 there). The assumptions made for LLRAP are graphs satisfying redundancy and one additional property termed *coexistence* there. The latter assures whenever three vertices are forming a connected triangle, all vertices inside the triangle will be connected to the triangle vertices. It is easy to see as written in Lemma 1 of the work introducing LLRAP that this is an additional structural property inherent to unit disk graphs.

1.3 Empirical Evidence for Log-Normal Shadowing

LLRAP and variants thereof were subject to different simulations studies based on *log-normal shadowing* (LNS) modeled graphs. The LNS model is a well established realistic physical layer model where a communication link exists between two vertices whenever a stochastically described distance dependent received signal strength value is above a given threshold.

---

[2] the term redundancy property was used there for the first time.

The LLRAP precursor CLDR described by Mathews and Frey (2011) removes links only if it is safe to do so, such that subgraph connectivity is assured. This is at the expense that possible intersections have to be tolerated in the solution. However, in simulation studies under log-normal shadowing performed in that work, only a small fraction of simulated graphs were not intersection-free. A similar simulation study repeated for LLRAP by Mathews and Frey (2012) even showed in the log-normal shadowing simulation settings used there that LLRAP produced intersection-free subgraphs in all cases. A more extensive simulation study was delivered at a later stage by Mathews [2012]. Here LLRAP was applied on overlay graphs resulting from geographical clustering. In the simulation studies based on log-normal shadowing modeled graphs the resulting subgraphs are almost always connected and intersection-free.

Though redundancy and coexistence are not assured in graphs pertaining to the log-normal shadowing model, the promising simulation results on LLRAP and its variants under log-normal shadowing motivated Neumann et al. (2016) to further study by simulation, how far redundancy and coexistence can be assumed for networks pertaining to that model. For the considered simulation settings the network graph satisfies coexistence and redundancy with a high relative frequency.

In conclusion, all empirical studies so far suggest that designing algorithms for graphs with redundancy and coexistence property is a promising link to narrow the gap between theoretic algorithmic research on constructing intersection-free subgraphs and applicability of such algorithms in realistic wireless multihop networks.

1.4 Contribution and Outline of This Work

The contribution of this work is two fold. We study the correctness proof of LLRAP and show that within the proof one additional assumption on the underlying network graph was implicitly made which assures that the intersection-free result of LLRAP is always connected. We construct an example with a few vertices dropping that implicit assumption. With that example we observe that connectivity depends on the order in which LLRAP is processing the links. Though the simple example could be resolved locally, we show a way to construct arbitrary large so called cyclic redundant paths (Theorem 1) which finally leads to the question if redundancy and coexistence of connected graphs is sufficient to assure that an intersection-free connected subgraph has to exist at all. Answering that question is the second contribution of this paper. First of all we show by an example that the class of unit disk graphs and the class of graphs satisfying redundancy and coexistence are not isomorphic, i.e. that we are facing a problem at all. We derive necessary conditions as building blocks to support a recursive construction of a connected intersection-free subgraph. This is then exploited in our main theorem (Theorem 2) which shows by an induction argument that such subgraph always exists.

The remainder of this paper is structured as follows. In the next section we define the terms and notation used throughout the paper. Then Sect. 3 is dedicated to analysis of LLRAP correctness. We derive the term of cyclic redundancy which leads to the general question on existence of intersection-free connected subgraphs. Existence is then affirmed in Sect. 4 by an induction proof. Finally, in Sect. 5 we conclude the relevance of our findings and point towards two main next research directions.

2   Terms and Notations

We consider *undirected network graphs* $G = (V, E)$ with a *finite vertex set V* and an *edge set E* of undirected pairs of vertices. The vertices are located in 2D euclidean space. We use u to refer to both, the address of that vertex and its position. We use the short hand notation uv to refer to edge $\{u, v\}$. Notation uv also stands for the straight line segment connecting vertices u and v. We use notation $u \in G$ and $uv \in G$ as synonyms for $u \in V$ and $uv \in E$. Removing vertices or edges from a graph G will be expressed by short hand notation $G \backslash u$ and $G \backslash uv$, respectively.

A *path* from u to v in G is denoted by $p(u; v)$. We denote the *concatenation* of two paths $p(u; v)$ and $p(v; w)$ by $p(u; v) + p(v; w)$. We say two *vertices are connected* in a graph if there exists at least one path between these two vertices in that graph. We say a *graph is connected* if each pair of its vertices are connected.

In a *unit disk graph* (UDG) two vertices are connected by an edge iff their euclidean distance is less or equal than a given unit disk radius. We say two edges uv and wx *intersect* if they have a point in common which is not an end vertex of both edges.

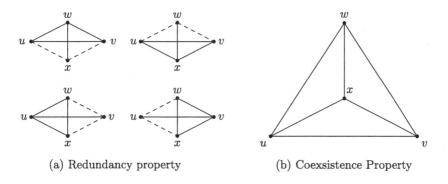

(a) Redundancy property   (b) Coexsistence Property

Fig. 1. Redundancy and Coexsistence property

A graph satisfies *redundancy property* if for all intersecting edges uv and wx at least one of the vertices $\{u, v, w, x\}$ is a neighbor of all other vertices in that set (see Fig. 1(a) where the dashed edges may exist or not). Three vertices of a graph are forming a triangle $\Delta(u, v, w)$ if all edges uv, vw and wu exist in that graph. A graph satisfies *coexistence property* if for each vertex x located in a triangle $\Delta(u, v, w)$ the edges ux, vx and wx exist (see Fig. 1(b)). A graph that satisfies both properties is called a *redundancy coexistence graph* (RCG).

Observe that the graph classes UDG and RCG are not *isomorphous* in the sense that for every graph from RCG vertices can be relocated such that redundancy and coexistence property are retained and all edges satisfy the unit disk graph property in addition. If that would be the case, obviously each connected graph from RCG could be transformed into a connected graph in UDG where existence of connected intersection-free subgraphs is well known. Retransformation of any such subgraph then yields a solution. The following example shows that it is not that simple, i.e. there are graphs in RCG which can not be transformed into graphs in UDG in the sense as mentioned before.

Corollary 1 (Quadrilateral property of UDGs). *Let u, v, w, x be vertices connected in a UDG forming a quadrilateral, without a triangle formed by 3 of the 4 vertices (see Fig. 2(a)). Each vertex z located inside the quadrilateral is connected by an edge to at least two of the vertices of the quadrilateral.*

Proof. Consider the quadrilateral formed by the edges uv, vw, wx and xu. Since uv and vw exist, the vertices u and w have to be located inside the unit disk around v. We term the vertex triple (u, v, w) a virtual triangle Δuvw (we term it virtual since the edge uw does not exist by assumption). The virtual triangle Δuvw is completely contained in the unit disk around v. The same holds for the virtual triangles Δvwx in the unit disk around w, Δwxu in the unit disk around x and Δxuv in the unit disk around u. Since each vertex z inside the quadrilateral is contained in at least two virtual triangles, it is also contained in at least two unit disks and therefore connected by an edge with at least two vertices of the quadrilateral.   □

The example in Fig. 2(b) shows a valid RCG with a quadrilateral and an additional triangle with one vertex of the quadrilateral and one located inside and the other one outside the quadrilateral, i.e. the quadrilateral property does not hold for the class of RCGs in general. Thus, the class of UDGs and RCGs are not isomorphous. However, since every UDG satisfies redundancy and coexistence as discussed, the class of UDGs is contained within the class of RCGs.

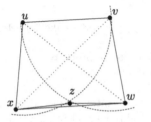

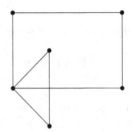

(a) quadrilateral property of UDGs   (b) An RCG which is no UDG

Fig. 2. Difference between RCG and UDG

3   LLRAP and Connectivity

The *Localized Link Removal and Addition based Planarization algorithm (LLRAP)* of Mathews and Frey (2012) is a localized topology control algorithm based on link removal for removing all intersections from an RCG. The algorithm is divided into two phases, the *local crosslink detection and removal* phase and the *local link addition* phase. In the first phase, all pairs of intersecting edges are detected in the original network graph G and removed according to the following rule. Each edge uv, which is intersected by an edge wx in G is deleted if either the path $p(u; w; v)$ containing the edges uw and wv or the path $p(u; x; v)$ containing the edges ux and xv exists in G. In the subsequent addition phase an edge uv is added to the graph again, if it does not intersect with an edge of the so far constructed graph G'. This leads to the graph $G'' = G' + uv$ in that step. Since all intersections are evaluated and removed in the removal phase and edges added in the addition phase only if they don't intersect with the intermediate result, the final resulting graph is obviously an intersection-free drawing. However, in the addition phase there is no specific order for adding edges. Therefore the case that an added edge blocks all other edges required to connect two disjoint components may occur (see Fig. 3). A first approach to solve this problem might be that we require for an added edge that it has to connect two disjoint components in the so far constructed graph. This might be a plausible approach, because adding an edge that connects two vertices of the same component will only block other possible edges which could be re-added to the graph, but is no improvement on the way to construct a connected graph. Unfortunately, there are still graphs were LLRAP does not work, even if we add the condition that an edge can only be added if it connects two unconnected components of the graph (see Fig. 3). Therefore there is no easy way to determine the order in which the edges should be re-added to the graph. However, this order is determining whether the algorithm finds a solution or not.

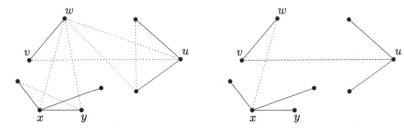

(a) Dotted edges are removed in the re-   (b) If the edge uv is added wx is
moval phase of LLRAP   blocked

Fig. 3. Example for a graph where LLRAP could fail

In this example the reason why the graph gets disconnected is that an edge wx is removed because there is an alternative path $p(w; y; x)$ containing the edges

wy and xy. However, the edge wy is also removed since there is an alternative path $p(w; x; y)$ containing the edges wx and xy. So the edges wx and wy are part of the alternative path for each other. However, such a dependence can also contain more than two edges and therefore arbitrary long cycles can occur. To show this we need to introduce the following notation. Let uv and wx be intersecting edges in an RCG and let v be the vertex that is connected by an edge to both end vertices of the intersecting edge wx. Then vw and vx are called *redundancy edges* for uv. If there is a sequence S of edges $e_1, \ldots, e_k$ such that e_i is a redundancy edge for e_{i-1} for $i \in 2, \ldots, k$ we call the sequence S *redundancy sequence*. If for a sequence e_1 is redundancy edge for e_k we call the sequence a *redundancy cycle* and its edges *cyclic redundant edges*. We define the distance $|uv, wx|$ between two edges uv and wx as the length of the shortest path connecting a vertex of the edge uv with a vertex of the edge wx.

Theorem 1 (Arbitrarily long redundancy cycles). *For each $n \in \mathbb{N}$, one can always construct a redundancy cycle R, such that for each edge $u_0 v_0 \in R$ holds, that another edge $u_i v_i \in R$ exists with $|u_0 v_0, u_i v_i| > n$.*

Proof. A graph containing an arbitrarily large redundancy cycle can be constructed by using the following scheme: Set two vertices v_0 and v_1 and the edge $v_0 v_1$. After that, add node v_2 and the edges $v_0 v_2$ and $v_1 v_2$ to the graph (see Fig. 4).

Then repeat the following for each $3 \leq i \leq 2m + 2, m \in \mathbb{N}$: Set v_i and x_i, such that $v_i x_i$ only intersects $v_{i-3} v_{i-1}$ and $v_{i-2} v_{i-1}$ and $\forall\, 2 \leq j \leq i$ holds that $\Delta v_{j-2} v_{j-1} v_j = \emptyset$ and $v_{i-1} v_i$ does not intersect $v_{j-2} v_{j-1}$. Then add the edge $v_{i-1} x_i$, to let G satisfy redundancy property (see Fig. 4(a)). It also holds that, $v_{2m} = v_0$, $v_{2m+1} = v_1$ and $v_{2m+2} = v_2$.

Each graph which is constructed this way satisfies redundancy property and

$$R = \{\{v_0, \ldots, v_{2m-1}\}, \{(v_0, v_1), (v_1, v_2), \ldots, (v_{2m-2}, v_{2m-1}), (v_{2m-1}, v_0)\}\}$$

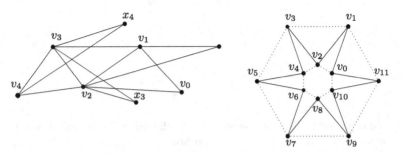

(a) Part of the redundancy cycle used in the proof of Theorem 1

(b) Resulting redundancy cycle without the additional intersecting edges

Fig. 4. The scheme to construct arbitrary long redundancy cycles

is a redundancy cycle with $|E_R| = 2m$. All edges (v_i, v_{i+2}) are not part of R. These edges form two envelopes: An outer envelope and an inner envelope (see Fig. 4(b)).

Due to the fact, that all v_i, v_{i+1}, v_{i+2} form triangles, edges (v_i, v_{i+2}) and (v_{i+1}, v_{i+3}) cannot be part of the same envelope. Hence, all of the edges (v_i, v_{i+2}) with even indices form one envelope, whereas all of these edges with odd indices form the other one. It follows, that each envelope contains m edges. It is also clear, that the shortest path between two cyclic redundant edges does not contain any other cyclic redundant edge, because every cyclic redundant edge has a vertex on each envelope. Hence, the maximum distance between two cyclic redundant edges is $\lfloor \frac{m}{2} \rfloor$.

Let a graph be constructed as described above with $m \geq 2(n+1)$. Then, for each edge $(v_i, v_{i+1}) \in R$ holds, that there exists another edge $(u_j, v_{j+1}) \in R, 0 \leq i, j \leq m - 1$ with $|(v_i, v_{i+1}), (v_j, v_{j+1})| > n$. □

The lemma shows that it is not possible to find out with local information if two edges are part of the same redundancy cycle. If such a redundancy cycle would not occur the LLRAP algorithm would work correctly, since for each deleted edge an alternative path would still exists in the graph.

Another question is now, is it possible that two cycles are intersecting and form and even bigger cycle that can never be broken? The answer is no, as we will state in the following section.

4   Existence of a Solution

To find a connected intersection-free drawing of an RCG we need to show three properties first. These are then used to show the main theorem of this paper.

Lemma 1 (Robustness against vertex deletion). *Deleting a vertex v in an RCG yields again an RCG $G' = G \backslash v$*

Proof. For the redundancy property assume there is an intersection of the edges uv and wx in G' but no of the four vertices u, v, w, x is connected by an edge to the other three. However, in G there has to be a vertex that is connected with all other three vertices. Assume wlog. this vertex is v and uv is not contained in G'. Then u or v are not contained in G' which is obviously a contradiction.

For the coexistence property assume that there is a triangle Δuvw and a vertex x in this triangle, but x is not connected to all three vertices of the triangle Δuvw. Let wlog. xw be the missing edge. Since the edge xw has to exist in G one of the vertices x or w have to be missing in G', a contradiction.

Therefore deleting a vertex from an RCG yields again an RCG. □

Lemma 2 (Clique property). *All vertices that are located inside a triangle form a clique.*

Proof. If there are no vertices inside a triangle Δuvw the statement is obviously true. So assume by induction that it holds for n vertices located in the triangle. Adding another vertex x yields by coexistence the existence of the edges ux vx and wx and therefore the triangles Δuvx, Δuwx and Δwvx have to exist.

Since all n vertices in the triangle Δuvw lie in (at least) one of the triangles Δuvx, Δuwx or Δwvx an edge from x to all of this vertices exists and these n vertices together with x as well as u, v and w form again a clique.   □

Lemma 3 (Reconnection property). *Let G be an RCG. Let F be a connected intersection-free subgraph of $G\backslash v$. Let uv be an edge in G which intersects with some edges w_ix_i of F. Consider for all w_ix_i,*

(1) w_1x_1 is closest to v and one of the edges vw_1 or vx_1 exist: then F can be transformed into a connected intersection-free subgraph F' with vertices of G that contains all edges of F and a path $p(v; w_1)$ or $p(v; x_1)$ that does not intersect with an edge of F and not with uv (see Fig. 5(a)).

(2) w_1x_1 is closest to u and one of the edges uw_1 or ux_1 exist: then F can be transformed into a connected intersection-free subgraph F' with vertices of $G\backslash v$ that contains all edges of F and a path $p(u; w_1)$ or $p(u; x_1)$ that does not intersect with an edge of F and not with uv (see Fig. 5(b) with one of the paths $p(u; w_1)$ or $p(u; x_1)$).

(3) w_1x_1 is closest to u and both edges uw_1 and ux_1 exist: then F can be transformed into a connected intersection-free subgraph F' with nodes of $G\backslash v$ which does not contain the edge w_1x_1 (see Fig. 5(b)).

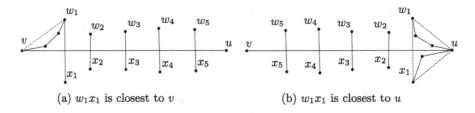

(a) w_1x_1 is closest to v (b) w_1x_1 is closest to u

Fig. 5. The situations of Lemma 3

Proof. Let the intersection point of uv and w_1x_1 be p (p is not a vertex).

(1) and (2): We show the case (1). The proof for case (2) is analogous. Assume that the edge w_1x_1 is the edge of F with intersection point closest to v and the edge vw_1 exists. By redundancy property at least one of the edges vx_1 or uw_1 has to exist also. Wlog. this is uw_1 and therefore the triangle Δvw_1u exists. Then regard the vertices that form the convex hull of the vertices inside triangle Δvpw_1 This leads to the situation that the triangle is divided in two parts, one containing all vertices in the triangle and another one that is empty. By Lemma 2 all vertices in the triangle Δvw_1u (and therefore also in Δvpw_1) are connected and therefore the path $p(v; w_1)$ on the boundary of the convex hull of the vertices inside the triangle Δvpw_1 exists in G.

This path cannot be intersected by another edge of F since otherwise the edge uv has to be intersected by another edge of F which has its intersection point closer to v or the edge w_1x_1 has to be intersected, which is both a contradiction. Therefore $F' = F + p(v; w_1)$ satisfies the condition.

(3): Now the triangle $\Delta(uw_1x_1)$ has to exist. The triangle Δuw_1x_1 can be split into two triangles Δupw_1 and Δupx_1. Then regard the vertices that form the convex hull of the vertices inside the triangle Δupw_1 and as well the vertices that form the convex hull of the vertices inside triangle Δupx_1. This leads to the situation that the triangles are divided in two parts, one containing all vertices in the triangle and another one that is empty. By Lemma 2 all vertices in the triangle Δuw_1x_1 (and therefore also in Δupw_1 and Δupx_1) are connected and therefore the path $p(u; w_1)$ on the boundary of the convex hull of the vertices inside the triangle Δupw_1 and the path $p(u; x_1)$ on the boundary of the convex hull of the vertices inside the triangle Δupx_1 exists in G.

Both paths cannot be intersected by another edge of F since otherwise the edge uv has to be intersected by another edge of F with intersection point closer to u or the edge w_1x_1 has to be intersected, which is both a contradiction. Therefore $F' = F \backslash w_1x_1 + p(u; w_1) + p(u; x_1)$ satisfies the condition.

Theorem 2 (Existence of connected intersection-free subgraphs). *For each connected RCG G there exists a spanning subgraph G' such that G' is connected and an intersection-free drawing.*

Proof. To find a connected intersection-free drawing of the given RCG G we follow a recursive approach by adding vertices to an empty initial solution and restructuring the existing graph with Lemma 3 whenever this is necessary.

To show correctness of that approach we apply an induction argument. Starting with an single-vertex graph it is clear that the properties are satisfied. We assume as induction hypothesis that every RCG with at most n vertices contains a intersection-free connected spanning subgraph G'. So we take for an arbitrary connected RCG with $n + 1$ vertices a spanning tree (not necessary an intersection-free drawing) and delete a leaf v of this tree, therefore $G \backslash v$ is still connected.

The graph $G \backslash v$ is by Lemma 1 still an RCG and by induction hypothesis there exists a connected intersection-free drawing F containing all vertices and a subset of edges of $G \backslash v$. If there is an edge that connects v to a vertex of $G \backslash v$ without intersecting an edge of F then we can add this edge and we are done.

So assume that all edges incident with v are intersected by an edge of F. Pick one edge uv and the first intersecting edge $wx \in F$, that is the edge that has its intersection point p closest to v (see Fig. 6). By redundancy property one of the four vertices u, v, w, x has to be connected by an edge to all others. If this vertex is not u then at least one of the edges vw or vx has to exist, say wlog. vw. By Lemma 3(1) a path $p(v; w)$ in the convex hull of the triangle Δvpw can be found and this path together with the edges of F forms an intersection-free drawing containing all vertices of G (see Fig. 6(a)). Other edges intersecting with uv can be ignored since they can not enter the triangle Δvpw.

Thus, we can assume that only the edges uw and ux exist. If there is no other edge of F intersecting with uv or for all other intersecting edges, u is connected by an edge to both end vertices of the intersecting edges, Lemma 3(3) can be applied multiple times and uv can be added to F. Therefore it can be assumed that there is an intersecting edge w_1x_1 where u is not connected by an edge with both end vertices of this edge.

Now we regard the edge $w_1x_1 \in F$, intersecting with uv, with intersection point closest to u, where u is not connected by an edge to both end vertices of the intersecting edge (see Fig. 6(b)). For all previous intersections we apply Lemma 3(3). Now we have to distinguish two cases. In the first case v is connected by an edge with both end vertices of w_1x_1. If w or x are inside the triangle Δw_1x_1v there has to exist one of the edges vw or vx by coexistence property in contradiction to the assumption. Otherwise the edges w_1v and wu as well as x_1v and xu are intersecting. Then by redundancy property either one of the edges vw or vx has to exist or both of the edges w_1u and x_1u. This is also a contradiction to the assumption (see Fig. 6(b)).

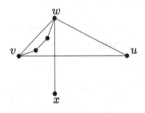
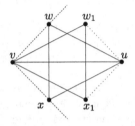

(a) The vertex v can be added to $G \setminus v$ by an path $p(v; w)$

(b) u is connected by an edge with w and x as well as v with w_1 and x_1

Fig. 6. The easy cases when u or v are connected to the intersecting edges

Thus, the only remaining case is that neither u nor v are connected by an edge with w_1 and x_1 (see Fig. 7). Then w_1 or x_1 have to be connected by an edge with u and v, say w_1. Since we took the first (remaining) intersecting edge starting from u with intersection point p_1, by Lemma 3(2) we can find a path $p(u; w_1)$ in the convex hull of the triangle Δup_1w_1 that is not intersected by an edge of F. However, it is not sure that such a path can also be constructed in the triangle Δw_1p_1v since there can be intersecting edges of F.

Now w_1 can be considered as the vertex u and the same procedure can be started according to the edge vw_1, while u is renamed in w_0. Regard the sequence S of edges vw_n which are constructed in this way. Since there are only a finite number of vertices and therefore also edges in G this procedure terminates at one point if there does not occur a cycle with $w_r = w_s$ for some $r \neq s$. So it is enough to show that such a cycle can not exist. If there was an edge vw_k that does not intersect with wx but all previous edges of the sequence did, then w or

x lie in the triangle $\Delta v w_k w_{k-1}$ and therefore by coexistence property the edge vw or vx would exist in contrast to the assumption (see Fig. 7(a)).

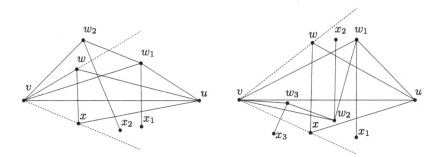

(a) Vertex w is located inside a triangle   (b) Edge wx is not the first intersecting edge with vw_2 starting in v

Fig. 7. Two situations of sequences of edges vw_k

Now assume an edge $w_k x_k \in F$ would intersect with vw_{k-1} and the intersection point p_k is located between v and the intersection point of the edges vw_{k-1} and wx, p_{k-1}. Then one of the vertices w_k or x_k, say w_k, has to be located in the triangle Δvpp_{k-1}, because otherwise the edge wx would be intersected or there would be an intersection point on the edge uv between v and p which is both a contradiction. Then w_k is also located in a triangle $\Delta v w_{j-1} w_j$ with $j < k$ and therefore an edge between v and w_k has to exist by coexistence property, in contradiction to the assumption that such an edge does not exist (see Fig. 7(b)). This means that all edges of the sequence S have to intersect with the edge wx and therefore the vertex that forms an edge with v has to be located in the cone C_1 formed by v, w and x, but outside the (virtual) triangle Δvwx.

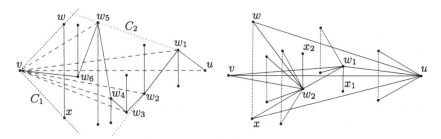

(a) Sequence of edges vw_k and cones   (b) Edge vw_2 can be added after re-
C_1 and C_2 (where w_r is w_1)   structuring the graph with Lemma 3

Fig. 8. Possible sequences of edges vw_k to illustrate the termination

If there would be an edge $w_t x_t \in F$ such that $w_t = w_r$ for $r < t$ then x_t has to be located outside the cone C_2 that contains w_r and all edges $w_s x_s \in F$ with $r < s < t$. Since vw_{t-1} is located inside C_2, $w_t x_t$ can not intersect with vw_{t-1} if x_t is located outside C_2, a contradiction (see Fig. 8(a)).

That means the process terminates at some time (see Fig. 8(b)), so the proof follows by induction.   □

5   Conclusion

We studied graphs obeying the redundancy and coexistence property and answered a so far open question that connected graphs obeying these two properties always contain a connected intersection-free subgraph. In proving this we also derived additional structural properties resulting from redundancy and coexistence. Moreover, we have demonstrated that cyclic redundancy which is possible in such graphs is the reason why so far existing solutions can not guarantee connectivity and intersection-free sub graph at the same time.

Our ongoing research is at two frontiers. (1) The proof of Theorem 2 for showing existence of an intersection-free connected subgraph also suggests how such a subgraph can be constructed recursively (just following the inductive construction). However, this is not a local solution. The goal of our research here is to find a local algorithm which is provably correct under redundancy and coexistence and which has low error rate in case these properties hold only with high probability. (2) We continue on substantiating that redundancy and coexistence describe a graph class way beyond the simplified unit disk assumption, also showing when and when not these properties can be assumed to hold very likely in practice. To show this we are conducting ongoing simulation studies and theoretical investigations based on stochastic point process theory.

References

Barrière, L., Fraigniaud, P., Narayanan, L., Opatrny, J.: Robust position-based routing in wireless ad hoc networks with irregular transmission ranges. Wireless Commun. Mob. Comput. **3**(2), 141–153 (2003)

Bose, P., Morin, P., Stojmenović, I., Urrutia, J.: Routing with guaranteed delivery in ad hoc wireless networks. Wireless Netw. **7**(6), 609–616 (2001)

Deng, Y., Stojmenovic, I.: Partial delaunay triangulations based data-centric storage and routing with guaranteed delivery in wireless ad hoc and sensor networks. In: 2009 Mexican International Conference on Computer Science, pp. 24–32 (2009)

Fang, Q., Gao, J., Guibas, L.J.: Locating and bypassing routing holes in sensor networks. In: IEEE INFOCOM 2004, vol. 4, pp. 2458–2468, March 2004

Frey, H.: Geographical cluster based multihop ad hoc network routing with guaranteed delivery. In: Proceedings of the 2nd IEEE International Conference on Mobile Adhoc and Sensor Systems (MASS), pp. 510–519. IEEE, November 2005

Frey, H., Görgen, D.: Planar graph routing on geographical clusters. Ad Hoc Netw. **3**(5), 560–574 (2005)

Frey, H., Simplot-Ryl, D.: Localized topology control algorithms for ad hoc and sensor networks. In: Nayak, A., Stojmenovic, I. (eds.) Handbook of Applied Algorithms, pp. 439–464. Wiley (2007)

Frey, H., Ingelrest, F., Simplot-Ryl, D.: Localized minimum spanning tree based multicast routing with energy-efficient guaranteed delivery in ad hoc and sensor networks. In: 2008 International Symposium on a World of Wireless, Mobile and Multimedia Networks, pp. 1–8, June 2008

Gao, J., Guibas, L.J., Hershberger, J., Zhang, L., Zhu, A.: Geometric spanner for routing in mobile networks. In: Proceedings of the 2nd ACM International Symposium on Mobile Ad hoc Networking & Computing - MobiHoc 2001 (2001)

Huang, Q., Lu, C., Roman, G.C.: Reliable mobicast via face-aware routing. In: IEEE INFOCOM 2004, vol. 3, pp. 2108–2118, March 2004

Karp, B., Kung, H.T.: GPSR: greedy perimeter stateless routing for wireless networks. In: Proceedings of the 6th Annual International Conference on Mobile Computing and Networking, pp. 243–254 (2000)

Kuhn, F., Wattenhofer, R., Zollinger, A.: Ad-hoc networks beyond unit disk graphs. In: Proceedings of the 2003 Joint Workshop on Foundations of Mobile Computing, DIALM-POMC 2003, pp. 69–78. ACM (2003)

Li, X.-Y., Calinescu, G., Wan, P.-J.: Distributed construction of a planar spanner and routing for ad hoc wireless networks. In: Proceedings of the 21st Annual Joint Conference of the IEEE Computer and Communications Society, INFOCOM 2002, vol. 3, pp. 1268–1277. IEEE Computer Society (2002)

Li, X., Deng, Y., Narasimhan, V., Nayak, A., Stojmenovic, I.: Localized address auto-configuration in wireless ad hoc networks. In: 2010 International Conference on Wireless Communications Signal Processing (WCSP), pp. 1–6 (2010)

Mathews, E.: Planarization of geographic cluster-based overlay graphs in realistic wireless networks. In: 2012 Ninth International Conference on Information Technology - New Generations, pp. 95–101, April 2012

Mathews, E., Frey, H.: A localized planarization algorithm for realistic wireless networks. In: Proceedings of the 11th IEEE International Symposium on a World of Wireless, Mobile and Multimedia Networks, WoWMoM (2011)

Mathews, E., Frey, H.: A localized link removal and addition based planarization algorithm. In: Proceedings of the 13th International Conference on Distributed Computing and Networking (ICDCN), pp. 337–350 (2012)

Mitton, N., Simplot-Ryl, D., Stojmenovic, I.: Guaranteed delivery for geographical anycasting in wireless multi-sink sensor and sensor-actor networks. IEEE INFOCOM 2009, 2691–2695 (2009)

Neumann, F., Estevao, D.V., Ockenfeld, F., Radak, J., Frey, H.: Short paper: structural network properties for local planarization of wireless sensor networks. In: Proceedings of the 15th International Conference on Ad-Hoc Networks and Wireless, ADHOC-NOW 2016, vol. 9724, pp. 229–233 (2016)

Philip, S.J.: Scalable location management for geographic routing in mobile ad hoc networks. Tech. rep. Computer Science Tech Report TR-2005-21, SUNY at Buffalo (2005)

Philip, S.J., Ghosh, J., Ngo, H.Q., Qiao, C.: Routing on overlay graphs in mobile ad hoc networks. In: Proceedings of the IEEE Global Communications Conference, Exhibition & Industry Forum, GLOBECOM 2006 (2006)

Ratnasamy, S., et al.: Data-centric storage in sensornets with GHT, a geographic hash table. Mob. Netw. Appl. 8(4), 427–442 (2003)

Sanchez, J.A., Ruiz, P.M., Liu, J., Stojmenovic, I.: Bandwidth-efficient geographic multicast routing protocol for wireless sensor networks. IEEE Sens. J. **7**(5), 627–636 (2007)

Seddigh, M., González, J.S., Stojmenovic, I.: RNG and internal node based broadcasting algorithms for wireless one-to-one networks. SIGMOBILE Mob. Comput. Commun. Rev. **5**(2), 37–44 (2001)

Stojmenovic, I.: Geocasting with guaranteed delivery in sensor networks. IEEE Wirel. Commun. **11**(6), 29–37 (2004)

Stojmenovic, I., Seddigh, M., Zunic, J.: Dominating sets and neighbor elimination-based broadcasting algorithms in wireless networks. IEEE Trans. Parallel Distrib. Syst. **13**(1), 14–25 (2002)

Tan, J.: A scalable graph model and coordination algorithms for mobile sensor networks. In: Li, Y., Thai, M.T., Wu, W. (eds.) Wireless Sensor Networks and Applications. Signals and Communication Technology, pp. 65–83. Springer, Boston (2008)

Tsai, H.-W., Chu, C.-P., Chen, T.-S.: Mobile object tracking in wireless sensor networks. Comput. Commun. **30**(8), 1811–1825 (2007)

Vertex-Connectivity for Node Failure Identification in Boolean Network Tomography

Nicola Galesi[1], Fariba Ranjbar[1], and Michele Zito[2(✉)]

[1] Universitá La Sapienza, Rome, Italy
[2] University of Liverpool, Liverpool, UK
`michele@liverpool.ac.uk`

Abstract. In this paper we study the node failure identification problem in undirected graphs by means of Boolean Network Tomography. We argue that vertex connectivity plays a central role. We show tight bounds on the maximal identifiability in a particular class of graphs, the Line of Sight networks. We prove slightly weaker bounds on arbitrary networks. Finally we initiate the study of maximal identifiability in random networks. We focus on two models: the classical Erdős-Rényi model, and that of Random Regular graphs. The framework proposed in the paper allows a probabilistic analysis of the identifiability in random networks giving a tradeoff between the number of monitors to place and the maximal identifiability.

1 Introduction

A central issue in communication networks is to ensure that the structure works reliably. To this end it is of the utmost importance to discover as quickly as possible those components that develop some sort of failure. Network Tomography is a family of distributed failure detection algorithms based on the spreading of end-to-end measurements [8,23] rather than directly measuring individual network components. Typically a network $G = (V, E)$ is given as a graph along with a collection of paths $\mathbb{P}$ in it and the goal is to take measurements along such paths to infer properties of the given network. Quoting from [12] "A key advantage of tomographic methods is that they require no participation from network elements other than the usual forwarding of packets. This distinguishes them from well-known tools such as `traceroute` and `ping`, that require ICMP responses to function. In some networks, ICMP response has been restricted by administrators, presumably to prevent probing from external sources. Another feature

The first two authors kindly acknowledge the partial support by the MIUR under the grant "Dipartimenti di eccellenza 2018–2022" of the Department of Computer Science of Sapienza University. The research was also partly supported by a visiting fellowship of the University of Liverpool and the Networks Sciences & Technologies (NeST) initiative of the University of Liverpool (https://www.liverpool.ac.uk/network-science-technologies/).

F. Dressler and C. Scheideler (Eds.): ALGOSENSORS 2019, LNCS 11931, pp. 79–95, 2019.
https://doi.org/10.1007/978-3-030-34405-4_5

of tomography is that probing and the recovery of probe data may be embedded within transport protocols, thus co-opting suitably enabled hosts to form impromptu measurement infrastructures". The approach is strongly related to group testing [11] where, in general, one is interested in making statements about individuals in a population by taking group measurements. The main concern is to do so with the minimum number of tests. In our setting, the connectivity structure of the network constrains the set of feasible tests. Graph-constrained group testing has been studied before, starting with [7]. We are interested in using structural graph-theoretic properties to make statements about the quality of the testing process.

Research in Network Tomography is vast. The seminal works of Vardi [23], and Coates et al. [8], or more recent surveys like [6] each have more that 500 citations, according to Google Scholar. Methods and algorithms vary dramatically depending on the network property of interest, or the measurements one has to rely on. Boolean Network Tomography (BNT) aims to identify corrupted components in a network using boolean measurements (i.e. assuming that elementary network components can be in one of two states: "working" or "not-working"). Introduced in [12], the paradigm has recently attracted a lot of interest [14,19] because of its simplicity. In this work we use BNT to identify failing nodes. Assume to have a set $\mathbb{P}$ of measurement paths over a node set V. We would like to know the state x_v (with $x_v = 0$ corresponding to "v in working order" and $x_v = 1$ corresponding to "v in a faulty state") of each node $v \in V$. The localization of the failing nodes in $\mathbb{P}$ is captured by the solutions of the system:

$$\bigwedge_{p\in\mathbb{P}} \left(\bigvee_{v\in p} x_v \equiv b_p \right) \tag{1}$$

where b_p models the (boolean) state of the path $p \in \mathbb{P}$. Of course, systems of this form may have several solutions and therefore, in general, the availability of a collection of end-to-end measurements does not necessarily lead to the unique identification of the failing nodes. We will investigate properties of the underlying network that facilitate the solution of this problem. In particular, we follow the approach initiated by Ma et al. [18] based on the notion of *maximal identifiability* (see Sect. 2 for a precise definition). The metric aims to capture the maximal number of simultaneously failing nodes that can be uniquely identified in a network by means of measurement along a given path system. It turns out that the network maximal identifiability is an interesting combinatorial measure and several studies [2,15,18,20] have investigated variants of this measure in connection with various types of path systems. However, it seems difficult to come up with simple graph-theoretic properties that affect the given network identifiability. We contend that the maximal identifiability using measures over the collection of all simple paths between two disjoint sets of vertices S and T enables us to make good progress on this issue. More specifically we show that the proposed approach provides an almost tight characterization of the maximal identifiability in *augmented hypergrids* (see definition in Sect. 2) and more general Line-of-Sight (LoS) networks. LoS networks were introduced by Frieze *et al.*

in [13] and have been widely studied (see for instance [9,10,21,22]) as models for communication patterns in a geometric environment containing obstacles. Like grids, LoS networks can be embedded in a finite cube of $\mathbb{Z}^d$, for some positive integer d. But LoS networks generalize grids in that edges are allowed between nodes that are not necessarily next to each other in the network embedding.

Using the network vertex-connectivity, $\kappa(G)$, (i.e. the size of the minimal set of nodes disconnecting the graph) we are able to prove the following:

Theorem 1. *Let $\mathcal{H}$ be an augmented hypergrid. For every pair of disjoint $S, T \subseteq V(\mathcal{H})$, the maximal identifiability of $\mathcal{H}$, $\mu(\mathcal{H})$ using measures over simple paths between S and T satisfies: $\mu(\mathcal{H}) \leq \kappa(\mathcal{H})$. Furthermore, there is a way to choose S and T that guarantees $\mu(\mathcal{H}) \geq \kappa(\mathcal{H}) - 1$.*

The result on hypergrids immediately suggests the related question about general graphs. In this work we prove upper and lower bounds on the maximal identifiability of any network G. The following statement summarizes our findings (here $\kappa_{ST}(G)$ is the size of smallest set of vertices separating S and T):

Theorem 2. *Let $G = (V, E)$ be an arbitrary graph. For every pair of disjoint $S, T \subseteq V(G)$, the maximal identifiability of G, $\mu(G)$ using measures over simple paths between S and T satisfies: $\mu(G) \leq \min(\delta(G), \kappa_{ST}(G))$. Furthermore, there is a way to choose S and T that guarantees $\mu(G) \geq \lfloor \kappa(G)/2 \rfloor - 1$.*

In both results, the upper bound is proved by showing that there are sets of $\kappa(G) + 1$ vertices that cannot be identified. The lower bounds which require the construction of paths separating large sets of nodes in the graph, are based on a well-known relationship between $\kappa(G)$ and the existence of collections of vertex-disjoint paths between certain sets of nodes in G. In fact a much higher lower bound can be proved for graphs with low connectivity. The following result applies to arbitrary LoS networks, and to many topologies studied in relation to communication problems including various types of grids, butterflies, hypercubes, and sparsely connected sensor networks.

Theorem 3. *Let $G = (V, E)$ be an arbitrary network with $\kappa(G) \leq |V|/3$. Let $\mu(G)$ denote the maximal identifiability of G using measures over simple paths between two disjoint sets of vertices S and T.*

1. For all pairs of disjoint $S, T \subseteq V$, $\mu(G) \leq \kappa(G)$.
2. There is a pair of disjoint $S, T \subseteq V(G)$ such that $\mu(G) \geq \kappa(G) - 2$.

Finally, we look at random networks (Erdős-Rényi and Random Regular Graphs). In these structures we are able to show a trade-off between the success probability of the relevant path construction processes and the size of the sets S and T defining the path set $\mathbb{P}$. Random graphs also give us alternative constructions of networks with large identifiability.

The rest of the paper is organized as follows. After a section devoted to preliminaries and important definitions, we have a section that focuses on Theorem 1. Section 4 focuses on arbitrary graphs. First we look at the proof of

Theorem 2. Then describe a different construction that leads to the proof of Theorem 3. Finally Sect. 5 is dedicated to the analysis of the maximal identifiability in random graphs. First we look at Erdős-Rényi graphs, then random regular graphs.

2 Preliminaries

Sets, Graphs, Paths, and Connectivity. If U and W are sets, $U \triangle W = (U \setminus W) \cup (W \setminus U)$ is the symmetric difference between U and W. Graphs (we will use the terms network and graph interchangeably) in this paper will be undirected, simple and loop-less. A path (of length k) in a graph $G = (V, E)$ from a node u to a node v is a sequence of nodes $p = u_1, u_2, \ldots, u_{k+1}$ such that $u_1 = u$, $u_{k+1} = v$ and $\{u_i u_{i+1}\} \in E$ for all $i \in [k]$. The path p is *simple* of no two u_i and u_j in p are the same. Any sub-sequence $u_x, \ldots, u_{x+y}$ ($x \in \{1, \ldots, k+1\}$, $y \in \{0, \ldots, k+1-x\}$) is said to be *contained in* p, and dually we say that p *contains* the sequence or *passes through* it. We say that path p and q *intersect* if they contain a common sub-sequence. The intersection of a path p and an arbitrary set of nodes W is the set of elements of W that are contained in p. When p intersect W sometimes we say that p *touches* W. For an arbitrary $U \subseteq V(G)$, $N(U)$ is the set of *neighbours* of $u \in U$. If $U = \{u\}$ we write $N(u)$ instead of $N(\{u\})$. The *degree* of u, $\deg(u)$, is the cardinality of $N(u)$, and let $\delta(G) = \min_{u \in V} \deg(u)$ be the minimum degree of G.

In what follows $\kappa(G)$ denotes the vertex-connectivity of the given graph $G = (V, E)$, namely $\kappa(G)$ is the size of the minimal subset K of V, such that removing K from G disconnects G. In particular it is well-known (see for example [16], Theorem 5.1, p. 43) that

$$\kappa(G) \leq \delta(G). \tag{2}$$

It will also be convenient to work with sets of vertices disconnecting particular parts of G. If $S, T \subseteq V$, then $\kappa_{ST}(G)$ is the size of the smallest vertex separator of S and T in G, i.e. the smallest set of vertices whose removal disconnects S and T (set $\kappa_{ST}(G) = \infty$ if $S \cap T \neq \emptyset$ or there are $s \in S$ and $t \in T$ such that $\{s, t\} \in E$). Notice that $\kappa_{ST}(G) \geq \kappa(G)$.

Grids and LoS Networks. For positive integers d, and $n \geq 2$, let $\mathbb{Z}_n^d$ be the d-dimensional cube $\{1, \ldots, n\}^d$. We say that distinct points P_1 and P_2 in a cube *share a line of sight* if their coordinates differ in a single place. A graph $G = (V, E)$ is said to be a *Line of Sight (LoS) network of size* n, *dimension* d, *and range parameter* ω if there exists an embedding $f_G : V \to \mathbb{Z}_n^d$ such that $\{u, v\} \in E$ if and only if $f_G(u)$ and $f_G(v)$ share a line of sight and the (Euclidean) distance between $f_G(u)$ and $f_G(v)$ is less than ω. In the rest of the paper a LoS network G is always given along with some embedding f_G in $\mathbb{Z}_n^d$ for some d and n, and with slight *abus de langage* we will often refer to the vertices of G, $u, v \in V$ in terms of their corresponding points $f_G(u), f_G(v), \ldots$ in $\mathbb{Z}_n^d$, and in fact the embedding f_G will not be mentioned explicitly. Note that d-dimensional hypergrids, $\mathcal{H}_{n,d}$, as defined in [15] are particular LoS networks with $\omega = 2$ and all possible n^d vertices. In the forthcoming sections we will study *augmented* hypergrids $\mathcal{H}_{n,d,\omega}$ (or simply $\mathcal{H}_{n,\omega}$ in the 2-dimensional case), namely d-dimensional LoS networks with range parameter $\omega > 2$ containing all possible n^d nodes. Fig. 1 gives an example of 2-dimensional augmented hypergrid, and a (more general) LoS network.

Paths, Monitors and Identifiability. In BNT one takes measurements along paths, and the quality of the monitoring scheme depends on the choice of such paths. Let $\mathbb{P}$ be a set of paths over some node set V. For a node $v \in V$, let $\mathbb{P}(v)$ be the set of paths in $\mathbb{P}$ passing through v. For a set of nodes U, $\mathbb{P}(U) = \bigcup_{u \in U} \mathbb{P}(u)$. Hence if $U \subseteq V$, $\mathbb{P}(U) \subseteq \mathbb{P}(V)$. Crucially, we identify two disjoint sets of vertices S and T, and assume that $\mathbb{P}$ is the set of all $S - T$ paths in G, i.e. simple paths with one end-point in S and the other one in T. This is similar to the CSP probing scheme analyzed in [17], but the scheme in that paper does not assume $S \cap T = \emptyset$.

Traditionally in Network Tomography all measurements originate and end at special *monitoring stations* that are connected to the structure under observation. For any tomographic process to have any chance of succeeding one has to assume that such *monitors* are infallible. It is therefore customary to assume that the monitors are external to the given network, but connected to it through a designated set of nodes. $S \cup T$ is such set in our case. We call the pair (S, T) a *monitor placement*. In this settings, two sets of vertices U and W are *separable* if $\mathbb{P}(U) \triangle \mathbb{P}(W) \neq \emptyset$. A set of vertices N is *k-identifiable* (with respect to the probing scheme $(\mathbb{P}, S, T)$) if and only if any $U, W \subseteq N$, with $U \triangle W \neq \emptyset$ and $|U|, |W| \leq k$, U are separable. The *maximal identifiability* of N with respect to $(\mathbb{P}, S, T)$, $\mu(N, \mathbb{P}, S, T)$, is the largest k such that N is k-identifiable. For a graph $G = (V, E)$, we write $\mu(G, \mathbb{P}, S, T)$ to indicate the maximal identifiability of the set of nodes in V which are used in at least a path of $\mathbb{P}$. In what follows we usually omit the dependency of μ on the probing scheme $(\mathbb{P}, S, T)$ when this is clear from the context.

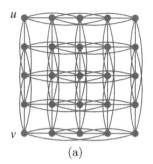 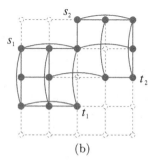

(a)   (b)

Fig. 1. On the left, the network $\mathcal{H}_{n,\omega}$ for $n = 5$ and $\omega = 4$ (note that vertices u and v are not adjacent); on the right a more general example of LoS network, having $\omega = 3$, embedded in $\mathbb{Z}_5^2$ (represented as a dashed grid).

Note that k-identifiability is monotone: if G is k-identifiable then it is k'-identifiable for any $k' < k$. This implies that to prove that $\mu(N) \leq k - 1$ it is sufficient to show that N is **not** k-identifiable. By the definition given above this boils down to showing the existence of two distinct node sets U and W in N of cardinality at most k that are not separable.

Conversely, if we want to prove that $\mu(N) \geq k$ for some k, then it is enough to argue that all distinct node sets U and W of cardinality $|U|, |W| \leq k$ are separable. To prove this we have to show that for any two distinct node sets U and W of cardinality at most k there exists a path in $\mathbb{P}$ intersecting exactly one between U and W.

3   Failure Identifiability in Augmented Hypergrids

Let $\omega > 2$ be an integer. In this section we analyze the maximal identifiability of augmented hypergrids. To maximize clarity, we provide full details for the special case of $\mathcal{H}_{n,\omega}$, the 2-dimensional augmented hypergrid. The proof of the result for d-dimensional structures, which we state at the end of this section, is left for the full version of this work.

In [15] two of us showed that $\mu(G) \leq \delta(G)$ for any $(\mathbb{P}, S, T)$. In $\mathcal{H}_{n,\omega}$ each node u has $\omega - 1$ edges for each one of the possible directions (north, south, east, west). Hence the minimal degree in $\mathcal{H}_{n,\omega}$ is reached at the corner nodes and it is $2(\omega - 1)$. Thus $\mu(\mathcal{H}_{n,\omega}) \leq 2(\omega - 1)$ for any $(\mathbb{P}, S, T)$. In the remainder of this section we pair this up with a tight lower bound for a specific monitor placement. Note that these results readily imply the upper bound in Theorem 1 as in augmented hypegrids the vertex connectivity is actually equal to the network's minimum degree. The rest of this section focuses on the second inequality in that theorem.

We say that nodes with coordinates $(1, j)$ in $\mathcal{H}_{n,\omega}$, for some $j \in \{1, \ldots, n\}$, are *on the north border* of $\mathcal{H}_{n,\omega}$. Analogously we can define nodes on the south, west and east borders of $\mathcal{H}_{n,\omega}$. Given a node u of $\mathcal{H}_{n,\omega}$, identified as a pair $(i, j) \in \mathbb{Z}_n^2$, and a positive integer k, we define:

$$SE_k(u) = \{(i', j') \in \mathbb{Z}_n^2 : i + k \geq i' \geq i \ \wedge \ j + k \geq j' \geq j\}$$

and

$$NW_k(u) = \{(i', j') \in \mathbb{Z}_n^2 : i - k \leq i' \leq i \ \wedge \ j - k \leq j' \leq j\}.$$

In particular we denote by $SE(u)$ (resp. $NW(u)$) the union of all $SE_k(u)$ (resp. $NW_k(u)$). Furthermore $\partial SE_k(u)$ (resp. $\partial NW_k(u)$) is the set of all points in $SE_k(u)$ (resp. $NW_k(u)$) with coordinates (i', j) or (i, j'). Expressions $\partial SE(u)$ and $\partial NW(u)$ are defined analogously. Also, we say that a direction X (north, south, west, east) is *W-saturated on u* all neighbours of u in direction X are in W.

Definition 1 *(W-unreachability).* Let $u = (i, j)$ be a node in $\mathcal{H}_{n,\omega}$ and W be a set of nodes in $\mathcal{H}_{n,\omega}$. A node $u' = (i', j')$ for $i' \geq i$ and $j' \geq j$ is W-unreachable from u if either $\partial SE(u) \subseteq W$ or $\partial NW(u') \subseteq W$. Otherwise we say that u' is W-reachable from u.

A *canonical monitor placement* for $\mathcal{H}_{n,\omega}$ is a pair (S, T), such that S is formed by the node $(1, 1)$ and its neighbours, and T formed by (n, n) and it neighbours. Hence $|S| = |T| = 2\omega - 1$. We are now ready to state the main result in this section.

Theorem 4. *Let $n, \omega \in \mathbb{N}$, $\omega > 2$ and $n > 3(\omega - 1)$. Let (S, T) be a canonical monitor placement for $\mathcal{H}_{n,\omega}$. Then $\mu(\mathcal{H}_{n,\omega}) \geq 2(\omega - 1) - 1$.*

Proof. We have to prove that for any pair of node sets U, and W of cardinality at most $2(\omega - 1) - 1$, with $U \triangle W \neq \emptyset$ we can build an $S - T$ path touching exactly one of them. Assume without loss of generality that $u \in U \setminus W$. Since $|S| = |T| = 2(\omega - 1)$ and $|W| < 2(\omega - 1)$, there is a node in $s \in S \setminus W$ and a node $t \in T \setminus W$. Assume without loss of generality that $s = (1, 1)$ (the case $s \neq (1, 1)$ is similar, and give even better results). Similarly for T, assume that $t = (n, n) \notin W$.

We build two *disjoint* paths i_u and o_u such that their concatenation is an $S - T$ path passing through u and not touching nodes in W. We show how to build i_u (o_u is analogous).

If $u = (i, j)$ and $\min(i, j) > \omega - 1$ and u is W-reachable from s we proceed by a careful induction on $|NW(u)|$. In the inductive step, two things can happen. If u is far from the north and west borders there is a at least a direction X between North and West which is not W-saturated. Hence there is a node $u' \in NW(u) \setminus W$ on direction X from u at distance less than ω. Hence there is an edge $\{u', u\} \in \mathcal{H}_{n,\omega}$. Since $NW(u') \subset NW(u)$ the inductive hypothesis applied on u', give us a path $i_{u'}$ and the path $i_u = i_{u'}, u$. Alternatively if u is close to s (i.e. $\min(i, j) \leq \omega - 1$) we know that u is W-reachable and this guarantees the existence of a neighbour u' of u in $NW(u)$ that is NOT in W and the inductive hypothesis can be applied to u' again to complete i_u.

The induction reaches a base case in one of two possible ways. If $|NW(u)| = 1$, then $u = s$ and we have done: i_u is s. Otherwise $|NW(u)| > 1$ but u is W-unreachable from s. In such case we proceed as follows (see also Fig. 2 for an example). Notice that in this case it must be that u has less than $\omega - 1$ neighbours either in direction North or West, for otherwise it would not be possible for W, which is of size at most $2(\omega - 1) - 1$, to cover $\partial NW(u)$ or $\partial SE(s)$. Let $u = (i, j)$, hence, by unreachability property, it must be that in $NW(u)$ there are at least $t = (i - 1) + (j - 1) \geq 2$ nodes in W. Let us look at the neighbours of u in $SE(u)$ which are South of u at distance at most $\omega - 1 - i$ from u and East of u at distance at most $\omega - 1 - j$. (Notice that these nodes are at distance at most $\omega - 1$ from the North and West borders). First we claim that either in direction South or direction East, there is a neighbour (say wlog direction South) $u' = (i', j)$ of u at distance at most $\omega - 1 - i$ from u such that both u' and $u'' = (i', 1)$ are not in W. This is because the sum of nodes at distance at most $\omega - i - 1$ from u in direction South and at distance at most $\omega - j - 1$ in direction East is at most $2\omega - i - j$. Hence there are at most $2\omega - i - j$ pairs of nodes of the type (u', u''), but only $2\omega - i - j - 1$ nodes in W (the latter is because $|W| \leq 2\omega - 3$ and $t = (i - 1) + (j - 1)$ nodes of W are already used in $NW(u)$). Then there is at least a pair (u', u'') such that neither u' nor u'' are in W. Hence the path $i_u = s, u'', u', u$ connecting s to u without touching W. This path i_u is ok, unless u' is already on the path we have built by induction so far. In that case we can cut i_u at u' and link it to the inductive path.

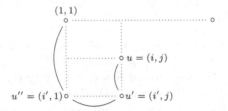

Fig. 2. An example of how to build i_u when u is not W-reachable and in $SE_k((1,1))$ for some $k < \omega - 1$.

The argument presented so far leaves a gap in che case when $u \in U \setminus W$ is close to s and it is W-unreachable. This case is in fact not very different from the last one we have considered. As in that case we consider the neighbours of u in $\partial SE_{\omega - i}(u)$ at distance $\omega - i$ in the South direction (instead of distance $\omega - i - 1$ as in the previous case) and at distance $\omega - j$ in the East direction (instead of $\omega - j - 1$). Exactly the same counting argument now justifies three pairs of nodes (u', u''), (v', v'') and (w', w'') such that none of $u', u'', v', v'', w', w''$ are in W (notice that as before, u'', v'' and w'' are nodes on the border of $\mathcal{H}_{n,\omega}$). If either one between v' and w', say wlog w', is exactly at distance $\omega - 1$ from u, then we can define a path i_u touching u and not touching W as $i_u = (1,1), u'', u', u, w'$ (see also Fig. 3). If both of v' and w'' are at distance $< \omega - 1$, then two among u', v' and w', say wlog u', and v' are on the same direction, say wlog South, and hence one of them, say wlog u' is northern of the other. In this case we define i_u as the path $(1,1), u'', u', u, v'$.

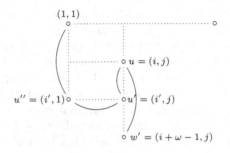

Fig. 3. An example where $u \in SE_k(1,1))$ for some $k < \omega - 1$ and w' is at South distance exactly $\omega - 1$ from u.

□

Theorem 4 generalizes to d-dimensional augmented hypergrids. We leave the details to the full version of this work.

Theorem 5. *Let $d, n, \omega \in \mathbb{N}$, $d, n \geq 2$ and $\omega > 2$. There is a monitor placement for $\mathcal{H}_{n,d,\omega}$ for which $\mu(\mathcal{H}_{n,d,\omega}, \mathbb{P}, S, T) \geq d(\omega - 1) - 1$.*

4   General Topologies

We now look at the maximal identifiability in arbitrary networks. Theorem 2 stated in Sect. 1 will be a consequence of two independent results. In [15] it was proved that $\mu(G) \leq \delta(G)$, for any monitor placement (S, T). Here we show that $\mu(G)$ can be upper bounded in terms of κ_{ST}, the size of the minimal node set separating S from T.

Theorem 6. *Let $G = (V, E)$ be a graph and (S, T) be a monitor placement. Then $\mu(G) \leq \kappa_{ST}(G)$.*

Proof. If there is no vertex set in G separating S and T, $\kappa_{ST}(G) = \infty$ and the result is trivial. Let K be the set witnessing the minimal separability of S from T in G. Hence $|K| = \kappa_{ST}(G)$. Let $N(K)$ be the set of neighbours of nodes in K and notice this cannot be empty since K is disconnecting G. Pick one $w \in N(K)$ and define $U := K$ and $W := U \cup \{w\}$. Clearly $\mathbb{P}(U) \subseteq \mathbb{P}(W)$. To see the opposite inclusion assume that there exists a path from S to T passing from w but not touching $U = K$. Then K is not separating S from T in G. Contradiction. $\square$

Note that, while in general $\kappa_{ST}(G)$ may be larger than $\delta(G)$, if S and T are separated by a set of $\kappa(G)$ vertices then, by inequality (2), the bound in Theorem 6 is at least as good as the minimum degree bound proved earlier by the first two authors [15]. This implies the upper bound in Theorem 2.

Moving to lower bounds, in this section we prove the following:

Theorem 7. *Let $G = (V, E)$ and (S, T) be a monitor placement for G. Then $\mu(G) \geq \min(\kappa(G) - 1, |S|, |T|) - 1$.*

The lower bound in Theorem 2 can be derived easily from Theorem 7. Let K be a vertex separator in G of size $\kappa(G)$, set S^K to be the first $\lfloor \kappa(G)/2 \rfloor$ elements of K and $T^K = K \setminus S^K$. By Theorem 7 the maximal identifiability of G is at least $|S^K| - 1 = \lfloor \kappa(G)/2 \rfloor - 1$.

The proof of Theorem 7 uses Menger's Theorem, a well-known result in graph theory (see [16, Theorem 5.10, p. 48] for its proof).

Theorem 8 *(Menger's Theorem).* *Let $G = (V, E)$ be a connected graph. Then $\kappa(G) \geq k$ if and only if each pair of nodes in V is connected by at least k node-disjoint paths in G.*

Menger's Theorem is central to the following Lemma which is used in the proof of Theorem 7.

Lemma 1. *Let $G = (V, E)$. Let $W \subseteq V$ such that $|W| \leq \kappa(G) - 2$. Then any pair of vertices in $V \setminus W$ is connected by at least two vertex-disjoint simple paths not touching W.*

Proof. By Menger's Theorem, for any pair of nodes u and v in $V \setminus W$ there are at least $\kappa(G)$ vertex-disjoint paths from u to v in G. Call $\mathbb{P}$ the set of such paths. Since $|W| \leq \kappa(G) - 2$, then the nodes of W can be in at most $\kappa(G) - 2$ of paths in $\mathbb{P}$. Hence there are at least two paths in $\mathbb{P}$ not touching W.   □

Proof of Theorem 7. Let $G = (V, E)$ be an undirected connected graph and (S, T) be a monitor placement in G. Note that without loss of generality $\min(\kappa(G) - 1, |S|, |T|) > 1$ (for otherwise there is nothing to prove).

Assume first that $|S| \geq \kappa(G) - 1$ and $|T| \geq \kappa(G) - 1$. We claim that

$$\mu(G) \geq \kappa(G) - 2.$$

We show that for any distinct non-empty subsets U and W of V of size at most $\kappa(G) - 2$, there is a path in $\mathbb{P}$ touching exactly one between U and W. Given such U and W, fix a node $u \in U \triangle W$ and assume w.l.o.g. that $u \in U$. Since $|W| \leq \kappa(G) - 2$ and $|S| \geq \kappa(G) - 1$ there is at least a node in $s \in S \setminus W$. By the Claim above applied to nodes s and u and to the set W, there are two vertex-disjoint simple paths π_1^s, π_2^s from s to u not touching W. The same reasoning applied to T, guarantees the existence of a node $t \in T \setminus W$ and two vertex-disjoint paths π_1^t, π_2^t from u to t not touching W. If at least one between π_1^s, and π_2^s only intersects one of π_1^t, and π_2^t at u then the concatenation of such paths is a (longer) simple path from s to t passing through u and not touching W. Otherwise the concatenation of one between π_1^s, and π_2^s with one between π_1^t, and π_2^t is a non simple path. In what follows we show that the subgraph of G induced by the four paths does contain a simple path from s to t passing through u and not touching W. In the construction below we exploit the fact that π_1^s, and π_2^s (resp. π_1^t, and π_2^t) are simple and vertex disjoint. Let p be a path from s to u. Define an order on the nodes of p as follows: $v \prec_p w$ if going from v to u we pass though w. From now on we will use $\prec$ instead of $\prec_p$ when the path under consideration will be clear from the context. Let Z_1^j be the nodes in $\pi_1^s \cap \pi_j^t$. Z_1^1 and Z_1^2 are disjoint but there will be a node in those sets, say z, which is minimal according to $\prec$. Without loss of generality let us say that $z \in Z_1^1$. The subpath $\pi_1^s[s \ldots z]$ of π_1^s going from s to z, is intersecting neither π_1^t nor π_2^t. Hence the concatenation of the following three disjoint paths defines a simple path from s to t passing through u avoiding W, hence a path in $\mathbb{P}$ with the required properties:

1. $\pi_1^s[s \ldots z]$, going form s to z;
2. $\pi_1^t[z \ldots u]$ a sub path of π_1^t going from u to z and traversed in the other direction;
3. π_2^t, connecting u to t.

Now assume that at least one between $|S|$ and $|T|$ is less than $\kappa(G) - 1$. Let $r = \min(|S|, |T|) - 1$. As before we prove that for all distinct non-empty U and W subsets of V of size at most r, there is an $S - T$ path in G, hence in $\mathbb{P}$, touching exactly one between U and W. Let $u \in U \triangle W$ and without loss of generality assume $u \in U$. Notice that $r+1 = \min(|S|, |T|)$, then both $|S| \geq r+1$ and $|T| \geq r + 1$. Since $|W| \leq r$, as before there are $s \in S \setminus W$ and $t \in T \setminus W$. Furthermore, since $\kappa(G) \geq \min(|S|, |T|)$, then by previous observation on $|S|$ and $|T|$, $\kappa(G) \geq r+1$ and, since $|W| \leq r$, then $\kappa(G) - |W| \geq 2$, that is $|W| \leq \kappa(G) - 2$. As in the previous case we can apply the Claim above once to s, u and W getting the vertex-disjoint paths π_1^s and π_2^s from s to u, and once to t, u and W getting the vertex-disjoint paths π_1^t and π_2^t from t to u. The proof then follows by the same steps as in the previous case. We then have proved that if $|S|$ or $|T|$ are smaller than $\kappa(G) - 1$, then $\mu(G) \geq \min(|S|, |T|) - 1$ and the proof of Theorem 7 is complete.   □

Proof of Theorem 3. We complete this section investigating a different way to relate the graph vertex connectivity to $\mu(G)$. It is easy to see that, in general, the bounds in Theorem 2 are not very tight, particularly when $\kappa(G)$ is large. However, if $\kappa(G)$ is small, we can do better.

In what follows let K be a minimal vertex separator in G. Let $G_i^K = (V_i^K, E_i^K)$, $i \in \{1, \ldots, r_K\}$ be the $r_K \geq 2$ connected components remaining in G after removing K. Since $\kappa(G) \leq \frac{n}{3}$, then $2\kappa(G) \leq n - \kappa(G)$ and one can define disjoint sets S, and T with $\kappa(G)$ vertices each in such a way that the smallest among the V_i^K's contains only elements of S. This can be done as follows: if the smallest V_i^K's has less than $\kappa(G) - \ell$ nodes, then assign all its nodes to S. Then use the other components G_j^K's to assign ℓ nodes to S and $\kappa(G)$ other nodes to T. If the smallest V_i^K has more than $\kappa(G)$ nodes, choose $\kappa(G)$ among them and put them in S. Choose $\kappa(G)$ nodes in other components and assign them to T.

We now prove that the set of simple paths between S and T defined as above allow a very high identifiability. The lower bound on $\mu(G)$ follows from Theorem 7 noticing that $|S| = |T| > \kappa(G) - 1$. We now prove that $\mu(G) \leq \kappa(G)$. Let G_i^K be the component where all the S-nodes are assigned. Let w be a node in $V_i^K \cap N(K)$. This node has to exists since G was connected and the removal of K is disconnecting G_i^K from K. Fix $U = K$ and $W = K \cup \{w\}$. We will show that $\mathbb{P}(U) = \mathbb{P}(W)$. It suffices to prove that $\mathbb{P}(\{w\}) \subseteq \mathbb{P}(K)$, since clearly $\mathbb{P}(U) \subseteq \mathbb{P}(W)$. Observe that no $S-T$ path p in G can live entirely inside G_i^K, i.e. have all of its nodes in V_i^K. This is because at least one end-point (that in T) it is necessarily missing in any path entirely living only in G_i^K. Hence a path touching w is either entering or leaving G_i^K. But outside of G_i^K w is connected only to K, since otherwise K would not be a minimal vertex separator. Hence it must be $\mathbb{P}(\{w\}) \subseteq \mathbb{P}(K)$. We have found U, W of size $\leq \kappa(G)$ such that $\mathbb{P}(U) = \mathbb{P}(W)$. The upper bound follows.

Arbitrary LoS networks have minimum degree, and hence also vertex connectivity at most $2d(\omega - 1)$. The next corollary follows directly from Theorem 3.

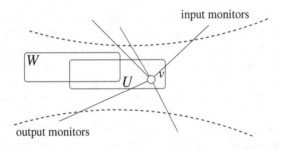

Fig. 4. A node $v \in U \Delta W$ and a possible way to connect it to S and T.

Corollary 1. *Let G be an arbitrary LoS network over n nodes and with fixed range parameter ω, independent of n, such that $n \geq \omega$. Then $\mu(G) \geq \kappa(G) - 2$.*

5   Random Networks and Tradeoffs

The main aim of this work is to characterize the identifiability in terms of the vertex connectivity. In this section we prove that tight results are possible in random graphs. Also we show an interesting trade-off between the success probability of the various random processes and the size of the sets S and T. Finally, random graphs give us constructions of networks with large identifiability.

5.1   Sub-linear Separability in Erdős-Rényi Graphs

We start our investigation of the identifiability of node failures in random graphs by looking at the binomial model $G(n, p)$, for fixed $p \leq 1/2$ (in this section only we follow the traditional random graph jargon and use p to denote the graph edge probability rather than a generic path). The following equalities, which hold with probability approaching one as n tends to infinity (that is *with high probability* (w.h.p.)), are folklore:

$$\kappa(G(n,p)) = \delta(G(n,p)) = np - o(n). \tag{3}$$

(see [5]). Here we describe a simple method which can be used to separate sets of vertices of sublinear size.

We assume, for now, that S and T are each formed by $\gamma = \gamma(n)$ nodes with $\kappa(G(n,p)) \leq \gamma < n/2$. Let $M = S \cup T$. Let U and W be two arbitrary subsets of $V \setminus M$ of size k (see Fig. 4). The probability that U and W are separable is at least the probability that an element v of $U \Delta W$ (w.l.o.g. assume $v \in U \setminus W$) is directly connected to a node in S and to a node in T. This event has probability $(1 - (1 - p)^\gamma)^2$. Hence the probability that U and W cannot be separated is at most $1 - (1 - (1 - p)^\gamma)^2 = 2(1 - p)^\gamma - (1 - p)^{2\gamma}$ and therefore the probability that some pair of sets U and W of size k (not intersecting M) fail is at most $2\binom{n-2\gamma}{2k}\binom{2k}{k}(1 - p)^\gamma$.

Theorem 9. *For fixed p with $p \leq 1/2$, under the assumptions above about the way monitors are placed in $G(n,p)$, the probability that $G(n,p)$ is not k-vertex separable is at most $2k\binom{n}{k}^2 e^{(2k-\gamma)p}$.*

Proof. The argument above works if both U and W contain no vertex in M. The presence of elements of vertices in M in U or W may affect the analysis in two ways. First v could be in M (say $v \in S$). In this case U and W are separable if v is directly connected to a vertex in T. This happens with probability $(1-(1-p)^\gamma) > (1-(1-p)^\gamma)^2$. Second, M might contain some elements of U and W different from v. In the worst case when v is trying to connect to M, it must avoid at most $2k$ element of such set. There is at most $\sum_{h \leq k} \binom{n}{h}^2 \leq k\binom{n}{k}^2$ pairs of U and W of size at most k. Thus the probability that $G(n,p)$ fails to be k-vertex separable is at most $2k\binom{n}{k}^2(1-p)^{\gamma-2k}$. and the result follows as $1 - p \leq e^{-p}$. $\square$

Note that the bound in Theorem 9 can only be small if $k = o(n)$ for otherwise the factor $e^{(2k-\gamma)p}$ is large. In fact it has to be $k = O(n^\epsilon)$ for sufficiently small positive ϵ otherwise the large factor $\binom{n}{k}^2$ is not "killed off" by the magnitude of the small exponential.

5.2 Linear Separability in Erdős-Rényi Graphs

The argument above cannot be pushed all the way up to $\kappa(G(n,p))$. When trying to separate vertex sets containing $\Omega(n)$ vertices the problem is that these sets can form a large part of M and the existence of direct links from v to $S \setminus W$ and $T \setminus W$ is not guaranteed with sufficiently high probability. However a different argument allow us to prove the following:

Theorem 10. *For fixed $p \leq 1/3$, $\kappa(G(n,p)) - 1 \leq \mu(G(n,p)) \leq \kappa(G(n,p))$ w.h.p.*

Full details of the proof are left to the final version of this paper, but here is an informal explanation. The upper bound follows immediately from (3) and Theorem 6. For the lower bound we claim that the chance that two sets of size at most $\kappa(G(n,p)) - 1$ are not vertex separable is small. First note that w.h.p. $G(n,p)$ has a single vertex of minimum degree. Choose S of size at least $n/3$ so that it contains such vertex. Choose T of size at least $n/3$ in $V \setminus (S \cup N(S))$ arbitrarily. To believe our claim pick two sets U and W, assume without loss of generality that $U \setminus W \neq \emptyset$ and remove, W from the graph. $G(n,p) \setminus W$ is still a random graph on at least $n - np = \Omega(n)$ vertices and constant edge probability. Results in [4] imply that $G(n,p) \setminus W$ has a Hamilton path starting at any $s \in S$ with probability at least $1 - o(2^{-n})$ (and in fact one can use well-known algorithmic techniques [1] to find one such path in polynomial time, w.h.p.). Such Hamiltonian path, by definition, contains a path from S to T passing through $v \notin W$, for every possible choice of v. This proves, w.h.p., the separability of sets of size up to $\kappa(G(n,p)) - 1$ (if $|W| = \kappa(G(n,p)) - 1$, v is the unique vertex of minimum degree and $W \subseteq N(v)$ then one needs to use a Hamiltonian path starting at v).

5.3   Random Regular Graphs

A standard way to model random graphs with fixed vertex degrees is Bollobas' configuration model [3]. There's n buckets, each with r free points. A random pairing of these free points has a constant probability of not containing any pair containing two points from the same bucket or two pairs containing points from just two buckets. These configurations are in one-to-one correspondence with r-regular n-vertex simple graphs. Denote by $\mathcal{C}_{n,r}$ the set of all configurations $C(n,r)$ on n buckets each containing r points, and let $G(r\text{-reg})$ be a random r-regular graph.

As before assume $|S| = |T| = \gamma$. The main result of this section is the following:

Theorem 11. *Let $r \geq 3$ be a fixed integer. $r - 2 - o(1) \leq \mu(G(r\text{-reg})) \leq r$ w.h.p.*

The result resembles Theorem 3 but its proof uses different techniques. The upper bound is true of any r-regular graph G as $\mu(G) \leq \delta(G) = r$. The lower bound is a consequence of the following:

Lemma 2. *Let $r \geq 3$ be a fixed integer. Two sets U and W with $U, W \subseteq V(G(r\text{-reg}))$ and $\max(|U|, |W|) \leq k$ are separable w.h.p. if $k = r - 2 - o(1)$.*

Proof. In what follows we often use graph-theoretic terms, but we actually work with a random configuration $C(n,r)$. Let U and W be two sets of k buckets. For simplicity assume that (the vertices corresponding to the elements of) both U and W are subsets of $V \setminus M$. The probability that U and W can be separated is at least the probability that a (say) random element v of $U \triangle W$ (w.l.o.g. $v \in U \setminus W$) is connected to S by a path of length at most ℓ_s and to T by a path of length at most ℓ_t, neither of which "touch" W. Figure 5 provides a simple example of the event under consideration. The desired paths can be found using algorithm PATHFINDER below that builds the paths and $C(n,r)$ at the same time.

PATHFINDER(v, ℓ_s, ℓ_t, W)

    SIMPLEPATHS(v, ℓ_s, ℓ_t, W). Starting from v, build a simple path p^s of length ℓ_s that avoids W. Similarly, starting from v, build a simple path p^t of length ℓ_t that avoids W.

    RANDOMSHOOTING(p^s, p^t). Pair up all un-matched points in p^s and p^t.

    Complete the configuration $C(n,r)$ by pairing up all remaining points.

Sub-algorithm SIMPLEPATHS can complete its constructions by pairing points starting from elements of the bucket v then choosing a random un-matched point in a bucket u, then picking any other point u and then again a random un-matched point and so on, essentially simulating two random walks RW$_s$ and RW$_t$ on the set of buckets. Note that the process may fail if at any point we revisit a previously visited bucket or if we hit W or even M. However the following can be proved easily.

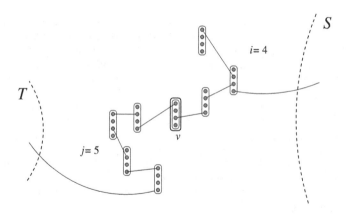

Fig. 5. Assume $r = 4$. The picture represents a bucket (i.e. vertex) $v \in U \triangle W$ and two possible "paths" (sequences of independent edges such that consecutive elements involve points from the same bucket) of length 3 and 5, respectively connecting it to S and T.

Claim. RW_s and RW_t succeed w.h.p. provided $\ell_s, \ell_t \in o(n)$.

As to RANDOMSHOOTING, the process succeeds if we manage to hit an element of S from p^s and an element of T from p^t.

Claim. RANDOMSHOOTING(q_s, q_t, S, T) succeeds w.h.p. if $\ell_s, \ell_t \in \omega(1)$.

Any un-matched point in p^s or p^t after SIMPLEPATHS is complete is called *useful*. Path p^s (resp. p^t) contains $q_s = (r - 2)\ell_s + 1$ (resp $q_t = (r - 2)\ell_t + 1$) useful points. During the execution of RANDOMSHOOTING a single useful point "hits" its target set, say S, with probability proportional to the cardinality of S. Hence the probability that none of the q_s useful points hits S is $(1 - \frac{\gamma}{n})^{q_s}$ and the overall success probability is $(1 - (1 - \frac{\gamma}{n})^{q_s})(1 - (1 - \frac{\gamma}{n})^{q_t})$.

Back to the proof of Lemma 2 Set $\ell_s = \ell_t = \ell$ and q the common value of q_s an q_t. The argument above implies that the success probability for U and W is asymptotically approximately $(1 - (1 - \frac{\gamma}{n})^q)^2$ and the rest of the argument (and its conclusion) is very similar to the $G(n, p)$ case (the final bound is slightly weaker, though). The chance that a random r-regular graph is not k-vertex separable is at most

$$O(n^{2k}) \times (1 - (1 - (1 - \frac{\gamma}{n})^q)^2) \leq O(n^{2k}) \times 2(1 - \frac{\gamma}{n})^q \leq O(n^{2k}) \times 2e^{-\frac{\gamma}{n}q},$$

which goes to zero as n^{-C} provided ℓ is at least logarithmic in n. The constraints on ℓ from the claims above imply that the parameter can be traded-off agains γ to achieve high identifiability. $\square$

References

1. Angluin, D., Valiant, L.G.: Fast probabilistic algorithms for Hamiltonian circuits and matchings. J. Comput. Syst. Sci. **18**, 155–193 (1979)

2. Bartolini, N., He, T., Khamfroush, H.: Fundamental limits of failure identifiability by Boolean network tomography. In: INFOCOM 2017. IEEE (2017)
3. Bollobás, B.: A probabilistic proof of an asymptotic formula for the number of labelled regular graphs. Eur. J. Comb. **1**, 311–316 (1980)
4. Bollobás, B., Fenner, T.I., Frieze, A.M.: An algorithm for finding Hamilton paths and cycles in random graphs. Combinatorica **7**, 327–341 (1987)
5. Bollobás, B.: Random Graphs. Cambridge Studies in Advanced Mathematics, vol. 73, 2nd edn. Cambridge University Press, Cambridge (2001)
6. Castro, R., Coates, M., Liang, G., Nowak, R., Yu, B.: Network tomography: recent developments. Stat. Sci. **19**(3), 499–517 (2004)
7. Cheraghchi, M., Karbasi, A., Mohajer, S., Saligrama, V.: Graph-constrained group testing. IEEE Trans. Inf. Theory **58**(1), 248–262 (2012)
8. Coates, M., Hero, A.O., Nowak, R., Yu, B.: Internet tomography. IEEE Signal Process. Mag. **19**, 47–65 (2002)
9. Czumaj, A., Wang, X.: Communication problems in random line-of-sight ad-hoc radio networks. In: Hromkovič, J., Královič, R., Nunkesser, M., Widmayer, P. (eds.) SAGA 2007. LNCS, vol. 4665, pp. 70–81. Springer, Heidelberg (2007). https://doi.org/10.1007/978-3-540-74871-7_7
10. Devroye, L., Farczadi, L.: Connectivity for line-of-sight networks in higher dimensions. Discrete Math. Theor. Comput. Sci. **15**(2), 71–86 (2013)
11. Du, D.-M., Hwang, F.K.: Combinatorial Group Testing and Its Applications. World Scientific, Singapore (2000)
12. Duffield, N.G.: Simple network performance tomography. In: Proceedings of the 3rd ACM SIGCOMM Internet Measurement Conference, IMC 2003, Miami Beach, FL, USA, 27–29 October 2003, pp. 210–215. ACM (2003)
13. Frieze, A.M., Kleinberg, J.M., Ravi, R., Debany, W.: Line-of-sight networks. In: Bansal, N., Pruhs, K., Stein, C. (eds.) Proceedings of the Eighteenth Annual ACM-SIAM Symposium on Discrete Algorithms, SODA 2007, New Orleans, Louisiana, USA, 7–9 January 2007, pp. 968–977. SIAM (2007)
14. Ghita, D., Karakus, C., Argyraki, K., Thiran, P.: Shifting network tomography toward a practical goal. In: Proceedings of the Seventh COnference on Emerging Networking EXperiments and Technologies, CoNEXT 2011, pp. 24:1–24:12. ACM, New York (2011)
15. Galesi, N., Ranjbar, F.: Tight bounds for maximal identifiability of failure nodes in boolean network tomography. In: 2018 IEEE 38th International Conference on Distributed Computing Systems, pp. 212–222. IEEE (2018)
16. Harary, F.: Graph Theory. Addison-Wesley, Reading (1969)
17. Ma, L., He, T., Leung, K.K., Swami, A., Towsley, D.: Inferring link metrics from end-to-end path measurements: identifiability and monitor placement. IEEE/ACM Trans. Netw. **22**(4), 1351–1368 (2014)
18. Ma, L., He, T., Swami, A., Towsley, D., Leung, K.K., Lowe, J.: Node failure localization via network tomography. In: Williamson, C., Akella, A., Taft, N. (eds.) Proceedings of the 2014 Internet Measurement Conference, IMC 2014, Vancouver, BC, Canada, 5–7 November 2014, pp. 195–208. ACM (2014)
19. Ma, L., He, T., Swami, A., Towsley, D., Leung, K.K.: Network capability in localizing node failures via end-to-end path measurements. IEEE/ACM Trans. Netw. **25**(1), 434–450 (2017)
20. Ren, W., Dong, W.: Robust network tomography: K-identifiability and monitor assignment. In: 35th Annual IEEE International Conference on Computer Communications, INFOCOM 2016, San Francisco, CA, USA, 10–14 April 2016, pp. 1–9. IEEE (2016)

21. Sangha, P., Wong, P.W.H., Zito, M.: Independent sets in restricted line of sight networks. In: Fernández Anta, A., Jurdzinski, T., Mosteiro, M.A., Zhang, Y. (eds.) ALGOSENSORS 2017. LNCS, vol. 10718, pp. 211–222. Springer, Cham (2017). https://doi.org/10.1007/978-3-319-72751-6_16
22. Sangha, P., Zito, M.: Finding large independent sets in line of sight networks. In: Gaur, D., Narayanaswamy, N.S. (eds.) CALDAM 2017. LNCS, vol. 10156, pp. 332–343. Springer, Cham (2017). https://doi.org/10.1007/978-3-319-53007-9_29
23. Vardi, Y.: Network tomography: estimating source-destination traffic intensities from link data. J. Am. Stat. Assoc. **91**(433), 365–377 (1996)

Reception Capacity: Definitions, Game Theory and Hardness

Michael Dinitz[1] and Naomi Ephraim[2(✉)]

[1] Johns Hopkins University, Baltimore, MD, USA
mdinitz@cs.jhu.edu
[2] Cornell University, Ithaca, NY, USA
nephraim@cs.cornell.edu

Abstract. The *capacity* of wireless networks is a classic and important topic of study. Informally, the capacity of a network is simply the total amount of information which it can transfer. In the context of models of wireless radio networks, this has usually meant the total number of point-to-point messages which can be sent or received in one time step. This definition has seen intensive study in recent years, particularly with respect to more accurate models of radio networks such as the SINR model. This paper is motivated by an obvious fact: radio antennae are (at least traditionally) omnidirectional, and hence point-to-point connections are not necessarily the best definition of the true *capacity* of a wireless network. To fix this, we introduce a new definition of *reception capacity* as the maximum number of messages which can be received in one round, and show that this is related to a new optimization problem we call the Maximum Perfect Dominated Set (MaxPDS) problem. Using this relationship we give a tight lower bound for approximating this capacity which essentially matches a known upper bound. As our main result, we analyze this notion of capacity under game-theoretic constraints, giving tight bounds on the average quality achieved at any coarse correlated equilibrium (and thus at any Nash). This immediately gives bounds on the average behavior of the natural distributed algorithm in which every transmitter uses online learning algorithms to learn whether to transmit.

1 Introduction

A fundamental quantity of a wireless network is its *capacity*, which informally is just the maximum amount of data which it can transfer. There is a large literature on analyzing and computing the capacity of wireless networks under various modeling assumptions, including models of how interference works and assumptions on how nodes are distributed in space. The last decade has witnessed a flurry of activity in this area, particularly for worst-case (rather than random)

M. Dinitz—Supported in part by NSF awards CCF-1464239 and CCF-1535887.
N. Ephraim—Supported in part by NSF Award SATC-1704788 and NSF Award IIS-1703846.

F. Dressler and C. Scheideler (Eds.): ALGOSENSORS 2019, LNCS 11931, pp. 96–115, 2019.
https://doi.org/10.1007/978-3-030-34405-4_6

node distributions, motivated by the ability to apply ideas from multiple areas of theoretical computer science (approximation algorithms and algorithmic game theory in particular) to these problems.

We continue that line of work in this paper, but with a new definition of capacity. Much of the research in the last decade (see, e.g., [2, 18–24]) has used a point-to-point definition of capacity: given a collection of disjoint pairs (s_i, t_i) of nodes (called the demands), and some model of interference, the point-to-point capacity is the maximum number of pairs which can simultaneously successfully transmit a message from s_i to t_i. This is sometimes motivated by its utility in scheduling: if we are trying to support many unicast demands in a wireless network, a natural thing to do is make as much progress as possible in each time step, i.e., maximize the number of successful transmissions.

But while well-motivated by scheduling, this is not the only possible definition of *capacity*. In particular, a natural notion of "capacity" is of the best case: what is the absolute limit on the usefulness of a network in even the best possible situation? With this intuition, there are two main issues with point-to-point capacity: the existence of demands, and the requirement for unicast communication. First, since we want to talk about the capacity of a network, why should the capacity be a function of any set of input demands (which are, after all, external to the network itself)? Instead we should allow any set of demands and take the best possible. So one might instead define the "capacity" of the network to be the maximum number of (s_i, t_i) pairs which can simultaneously successfully transmit a message, but not restrict (s_i, t_i) to come from any particular input subset (or equivalently, require the set of input demands to always be $V \times V$ where V is the set of nodes).

Even if we remove the demands, though, there is still something restrictive about this notion of capacity: it only allows unicast, point-to-point communication. One of the defining features of traditional wireless networks is that antennas are omnidirectional. Thus, if we want to truly understand the "capacity" of a given wireless network, we should surely take into account the ability for a single node to successfully send the same message to many other nodes in one time slot, since in the best case we can obtain significant benefits from this ability.

For example, suppose we are in a classical radio network represented by a communication graph, where each node is a transmitter who can communicate with its neighboring nodes. In this model, interference is destructive: u will receive a message from v if v sends a message, u does not send a message, and no other neighbor of u sends a message. Suppose that we are given a star topology with r as the center and leaves $x_1, \ldots, x_n$. What is the capacity of this network? Traditionally, the answer would be 1: only one of the unicast links can be successful, since r can only send or receive one message at a time. On the other hand, if r really only has a single message which it is trying to send to all of its neighbors, then there can be n successful receptions in a single round, and hence the capacity should be n.

Motivated by this, we define a new notion of capacity in radio networks which we call the *reception capacity*. Informally, this is simply the maximum number of successful message receptions in a single round. Note that there are no demands, and there is no requirement that different receptions correspond to different messages. Hence this definition is the true limit on the single-step "usefulness" of the network. We emphasize that there are many notions of capacity, each of which is appropriate and interesting in different contexts, and we are not claiming that reception capacity is the *right* definition. We are merely claiming that it is a natural definition of "best-case usefulness", so bounds on it are bounds on the utility of a network even in the best possible situation.

In this paper we study this notion of capacity in radio networks. We first show that maximizing this capacity is equivalent to a new optimization problem we call the *Maximum Perfect Dominated Set* (MaxPDS) problem. While this problem as defined is new, we show that the classical Decay protocol of [4] gives an $O(\log n)$-approximation algorithm. We also give a tight lower bound on its approximability which matches this upper bound, under plausible complexity assumptions. Both of these results are with respect to networks defined by general communication graphs (the networks are not restricted to having any specific structure). Together, these two bounds give us a tight understanding of the approximability of maximizing the reception capacity.

The main technical contribution of this paper, though, is the study of the capacity achieved by *self-interested* agents. What if every transmitter has its own goals, which do not necessarily align with the global objective of maximizing the reception capacity? While there are many ways to model this, we take a first step by considering a natural model in which every transmitter wants to broadcast its message to as many of its neighbors as possible, but is penalized for unsuccessful transmissions. This intuitively corresponds to a setting where transmitters want to get their message out to many of their neighbors (e.g., if it is an important piece of information which the transmitter wants to disseminate) but are discouraged from placing an unnecessary load on the network if there will be many unsuccessful transmissions.

This type of setting is naturally modeled as a game, where each transmitter is a player that is trying to maximize its own utility. In such a game, what can we say about the *achieved* reception capacity? Does the selfishness of the transmitters mean the network is being underutilized, or do they naturally arrive at an equilibrium with close to optimal reception capacity? In the unicast setting, Dinitz [9] showed that equilibria of the related unicast-specific game can be arbitrarily far from optimal: can the same thing happen with reception capacity?

We completely characterize the behavior of a broad class of equilibria known as ϵ-*coarse correlated equilibria* (ϵ-CCE), which both generalize Nash equilibria and to which natural distributed online learning algorithms (known as no-regret algorithms) will converge [5]. In particular, for a network with n nodes, we prove that at *every* ϵ-CCE the achieved reception capacity of the transmitters is at least $\Omega(1/\sqrt{n})$ of the true reception capacity (unlike the unicast setting), and moreover there exist instances in which *every* ϵ-CCE achieves reception capacity that is at most $O(1/\sqrt{n})$ of the true reception capacity.

1.1 Modeling

To model the notion of reception capacity, we consider the classical *radio network model*. In this model there is a communication graph $G = (V, E)$, and each node in V can act as either a transmitter or a receiver. In a given unit of time (we make the standard assumption of synchronous rounds), each node can either broadcast a message to all of its neighbors, or choose to not broadcast and thus act as a receiver. Interference is modeled by requiring that a receiver can only receive one message in each round, or else the messages interfere and cannot be decoded. In other words, a vertex i can successfully decode a message from a neighbor j if and only if i is not broadcasting (and so is acting as a receiver), j is broadcasting, and no other neighbor of i is broadcasting. If multiple neighbors of i are broadcasting then their messages all interfere with each other at i, and so i would not receive any message.

In this model, the equivalent of the unicast notion of "capacity" used in recent work would be a maximum induced matching (or if there is a set of input demands, a maximum induced matching subject to being a subset of the demands). This is because, in the unicast setting, each node can only transmit to a single neighbor or receive a message from a single broadcasting neighbor. Therefore, maximizing the unicast capacity is equivalent to finding a set S of broadcasters and a set T of receivers such that the bipartite subgraph induced by S and T is a matching, and maximizing the size of this matching.

However, this may be significantly smaller than the number of nodes which can successfully hear a message, as the star example shows. So we will instead adopt a different notion of capacity:

Definition 1. *The* reception capacity *of a wireless network is the maximum number of nodes which can simultaneously successfully receive a message.*

We note that this differs from the traditional unicast or multicast setting because there are no demands from broadcasters to receivers. The reception capacity is rather the total number of messages that can be received in one round, without any assumptions on whether one node "wants" to send a message to another node. Thus it is a true upper bound on the "capacity" (usefulness) of the network.

2 Our Results

2.1 MaxPDS and Approximability

We first observe that it is straightforward to relate reception capacity to reasonably well-studied notions in graph theory. In particular, since each node successfully receives a message if and only if it does not broadcast and exactly one of its neighbors does broadcast, we would like each receiver to be *perfectly dominated* by the set of broadcasting nodes.

Definition 2. *Given a graph* $G = (V, E)$ *and a set* $S \subseteq V$, *we say that a node* $v \in V \setminus S$ *is perfectly dominated by* S *if there exists exactly one node* $u \in S$ *such that* u *is a neighbor of* v.

For every subset $S \subseteq V$, let $D(S) = \{v : v$ is perfectly dominated by $S\}$. This immediately lets us relate the reception capacity to perfect domination.

Lemma 1. *The reception capacity of a wireless network* $G = (V, E)$ *is exactly* $\max_{S \subseteq V} |D(S)|$.

Proof. Let $S \subseteq V$. If every node in S broadcasts a message, by the definition of the radio network model, a node receives a message if and only if it is in $D(S)$. Hence the reception capacity is at least $\max_{S \subseteq V} |D(S)|$. On the other hand, let S be the set of nodes who transmit when the reception capacity is achieved, and suppose that v receives a message. Then $v \in D(S)$, and hence the reception capacity is at most $\max_{S \subseteq V} |D(S)|$.   □

Thus computing the reception capacity of a network is equivalent to the following optimization problem.

Definition 3. *Given a graph* $G = (V, E)$, *the* MAXIMUM PERFECT DOMINATED SET PROBLEM *(*MAXPDS*) is to find a set* $S \subseteq V$ *which maximizes* $|D(S)|$.

This problem seems to be new, despite the vast literature on variations of dominating sets. It is superficially similar to the well-studied MINIMUM PERFECT DOMINATING SET problem [27,28], in which the goal is to find the set S of minimum size such that $D(S) = V \setminus S$ (note that some such S always exists since we could set $S = V$). Despite their superficial similarity, though, the problems are quite different: in MAXPDS nodes not in S may still not be perfectly dominated, so both the feasible solutions and the objective functions of the two problems are quite different.

Therefore, our first goal is to characterize the hardness of MAXPDS. We observe that the classical *Decay protocol* [4] can be used to obtain a simple $O(\log(n))$ approximation algorithm for MAXPDS. We compliment this with an essentially matching lower bound for MAXPDS. The precise lower bound depends on the hardness assumption, but all are essentially polylogarithmic.

Theorem 1. MAXPDS *cannot be approximated to better than a polylogarithmic factor. More precisely:*

- *Let* $\varepsilon > 0$ *be an arbitrary small constant. Suppose that* $NP \not\subseteq BPTIME(2^{n^\varepsilon})$. *Then there is no polynomial time algorithm which approximates* MAXPDS *to within* $O(\log^\sigma n)$ *for some constant* $\sigma = \sigma(\varepsilon)$.
- *Under Feige's Random 3SAT Hypothesis [14], no polynomial time algorithms approximates* MAXPDS *to within* $O(\log^{1/3-\sigma} n)$ *for arbitrarily small constant* $\sigma > 0$.
- *Under the assumption that the Balanced Bipartite Independent Set Problem (BBIS) cannot be approximated better than* $O(n^\varepsilon)$ *for some constant* $\varepsilon > 0$ *(Hypothesis 3.22 of [8]), there is no polynomial time algorithm which approximates* MAXPDS *to within* $o(\log n)$.

This lower bound is obtained through a connection to the *Unique Coverage Problem* (UCP). Informally, UCP is a variation of Maximum Coverage with a similar uniqueness requirement as in MAXPDS (an element only counts as covered if it is contained in exactly one chosen set). Upper and lower bounds for UCP are known [8], so we derive our lower bound by reducing from UCP to MAXPDS (in particular, the different lower bounds and their hardness assumptions are all direct from equivalent bounds and assumptions for UCP). The lower bound is given in Sect. 3 and the upper bound is given in Appendix A.

2.2 Reception Capacity with Self-interested Agents

The above algorithmic results provide us with a comprehensive understanding of the problem of maximizing the reception capacity in arbitrary radio networks. However, they do not imply bounds on the usability of these networks with respect to their reception capacity. That is, for a given network, we would like to investigate the capacity that is utilized under reasonable behavioral assumptions. We focus on the model of self-interested agents due to the competitive nature of a network with fully destructive interference, and because it is a tractable and standard model in the literature on algorithmic game theory.

Therefore, the main focus of this paper is a natural game-theoretic formalization which we call the *reception capacity game*. Informally, this is a game in which the nodes are self-interested players, and the utility of each node is 0 if it does not transmit, and otherwise is a linear function of the number of neighbors who successfully heard its message and the number who did not (we define this game formally in Sect. 4). In other words, each node gets some positive utility from successfully transmitting its message to a neighbor, but pays a price for an unsuccessful transmission.

While this game may seem somewhat arbitrary, it is quite natural. Clearly there has to be some penalty for unsuccessful transmissions, or else the only equilibrium is for all nodes to broadcast all the time. This motivated the previous work on unicast capacity in which a similar game is analyzed [2,3,9], and in fact our game is the obvious generalization of the earlier unicast capacity game. It also motivated previous work on clique networks [15], where they analyzed equilibria in which all nodes were required to transmit with probability strictly smaller than 1. Thus, while it may not be a perfect model of the incentives of selfish transmitters, it is reasonable in at least some situations (e.g., if every transmitter is trying to broadcast an advertisement of some kind). More importantly, it provides insight into the limits of the performance of radio networks in the presence of self-interested agents.

When we analyze behavior in a game, the natural approach is to study the quality of the solution at some notion of equilibrium (this is the well-studied notion of *inefficiency of equilibrium* in algorithmic game theory). While the most popular notion of equilibrium to study is the famous Nash equilibria, we provide stronger results by studying *coarse-correlated equilibria (CCE)*, or more precisely, approximate versions known as ϵ-CCE. We define these formally in Sect. 4, but CCE are generalizations of Nash equilbria, and hence if we can prove that all CCE are close to optimal, or if we can prove that all CCE are far from optimal, then these bounds immediately hold for Nash equilibria as well. Moreover, CCE are an important class of equilibria in a distributed context since (unlike Nash equilibria) natural distributed learning algorithms will have an empirical distribution of play which converges to a CCE, and thus CCEs can be computed efficiently even in distributed settings. We note that these equilibria are precisely those analyzed and used in [3,9] to design distributed algorithms for unicast capacity. However, it was shown in [9] that in *arbitrary* graphs, no nontrivial bounds were possible: there are examples in which there is a solution with $\Omega(n)$ successful transmissions, while any CCE has an average of at most $O(1)$ successful transmissions. On the other hand, we will prove that even in arbitrary graphs, the expected number of receptions in any CCE is at most an $O(\sqrt{n})$ factor worse than OPT (the true reception capacity). We will also show that this is tight by designing instances in which *all* CCE are $\Omega(\sqrt{n})$ worse than OPT. More formally, we prove the following theorems.

Theorem 2. *In any instance of the reception capacity game, the expected number of successful receptions in any ϵ-CCE is at least $OPT \cdot \Omega\left(\frac{1}{\sqrt{n}} - \epsilon\right)$.*

Theorem 3. *There is an instance of the reception capacity game in which in every ϵ-CCE, the expected number of successful receptions is at most $OPT \cdot O((1 + \epsilon)/\sqrt{n})$.*

Note that since every Nash equilibrium is a 0-CCE, our bounds immediately imply bounds on the more classical Price of Anarchy/Stability, in which we compare the optimal solution to the worst/best Nash. We prove Theorem 2 in Sect. 4.2 and Theorem 3 in Sect. 4.3.

Interestingly, like the unicast capacity game studied in [2,3,9] but unlike most algorithmic game theory settings, our notion of "quality" is *not* the social welfare, i.e., it is not just the sum of the utilities of the players. Our notion of quality is number of successful receptions, which can be dramatically different from the social welfare. This means that standard techniques such as *smoothness* [26] cannot be used to analyze this game.

2.3   Related Work

Capacity in Wireless Networks. As discussed earlier, this paper follows an extensive line of work on computing the capacity of wireless networks. There has been a particular focus on the SINR or physical model, in which we explicitly reason about the signal strength and interference at each receiver. However, there has also been significant work directly on graph-based models (e.g., [9]) and on the relationship between graph models and the SINR model [23] (which shows in particular that graphs can do a surprisingly good job of representing the physical model, motivating continued study of graph models).

From the perspective of computing the capacity, the most directly related work (and much of the inspiration for this paper) are [2] and [19], which to a large extent introduced the unicast capacity problem for worst-case inputs and gave the first approximation bounds. These bounds were improved in a series of papers, most notably including a constant-factor approximation [24], and have been generalized to even more general models and metrics, e.g. [20,22].

Much of this paper focuses on analyzing a natural game-theoretic version of reception capacity. This is directly inspired by a line of work on a related game for unicast capacity, initiated by [2] and continued in [3,9]. These papers study various equilibria for the unicast capacity game (Nash equilibria in [2], coarse correlated equilibria in [3,9]) and prove what are essentially price of anarchy or total anarchy bounds (upper bounds on the gap between the optimal capacity and the capacity at equilibrium).

Radio Networks. There is a long line of research on the radio network model under various assumptions. Much of this work focuses on the *radio broadcast problem* [6,7], in which there is a graph representing the network and a source node s. The problem is to minimize the number of rounds that it takes for a message, originating at s, to be successfully propogated through the network.

The literature on this model includes many algorithmic results. NP-hardness results were shown in [7,13], approximation algorithms were given by [4,6,11,16, 17], and inaproximability results were given in [1,10,12,25]. Despite the vast work on this problem, reception capacity differs from the radio broadcast problem in that there we are trying to determine the optimal set of broadcasters in each round, rather than determining a broadcasting schedule given a set of nodes who are allowed to transmit.

Nevertheless, some results in the radio network models apply to the case of reception capacity. In particular, the Decay protocol, introduced as a means of giving an approximation algorithm to the radio broadcast problem, yields an approximation algorithm for MAXPDS [4] (given in Appendix A). Another line of work which focuses on testing communication lines between nodes in networks provides results which imply that MAXPDS is NP-hard. In particular, Even et al. show a reduction from a similar setting to a variant of the Exact Cover problem (which is a variant of Set Cover in which each element must be covered by exactly one set) [13]. Their proof can be used to show that the MAXPDS on bipartite graphs is NP-hard, thus implying hardness for the general case.

A notable variant of the radio broadcast problem is that of *gossiping* in radio networks, which is sometimes called all-to-all communication [17]. This problem studies the number of rounds for n messages, one originating at each of n nodes, to be propagated through the network. While this problem shares a closer resemblance to MAXPDS than that of radio broadcasting, we are not aware of any results that directly imply results for MAXPDS.

2.4   Notation

Given any graph $G = (V, E)$, we refer to undirected graphs with $|V| = n$. Additionally, for any vertex $v \in V$, we define $N(v)$ as the open neighborhood of v, that is, $N(v) = \{u \in V : \{v, u\} \in E\}$, and we let $d(v)$ denote the degree of v.

3   Hardness of Approximation

In this section, we present our hardness of approximation result for the MAXI-
MUM PERFECT DOMINATED SET PROBLEM. We begin by defining the Unique
Coverage Problem [8].

Definition 4 ([8]). *Given a universe U of elements and a collection S of subsets
of U, the* UNIQUE COVERAGE PROBLEM *(UCP) is to find a subcollection $S \subseteq \mathcal{S}$
of subsets which maximizes the number of elements that are uniquely covered,
i.e., are in exactly one set of S.*

Demaine et al. [8] proved the equivalent of Theorem 1 for UCP (all bounds
and assumptions are exactly the same, just for UCP rather than MAXPDS) and
an $O(\log n)$-approximation for UCP. Because of the similarity between UCP and
MAXPDS, we base our lower approximability bound on UCP, and in particular,
show an approximation-preserving reduction from UCP to MAXPDS.

Theorem 4. *Assuming UCP cannot be approximated to within $O(\log^c(n))$ for
some constant c satisfying Theorem 1, then MAXPDS is hard to approximate to
within $O(\log^c(n))$.*

Proof. Consider an instance of UCP with a universe U of elements and a collection $\mathcal{S}$ of subsets of U. For specified parameters α', β', given a subcollection
$\mathcal{S}' \subset \mathcal{S}$, we define the following two cases.

1. $\mathcal{S}'$ is a Yes-instance of UCP if the number of elements uniquely covered is at
   least α'.
2. $\mathcal{S}'$ is a No-instance of UCP if the number of elements uniquely covered is less
   than β'.

Given an instance of this problem, construct an undirected bipartite graph
$G' = (V', E')$ such that V' consists of a vertex s_i for each set $S_i \in \mathcal{S}$ and a
vertex x_i for each element $e_i \in U$. Let $\{s_i, x_j\} \in E'$ if $e_j \in S_i$. Let A denote
the set of vertices s_i corresponding to sets in $\mathcal{S}$, and let B denote the vertices
corresponding the elements in U.

Construct a new bipartite graph $G = (V, E)$ such that V consists of A and
k copies of B, denoted $B_1, B_2, \ldots, B_k$. Let V have an additional vertex v that
is adjacent to all vertices in A. Let E consist of k copies of E', one for each
bipartite subgraph over (A, B_i) for all $i \in [k]$.

Consider some solution $\mathcal{S}'$ to the UCP instance. Define $D = \{s_i : S_i \in
\mathcal{S}'\} \cup \{v\}$. If $\mathcal{S}'$ is a Yes-instance of UCP, then the number of vertices perfectly
dominated by D is $\alpha \geq \alpha'k$, because in each of the B_i, there are at least α'
perfectly dominated vertices. On the other hand, if $\mathcal{S}'$ is a No-instance of UCP,
then there are only $\beta < |\mathcal{S}| + k\beta'$ vertices perfectly dominated by D, because
$\{s_i : S_i \in \mathcal{S}'\}$ perfectly dominates less than $k\beta'$ of the vertices in the B_i and v
perfectly dominates the $|\mathcal{S}|$ vertices in A.

Now, set $k = |\mathcal{S}|$. Then $\alpha \geq \alpha' |\mathcal{S}| = \alpha'k$ and $\beta < |\mathcal{S}| + |\mathcal{S}| \beta' = k + k\beta' =
k(\beta' + 1)$. Therefore, the approximation ratio for MAXPDS in this setting is

$\frac{\alpha}{\beta} > \frac{\alpha' k}{k(\beta'+1)} = \frac{\alpha'}{\beta'+1} \geq \frac{\alpha'}{2\beta'}$ when $\beta' \geq 1$, which is trivially true. Since all we have done is create $|\mathcal{S}|$ repetitions of B, this can be done in polynomial time.

Therefore, this reduction begins with an instance of UCP with an approximation ratio of $\frac{\alpha'}{\beta'}$ and transforms the problem into an instance of MAXPDS with an approximation ratio of $\frac{\alpha}{\beta}$. Let n' be the size of the input to this reduction, and let n be the size of the resulting instance of MAXPDS. By assumption, $\frac{\alpha'}{\beta'} = \Omega(\log^c(n'))$. Therefore, we want to show that $\frac{\alpha}{\beta} = \Omega(\log^c(n))$. We start with $n' = |\mathcal{S}| + |E'|$ and we end with $n = |\mathcal{S}| + k|E'|$. Then $n = |\mathcal{S}| + k|E'| = |\mathcal{S}| + |\mathcal{S}||E'| = |\mathcal{S}|(1+|E'|) \leq 2|\mathcal{S}||E'| < 2(n')^2$, and hence $\log^c(n) \leq \log^c(2(n')^2) \leq 4^c \log^c(n')$, implying that $\log^c(n') \geq \frac{1}{4^c}\log^c(n)$. Therefore, $\frac{\alpha}{\beta} \geq \frac{\alpha'}{2\beta'} \geq \frac{1}{2}\log^c(n') \geq \frac{1}{4^{c+1}}\log^c(n) = \Omega(\log^c(n))$ as desired, thus showing that MAXPDS is hard to approximate to within $O(\log^c(n))$. $\square$

This reduction from UCP to MAXPDS shows that MAXPDS is hard to approximate to within $O(\log^c(n))$ under any hardness assumption for which UCP is hard to approximate to within $O(\log^c(n))$. In particular, this holds for the three different hardness assumptions used to show the hardness of approximating UCP in [8], thus proving Theorem 1.

4   The Reception Capacity Game

In this section, we study reception capacity as a game in a distributed setting with self-interested players. Formally, an instance of the *reception capacity game* is represented by a graph $G = (V, E)$, where we let $V = [n]$ represent the players. Each player has two actions: broadcast (represented by 1) or be silent (represented by 0). Let $S = \{0,1\}^n$ be the strategy space, where for each $s \in S$, s_i represents the action of player i for each $i \in [n]$. For any s, if $s_i = 1$ define $r_i(s) = \left| \left\{ j \in N(i) : s_j = 0 \wedge \sum_{k \in N(j)} s_k = 1 \right\} \right|$ as the number of neighbors of i not broadcasting and receiving exactly one message under s, and if $s_i = 0$, let $r_i(s) = 0$. That is, when i broadcasts, $r_i(s)$ is the number of neighbors of i that successfully receive its message, and $|N(i)| - r_i(s)$ is the number of neighbors of i that are either broadcasting or receiving multiple messages, and thus result in a failure for i. With this notation, we can define the reception capacity game.

Definition 5. *For constants $c, d \geq 1$, an instance of the* reception capacity game *is given by a graph $G = (V, E)$. The utility for player i is $u_i : S \to \mathbb{Z}$, defined by $u_i(s) = c \cdot r_i(s) - d \cdot (|N(i)| - r_i(s))$ if $s_i = 1$, and $u_i(s) = 0$ otherwise.*

This game intuitively models the fact that each node would like to send its message to its neighbors, and gets a benefit proportional to the number of successes but with a penalty for failures (possibly due to either the cost of wasting the transmission power, or more altruistically, a payment for the interference caused). The parameters c and d provide a means by which to model a difference between the reward of a successful broadcast and the cost of a failure (in the simplest case we can think of $c = d = 1$).

Definition 6. *A* coarse correlated equilibrium (CCE) *is a distribution over S such that in expectation, no player has any incentive to deviate. Formally, p is a CCE if for any $i \in [n]$ and any $s_i' \in \{0, 1\}$, $\mathbb{E}_{s \sim p}[u_i(s)] \geq \mathbb{E}_{s \sim p}[u_i(s_{-i}, s_i')]$, where s_{-i}, s_i' is a vector formed by replacing the i'th coordinate of s with s_i'.*

Clearly any Nash equilibrium is a CCE, but a CCE is not necessarily a Nash since every Nash is a product distribution over S while a CCE does not have to be a product distribution. This definition can be relaxed to that of an approximate CCE. In particular, we say that p is an ϵ-CCE if for any $i \in [n]$ and any $s_i' \in \{0, 1\}$, it holds that $\mathbb{E}_{s \sim p}[u_i(s)] \geq \mathbb{E}_{s \sim p}[u_i(s_{-i}, s_i')] - \epsilon$. Note that a true CCE is a 0-CCE, and in the reception capacity game, every distribution over S is a $(c + d)n$-CCE.

4.1   Notation

In the following sections, we let $G = (V, E)$ with $V = [n]$ be an instance of the reception capacity game. Without loss of generality we assume that G is connected, since the results below directly extend to the case where G is disconnected by applying the upper and lower bound to each connected component. We next define a few important sets and quantities.

For every $s \in S$, we will let $B(s) = \{i \in [n] : s_i = 1\}$ be the vertices which are broadcasting, $R(s) = \{i \in [n] : s_i = 0 \wedge \sum_{j \in N(i)} s_j = 1\}$ be the vertices which are successfully receiving a transmission, $F(s) = \{i \in [n] : s_i = 0 \wedge \sum_{j \in N(i)} s_j \geq 2\}$ be the vertices which are receiving at least two transmissions (and thus are failing to successfully receive any transmission), and $A(s) = \{i \in [n] : s_i = 0 \wedge \sum_{j \in N(i)} s_j = 0\}$ be the vertices which are neither broadcasting nor receiving any message.

Let p be a distribution over S which is an ϵ-CCE. Note that $\epsilon \geq 0$ without loss of generality, since if $\epsilon \leq 0$ then we are at a true CCE and so are at a 0-approximate CCE. With respect to p, we can define $B = \sum_{s \in S} p(s)|B(s)|$ as the expected number of broadcasters, $R = \sum_{s \in S} p(s)|R(s)|$ as the expected number of successful receptions (note that this is the quantity which we are trying to compare to OPT), $F = \sum_{s \in S} p(s)|F(s)|$ as the expected number of failures, and $A = \sum_{s \in S} p(s)|A(s)|$ as the expected number of nodes who neither broadcast nor hear a transmission.

4.2   Lower Bound on Successful Receptions

In this section we prove Theorem 2 by showing a lower bound on the expected number of successful receptions in any ϵ-CCE, i.e., showing that the quality of any CCE is not too far from OPT.

We begin with some lemmas that let us relate B and F to R, but for which we need some more notation. Recall that for every $s \in S$ and $i \in [n]$, we defined $r_i(s) = |R(s) \cap N(i)|$ if $s_i = 1$ and $r_i(s) = 0$ if $s_i = 0$. In other words, if i is broadcasting in s, then $r_i(s)$ is the number of its neighbors that successfully receive its message, and otherwise $r_i(s)$ is 0. Similarly, let $f_i(s) = |F(s) \cap N(i)|$

if $s_i = 1$ and let $f_i(s) = 0$ if $s_i = 0$, and let $b_i(s) = |B(s) \cap N(i)|$ if $s_i = 1$ and let $b_i(s) = 0$ if $s_i = 0$.

Since p is an ϵ-CCE we know that every vertex i gets expected utility that is at least $-\epsilon$, since otherwise it would have incentive to get utility 0 by never broadcasting. The expected utility of vertex i under p is precisely $\sum_{s \in S} p(s) (c \cdot r_i(s) - d(f_i(s) + b_i(s)))$, since if $s_i = 0$ then $c \cdot r_i(s) - d(f_i(s) + b_i(s)) = 0$ which is the utility obtained by i by not broadcasting, while if $s_i = 1$ then $r_i(s)$ is exactly the number of neighbors that successfully receive i's message, and $f_i(s) + b_i(s)$ is the number of neighbors of i that are either broadcasting or receiving multiple messages, and thus do not successfully receive i's transmission. Thus, for every $i \in [n]$ it holds that

$$\sum_{s \in S} p(s) (c \cdot r_i(s) - d(f_i(s) + b_i(s))) \geq -\epsilon. \tag{1}$$

We proceed by using this to relate B and F to R.

Lemma 2. $B \leq \frac{c+d}{d} \cdot R + \frac{\epsilon n}{d}$.

Proof. For any $s \in S$ and $i \in [n]$, clearly if $s_i = 1$ then $r_i(s) + f_i(s) + b_i(s) = |N(i)|$ (since every neighbor of i either successfully receives i's transmission or fails because it is broadcasting or also receiving another transmission). Therefore, (1) implies that $\sum_{s \in S} p(s) s_i (c \cdot r_i(s) - d(|N(i)| - r_i(s))) \geq -\epsilon$, and thus $\sum_{s \in S} p(s) s_i ((c + d) r_i(s) - d) \geq -\epsilon$ (since $|N(i)| \geq 1$). Rearranging, we get that

$$(c + d) \sum_{s \in S} p(s) r_i(s) = (c + d) \sum_{s \in S} p(s) s_i r_i(s) \geq d \sum_{s \in S} p(s) s_i - \epsilon.$$

We can now use this to bound the expected number of broadcasters:

$$
\begin{aligned}
B &= \sum_{s \in S} p(s)|B(s)| = \sum_{s \in S} p(s) \sum_{i=1}^{n} s_i = \sum_{i=1}^{n} \sum_{s \in S} p(s) s_i \\
&\leq \sum_{i=1}^{n} \left(\frac{c + d}{d} \sum_{s \in S} p(s) r_i(s) + \frac{\epsilon}{d} \right) \\
&= \frac{c + d}{d} \sum_{i=1}^{n} \sum_{s \in S} p(s) r_i(s) + \frac{\epsilon n}{d} = \frac{c + d}{d} \sum_{s \in S} p(s) \sum_{i=1}^{n} r_i(s) + \frac{\epsilon n}{d}.
\end{aligned}
$$

Since every successful reception can be uniquely attributed to a single transmitter, we know that $\sum_{i=1}^{n} r_i(s) = |R(s)|$ for every $s \in S$. Thus we get that $B \leq \frac{c+d}{d} \sum_{s \in S} p(s)|R(s)| + \frac{\epsilon n}{d} = \frac{c+d}{d} \cdot R + \frac{\epsilon n}{d}$, as claimed. □

Lemma 3. $F \leq \frac{c}{2d} \cdot R + \frac{\epsilon n}{2d}$.

Proof. For any $s \in S$, note that every failure is due to a collision between at least two messages. Thus $|F(s)| \leq \frac{1}{2} \sum_{i=1}^{n} f_i(s)$. Moreover, we know from (1) that

$\sum_{s \in S} p(s) \cdot d \cdot f_i(s) \leq \sum_{s \in S} p(s)(c \cdot r_i(s) - d \cdot b_i(s)) + \epsilon \leq \sum_{s \in S} p(s) \cdot c \cdot r_i(s) + \epsilon$
for all $i \in [n]$. Putting this together, we get that

$$F = \sum_{s \in S} p(s)|F(s)| \leq \frac{1}{2}\sum_{s \in S} p(s)\sum_{i=1}^{n} f_i(s) = \frac{1}{2}\sum_{i=1}^{n}\sum_{s \in S} p(s)f_i(s)$$

$$\leq \frac{1}{2}\sum_{i=1}^{n}\frac{1}{d}\left(\sum_{s \in S} c \cdot p(s)r_i(s) + \epsilon\right) = \frac{c}{2d}\sum_{i=1}^{n}\sum_{s \in S} p(s)r_i(s) + \frac{\epsilon n}{2d}$$

$$= \frac{c}{2d}\sum_{s \in S} p(s)\sum_{i=1}^{n} r_i(s) + \frac{\epsilon n}{2d} = \frac{c}{2d}\sum_{s \in S} p(s)|R(s)| + \frac{\epsilon n}{2d} = \frac{c}{2d}R + \frac{\epsilon n}{2d}.$$

$\square$

The quantity A is more difficult to bound, and will require us to split the nodes into two sets: nodes with large contribution to A, and nodes whose contribution to A is bounded. In particular, define $a = (d + \frac{2}{3}c + \epsilon)/(c+d)$, which will be the threshold. Let $X = \left\{i \in [n] : \sum_{s \in S: i \in A(s)} p(s) > a\right\}$ be the nodes which contribute a significant amount to A. Note that if $\epsilon > \frac{1}{3}c$ then X is empty. Let $Y = V \setminus X$. Let $d_i^X = |N(i) \cap X|$ and let $d_i^Y = |N(i) \cap Y|$. We begin with a simple equation which follows directly from the fact that p is an ϵ-CCE.

Lemma 4. *For every $i \in [n]$, it holds that $c \cdot \sum_{j \in N(i)} \sum_{\substack{s \in S: \\ s_i = 0 \wedge j \in A(s)}} p(s) \leq d \cdot \sum_{j \in N(i)} \sum_{\substack{s \in S: \\ s_i = 0 \wedge j \notin A(s)}} p(s) + \epsilon$.*

Proof. Let $i \in [n]$. Note that for any $s \in S$ with $s_i = 0$, if node i were to transmit, then every neighbor in $A(s)$ would result in a successful reception while every neighbor that is not in $A(s)$ (i.e., every neighbor in $B(s) \cup R(s) \cup F(s)$) would result in a failed reception. Formally, we have that $\mathbb{E}_{s \sim p}[u_i(s_{-i}, 1)] = \sum_{s \in S: s_i = 0} p(s)(c \cdot |N(i) \cap A(s)| - d \cdot |N(i) \setminus A(s)|) + \sum_{s \in S: s_i = 1} p(s)u_i(s)$, and the second summations is equal to $\mathbb{E}_{s \sim p}[u_i(s)]$, because i gets utility 0 if $s_i = 0$. By the definition of an ϵ-CCE we know that $\mathbb{E}_{s \sim p}[u_i(s_{-i}, 1)] - \mathbb{E}_{s \sim p}[u_i(s)] \leq \epsilon$, and thus $c \cdot \sum_{s \in S: s_i = 0} p(s)|N(i) \cap A(s)| \leq d \cdot \sum_{s \in S: s_i = 0} p(s)|N(i) \setminus A(s)|) + \epsilon$. Rearranging each sum gives the lemma. $\square$

Now we can use this lemma to prove some relationships between X and Y.

Lemma 5. *For every $i \in [n]$, it holds that $d \cdot d_i^Y \geq d_i^X(a(c+d) - d) - \epsilon$.*

Proof. We bound both sides of the inequality in Lemma 4. First, we have that

$$\sum_{\substack{j \in N(i)}} \sum_{\substack{s \in S: \\ s_i = 0 \\ \wedge j \in A(s)}} p(s) \geq \sum_{\substack{j \in N(i) \cap X}} \sum_{\substack{s \in S: \\ s_i = 0 \\ \wedge j \in A(s)}} p(s)$$

$$= \sum_{\substack{j \in N(i) \cap X}} \sum_{\substack{s \in S: \\ j \in A(s)}} p(s) \geq \sum_{\substack{j \in N(i) \cap X}} a = a \cdot d_i^X,$$

where we used the fact that for $j \in N(i)$, if $j \in A(s)$ for some $s \in S$ then $s_i = 0$. On the other hand,

$$\sum_{j \in N(i)} \sum_{\substack{s \in S: \\ s_i = 0 \wedge j \notin A(s)}} p(s) = \sum_{j \in N(i) \cap X} \sum_{\substack{s \in S: \\ s_i = 0 \wedge j \notin A(s)}} p(s) + \sum_{j \in N(i) \cap Y} \sum_{\substack{s \in S: \\ s_i = 0 \wedge j \notin A(s)}} p(s)$$

$$\leq \sum_{j \in N(i) \cap X} \sum_{\substack{s \in S: \\ j \notin A(s)}} p(s) + \sum_{j \in N(i) \cap Y} 1$$

$$< \sum_{j \in N(i) \cap X} (1 - a) + d_i^Y = (1 - a) \cdot d_i^X + d_i^Y.$$

Therefore, we can combine these two inequalities with Lemma 4 to get that $ac \cdot d_i^X \leq d(1-a)d_i^X + d \cdot d_i^Y + \epsilon$. Therefore, we get that $d \cdot d_i^Y \geq d_i^X(a(c+d)-d) - \epsilon$, which concludes the proof. $\square$

Lemma 6. *Let $i \in X$. Then $d_i^Y \geq 1$.*

Proof. Let $i \in X$. Suppose that $d_i^Y = 0$. Lemma 5 then implies that $\epsilon \geq |N(i)| (a(c + d) - d) \geq \frac{2}{3}c + \epsilon$ because $|N(i)| \geq 1$, which is a contradiction. $\square$

With these lemmas we can now show that R must be large.

Theorem 5. $R \geq \Omega \left(\frac{cd}{(c+d)^{5/2}} \sqrt{n} - \frac{\epsilon}{c+d}n \right)$.

Proof. The theorem is trivially true when $\epsilon \geq \frac{1}{6}c$, since for sufficiently large n the right hand side becomes negative. Thus we will assume that $\epsilon < \frac{1}{6}c$ (which implies that $a < 1$).

Our first step is to bound $|Y|$. We get that

$$n = |Y| + |X| \leq |Y| + \sum_{i \in X} d_i^Y = |Y| + \sum_{i \in Y} d_i^X \qquad \text{(by Lemma 6)}$$

$$\leq |Y| + \sum_{i \in Y} \left(\frac{d}{a(c+d) - d} \cdot d_i^Y + \frac{\epsilon}{a(c+d) - d} \right) \qquad \text{(by Lemma 5)}$$

$$\leq \frac{a(c+d) + \epsilon}{a(c+d) - d} |Y|^2 = \frac{\frac{2}{3}c + d + 2\epsilon}{\frac{2}{3}c + \epsilon} |Y|^2 < O \left((c+d) |Y|^2 \right)$$

and thus $|Y| \geq \Omega \left(\sqrt{\frac{n}{c+d}} \right)$. We now relate $|Y|$ to R. Note that for every node $i \in Y$, it holds that $\sum_{s \in S: i \notin A(s)} p(s) > 1 - a$. Thus

$$(1 - a)|Y| \leq \sum_{i \in Y} \sum_{s \in S: i \notin A(s)} p(s) \leq \sum_{i \in [n]} \sum_{s \in S: i \notin A(s)} p(s) = \sum_{s \in S} (n - |A(s)|) \cdot p(s)$$

$$= \sum_{s \in S} (|B(s)| + |R(s)| + |F(s)|) \cdot p(s) = B + R + F$$

$$\leq \left(\frac{c+d}{d} + 1 + \frac{c}{2d}\right) R + \frac{2\epsilon n}{d} = \frac{3c + 4d}{2d} \cdot R + \frac{2\epsilon n}{d},$$

where we use Lemma 2 to bound B and Lemma 3 to bound F. Therefore $R = \Omega\left(\frac{d(1-a)}{c+d}|Y| - \frac{\epsilon n}{c+d}\right) = \Omega\left(\frac{cd}{(c+d)^2}|Y| - \frac{\epsilon n}{c+d}\right) = \Omega\left(\frac{cd}{(c+d)^{5/2}}\sqrt{n} - \frac{\epsilon}{c+d}n\right)$, as claimed. □

This immediately gives Theorem 2: since $\mathsf{OPT} \leq n$ and c and d are constants, Theorem 5 implies that $R \geq \Omega\left(n\left(\frac{1}{\sqrt{n}} - \epsilon\right)\right) \geq \Omega\left(\mathsf{OPT}\left(\frac{1}{\sqrt{n}} - \epsilon\right)\right)$.

4.3   Upper Bound on Successful Receptions

We now prove Theorem 3 by upper bounding the expected number of successful receptions in any ϵ-CCE in a specific instance of the reception capacity game.

Theorem 6. *There exists an instance of the reception capacity game with $R \leq O\left((c + d + \epsilon)\sqrt{n}\right)$.*

Proof. For any $q \in \mathbb{N}$, let $G = (V, E)$ be a graph composed of $n = dq(3cq + 1) + 3cq + 1 = 3cdq^2 + dq + 3cq + q + 1$ vertices, defined as follows. Let $V = K \cup L$ and $L = \bigcup_{i \in [3cq+1]} L_i$, where K is a clique on $3cq + 1$ vertices, and for each $i \in K$, the set L_i is an independent set of size dq such that v_i is adjacent to each vertex in L_i.

We proceed by bounding the value of any ϵ-CCE. More formally, if p is a distribution over S which is an ϵ-CCE, we need to bound $R = \sum_{s \in S} p(s)|R(s)|$. It is easy to see that a vertex in L_i successfully receives a message if and only if it does not broadcast and vertex $i \in K$ does broadcast, and thus

$$\sum_{s \in S} p(s)|R(s)| \leq \sum_{s \in S} p(s)\left(|K| + \sum_{i \in K} |L_i|s_i\right) = \sum_{s \in S} p(s)\left(3cq + 1 + \sum_{i \in K} dqs_i\right)$$

$$= 3cq + 1 + dq \sum_{i \in K} \sum_{s \in S} p(s)s_i,$$

so we just need to bound $\sum_{i \in K} \sum_{s \in S} p(s)s_i$. To do this, we partition the strategy vectors into "good" vectors (where i might have positive utility), "bad" vectors (where i has negative utility), and "irrelevant" vectors (where i has zero utility). Formally, we partition S into the following three sets:

$$G_i = \{s \in S : s_i = 1 \wedge \sum_{j \in K} s_j = 1\}$$

$$B_i = \{s \in S : s_i = 1 \wedge \sum_{j \in K} s_j \geq 2\}$$

$$I_i = \{s \in S : s_i = 0\}$$

If $s \in G_i$ then i broadcasts a message which is successfully heard by all K and by at most all nodes in L_i. On the other hand, if $s \in B_i$, then i broadcasts a message which may be heard successfully by all nodes in L_i but which results in a failure at all nodes in $K \setminus \{i\}$. Thus the expected utility of i under ϵ-CCE p is at most

$$\sum_{s \in G_i} p(s)(3cq + dq)c + \sum_{s \in B_i} p(s)(-3cqd + dqc)$$

$$= (3c + d)cq \sum_{s \in G_i} p(s) - 2cqd \sum_{s \in B_i} p(s).$$

Since p is an ϵ-CCE we know that this expected utility must be at least $-\epsilon$, since i can receive utility 0 by not broadcasting. Then we can rearrange to get $\sum_{s \in B_i} p(s) \leq \frac{3c+d}{2d} \sum_{s \in G_i} p(s) + \frac{\epsilon}{2cdq}$. We can now use this inequality to get our desired bound:

$$\sum_{i \in K} \sum_{s \in S} p(s)s_i = \sum_{i \in K} \left(\sum_{s \in G_i} p(s) + \sum_{s \in B_i} p(s) \right)$$

$$\leq \sum_{i \in K} \left(\frac{\epsilon}{2cdq} + \left(\frac{3c + d}{2d} + 1 \right) \sum_{s \in G_i} p(s) \right)$$

$$= \frac{\epsilon \cdot (3cq + 1)}{2cdq} + \frac{3c + 3d}{2d} \sum_{i \in K} \sum_{s \in G_i} p(s) \leq \frac{\epsilon \cdot (3cq + 1)}{2cdq} + \frac{3(c + d)}{2d}.$$

The last inequality is because $G_i \cap G_j = \emptyset$ for $i, j \in K$ with $i \neq j$ by the definition of G_i and G_j, and thus $\sum_{i \in K} \sum_{s \in G_i} p(s) \leq 1$. Therefore, we get that

$$R \leq 3cq + 1 + dq \left(\frac{\epsilon \cdot (3cq + 1)}{2cdq} + \frac{3(c + d)}{2d} \right)$$

$$= 3cq + 1 + \frac{\epsilon(3cq + 1)}{2c} + \frac{3}{2}q(c + d) = \frac{9}{2}cq + 1 + \frac{3}{2}q\epsilon + \frac{\epsilon}{2c} + \frac{3}{2}dq.$$

Since $n \geq 3cdq^2$ we know that $q \leq \sqrt{n}$, and thus this shows that any ϵ-CCE has value at most $O((c + d + \epsilon)\sqrt{n}) = O((c + d + \epsilon)\sqrt{n})$.   □

This immediately implies Theorem 3 as a corollary.

5   Open Questions

We hope that this is only the beginning of analyzing the reception capacity of wireless networks. Many interesting open questions remain, paralleling the work on unicast capacity. For example, what if we consider restricted classes of graphs, such as unit-disc graphs, which are typically used to model wireless networks? Does MAXPDS become easier, and are equilibria in the reception capacity game closer to optimum? And what happens if we work in the SINR model rather than the graph model? For the unicast capacity game, [9] showed that arbitrary graphs are very easy to analyze but the SINR setting is more complicated. Can we analyze the Price of Anarchy of the reception capacity game in the SINR model?

A   Approximation Algorithm for MaxPDS

In this section, we give an approximation algorithm for MAXPDS. Despite the similarities between MAXPDS and UCP, we remark that degenerate cases prevent us from presenting it as a black-box reduction to UCP by invoking the approximation algorithm given by Demaine et al. for UCP. Nevertheless, we observe that the classical decay protocol of Bar-Yehuda et al. for transmitting in radio networks [4] yields a simple approximation algorithm for MAXPDS. We note that the resulting algorithm is also a straightforward adaptation of that of [8] for UCP.

The decay protocol is given in the classical radio broadcasting setting, where transmissions occur over multiple rounds, and there is a subset B of nodes that have already received the message. The decay protocol, for every node in B, is the following: for each round i, broadcast to all neighbors; then, with probability $\frac{1}{2}$, continue to the next round and otherwise stop transmitting. In [4], they observe that for any node v, with constant probability there is a round in which exactly one of v's neighbors will broadcast, and thus v will successfully receive the message (with high probability). This can be modified to a single-round protocol by having each node broadcast with probability $1/2^i$ for some $i \in [\log(n)]$. By setting i appropriately, we obtain an $O(\log(n))$ randomized approximation algorithm.

For completeness, we prove the following theorem.

Theorem 7. *There is a polynomial time $O(\log(n))$-approximation algorithm for* MAXPDS.

Proof. Let $G = (V, E)$ be an instance of MAXPDS with $|V| = n$. For any set S of vertices, let $f(S) = |D(S)|$ denote the number of perfectly dominated vertices by S. Let ALG be an initially empty set and let OPT denote the optimal set of dominating vertices in the above instance.

Partition the vertices into $\log(n)$ groups G_i such that $v \in G_i$ if $2^i \leq d(v) < 2^{i+1}$. Then there must exist a group $i^\star$ such that $|G_{i^\star}| \geq \frac{1}{\log(n)} \cdot n \geq \frac{1}{\log(n)} \cdot f(\text{OPT})$ since $f(\text{OPT}) \leq n$.

Our solution ALG is now constructed by randomly adding each vertex v to ALG independently with probability $\frac{1}{2^{i^\star}}$ when $i^\star > 0$, and with probability $\frac{1}{2}$ when $i^\star = 0$.

Let $S \subset V$ be the vertices that are perfectly dominated by ALG. For any vertex $v \in G_{i^\star}$, let $d = d(v) \in [2^{i^\star}, 2^{i^\star+1})$. Then, the probability that v is perfectly dominated by ALG is the probability that exactly one of $N(v)$ is in ALG and the remaining vertices in $N(v)$ are not in ALG. Since each vertex is chosen to be in ALG independently, when $i^\star > 0$ we have that

$$\Pr\left[v \in S\right] = \left(d \cdot \frac{1}{2^{i^\star}}\right)\left(1 - \frac{1}{2^{i^\star}}\right)^{d-1} \geq \left(1 - \frac{1}{2^{i^\star}}\right)^{2^{i^\star+1}-1}$$

$$\geq \left(1 - \frac{1}{2^{i^\star}}\right)^{2^{i^\star+1}} \geq \frac{1}{e^4}.$$

When $i^\star = 0$, then $d = 1$ and $\Pr[v \in S] = \left(d \cdot \frac{1}{2}\right)\left(1 - \frac{1}{2}\right)^{d-1} = \frac{1}{2} \cdot \left(\frac{1}{2}\right)^0 = \frac{1}{2}$.
Therefore,

$$\mathbb{E}\left[f(\mathsf{ALG})\right] = \sum_{v \in V} \Pr[v \in S] \geq \sum_{v \in G_{i^\star}} \Pr[v \in S] \geq \min\left\{\frac{1}{e^4}, \frac{1}{2}\right\} |G_{i^\star}|$$

$$\geq \frac{1}{e^4 \log(n)} f(\mathsf{OPT}).$$

Therefore, $\frac{f(\mathsf{OPT})}{\mathbb{E}[f(\mathsf{ALG})]} = O(\log(n))$ as desired.

Note that while the above algorithm is randomized, it is straightforward to derandomize in polynomial time using the standard method of conditional expectations. $\square$

References

1. Alon, N., Bar-Noy, A., Linial, N., Peleg, D.: A lower bound for radio broadcast. J. Comput. Syst. Sci. **43**(2), 290–298 (1991)
2. Andrews, M., Dinitz, M.: Maximizing capacity in arbitrary wireless networks in the SINR model: complexity and game theory. In: Proceedings of IEEE INFOCOM, pp. 1332–1340. IEEE (2009)
3. Asgeirsson, E.I., Mitra, P.: On a game theoretic approach to capacity maximization in wireless networks. In: Proceedings of IEEE INFOCOM, pp. 3029–3037. IEEE (2011). https://doi.org/10.1109/INFOCOM.2011.5935146. http://dx.doi.org/10.1109/INFOCOM.2011.5935146
4. Bar-Yehuda, R., Goldreich, O., Itai, A.: On the time-complexity of broadcast in multi-hop radio networks: an exponential gap between determinism and randomization. J. Comput. Syst. Sci. **45**(1), 104–126 (1992)
5. Blum, A., Hajiaghayi, M., Ligett, K., Roth, A.: Regret minimization and the price of total anarchy. In: Dwork, C. (ed.) Proceedings of the 40th Annual ACM Symposium on Theory of Computing, Victoria, British Columbia, Canada, 17–20 May 2008, pp. 373–382. ACM (2008)
6. Chlamtac, I.: The wave expansion approach to broadcasting in multihop radio networks. IEEE Trans. Commun. **39**(3), 426–433 (1991)
7. Chlamtac, I., Kutten, S.: On broadcasting in radio networks-problem analysis and protocol design. IEEE Trans. Commun. **33**(12), 1240–1246 (1985)
8. Demaine, E., Feige, U., Hajiaghayi, M., Salavatipour, M.: Combination can be hard: approximability of the unique coverage problem. SIAM J. Comput. **38**(4), 1464–1483 (2008)
9. Dinitz, M.: Distributed algorithms for approximating wireless network capacity. In: Proceedings of IEEE INFOCOM, pp. 1–9, March 2010. https://doi.org/10.1109/INFCOM.2010.5461905
10. Elkin, M., Kortsarz, G.: Logarithmic inapproximability of the radio broadcast problem. J. Algorithms **52**(1), 8–25 (2004)
11. Elkin, M., Kortsarz, G.: Improved schedule for radio broadcast. In: Proceedings of the Sixteenth Annual ACM-SIAM Symposium on Discrete Algorithms, pp. 222–231. Society for Industrial and Applied Mathematics (2005)

12. Elkin, M., Kortsarz, G.: Polylogarithmic additive inapproximability of the radio broadcast problem. SIAM J. Discrete Math. **19**(4), 881–899 (2005)
13. Even, S., Goldreich, O., Moran, S., Tong, P.: On the np-completeness of certain network testing problems. Networks **14**(1), 1–24 (1984)
14. Feige, U.: Relations between average case complexity and approximation complexity. In: Proceedings of the Thiry-Fourth Annual ACM Symposium on Theory of Computing, STOC 2002, pp. 534–543. ACM, New York (2002). https://doi.org/10.1145/509907.509985. http://doi.acm.org/10.1145/509907.509985
15. Fiat, A., Mansour, Y., Nadav, U.: Efficient contention resolution protocols for selfish agents (2007)
16. Gaber, I., Mansour, Y.: Centralized broadcast in multihop radio networks. J. Algorithms **46**(1), 1–20 (2003)
17. Gasieniec, L., Peleg, D., Xin, Q.: Faster communication in known topology radio networks. In: Proceedings of the Twenty-Fourth Annual ACM Symposium on Principles of Distributed Computing, pp. 129–137. ACM (2005)
18. Goussevskaia, O., Halldórsson, M.M., Wattenhofer, R.: Algorithms for wireless capacity. IEEE/ACM Trans. Netw. **22**(3), 745–755 (2014). https://doi.org/10.1109/TNET.2013.2258036. http://dx.doi.org/10.1109/TNET.2013.2258036
19. Goussevskaia, O., Wattenhofer, R., Halldórsson, M.M., Welzl, E.: Capacity of arbitrary wireless networks. In: Proceedings of IEEE INFOCOM, pp. 1872–1880. IEEE (2009). https://doi.org/10.1109/INFOCOM.2009.5062108. http://dx.doi.org/10.1109/INFOCOM.2009.5062108
20. Halldórsson, M.M., Mitra, P.: Wireless capacity with oblivious power in general metrics. In: Proceedings of the Twenty-Second Annual ACM-SIAM Symposium on Discrete Algorithms, SODA 2011, pp. 1538–1548. Society for Industrial and Applied Mathematics, Philadelphia (2011). http://dl.acm.org/citation.cfm?id=2133036.2133155
21. Halldórsson, M.M., Mitra, P.: Wireless connectivity and capacity. In: Proceedings of the Twenty-Third Annual ACM-SIAM Symposium on Discrete Algorithms, SODA 2012, pp. 516–526. Society for Industrial and Applied Mathematics, Philadelphia (2012). http://dl.acm.org/citation.cfm?id=2095116.2095160
22. Halldórsson, M.M., Mitra, P.: Wireless capacity with arbitrary gain matrix. Theor. Comput. Sci. **553**, 57–63 (2014). https://doi.org/10.1016/j.tcs.2013.09.035. http://dx.doi.org/10.1016/j.tcs.2013.09.035
23. Halldorsson, M.M., Tonoyan, T.: How well can graphs represent wireless interference? In: Proceedings of the Forty-Seventh Annual ACM Symposium on Theory of Computing, STOC 2015, pp. 635–644 ACM, New York (2015). https://doi.org/10.1145/2746539.2746585. http://doi.acm.org/10.1145/2746539.2746585
24. Kesselheim, T.: A constant-factor approximation for wireless capacity maximization with power control in the SINR model. In: Randall, D. (ed.) Proceedings of the Twenty-Second Annual ACM-SIAM Symposium on Discrete Algorithms (SODA), pp. 1549–1559. SIAM (2011). https://doi.org/10.1137/1.9781611973082.120. http://dx.doi.org/10.1137/1.9781611973082.120
25. Kushilevitz, E., Mansour, Y.: An $\omega(d\backslash\log(n/d))$ lower bound for broadcast in radio networks. SIAM J. Comput. **27**(3), 702–712 (1998)
26. Roughgarden, T.: Intrinsic robustness of the price of anarchy. J. ACM **62**(5), 32:1–32:42 (2015). https://doi.org/10.1145/2806883. http://doi.acm.org/10.1145/2806883

27. Weichsel, P.M.: Dominating sets in n-cubes. J. Graph Theory **18**(5), 479–488 (1994). https://doi.org/10.1002/jgt.3190180506. http://dx.doi.org/10.1002/jgt.3190180506

28. Yen, C.C., Lee, R.: The weighted perfect domination problem. Inf. Process. Lett. **35**(6), 295–299 (1990). https://doi.org/http://dx.doi.org/10.1016/0020-0190(90)90031-R. http://www.sciencedirect.com/science/article/pii/002001909090031R

Wireless Communication

Collaborative Broadcast in $\mathcal{O}(\log \log n)$ Rounds

Christian Schindelhauer[1]([✉])[iD], Aditya Oak[2][iD], and Thomas Janson[1][iD]

[1] University of Freiburg, Georges-Köhler-Allee 51, 79110 Freiburg im Breisgau, Germany
schindel@tf.uni-freiburg.de
[2] Technical University of Darmstadt, Hochschulstraße 10, 64289 Darmstadt, Germany
oak@st.informatik.tu-darmstadt.de

Abstract. We consider the multihop broadcasting problem for n nodes placed uniformly at random in a disk and investigate the number of hops required to transmit a signal from the central node to all other nodes under three communication models: Unit-Disk-Graph (UDG), Signal-to-Noise-Ratio (SNR), and the wave superposition model of multiple input/multiple output (MIMO).

In the MIMO model, informed nodes cooperate to produce a stronger superposed signal. We do not consider the problem of transmitting a full message nor do we consider interference with other messages. In each round, the informed senders try to deliver to other nodes the required signal strength such that the received signal can be distinguished from the noise.

We assume a sufficiently high node density $\rho = \Omega(\log n)$ in order to launch the broadcasting process. In the unit-disk graph model, broadcasting takes $\mathcal{O}(\sqrt{n/\rho})$ rounds. In the other models, we use an Expanding Disk Broadcasting Algorithm, where in a round only triggered nodes within a certain distance from the initiator node contribute to the broadcasting operation.

This algorithm achieves a broadcast in only $\mathcal{O}\left(\frac{\log n}{\log \rho}\right)$ rounds in the SNR-model. Adapted to the MISO model, it broadcasts within $\mathcal{O}(\log \log n - \log \log \rho)$ rounds. All bounds are asymptotically tight and hold with high probability, i.e. $1 - n^{-\mathcal{O}(1)}$.

1 Introduction

Understanding the limits of multi hop communications and broadcasting is important for the development of new technologies in the wireless communication sector. In the recent decades, ever more realistic models for communication have been considered. First, graph models have been used to describe the communication between wireless communication nodes, resulting in the Radio Broadcast model [29]. However, this model neglects the communication range, which has led to a geometric graph model, the Unit-Disk Graph (UDG) [2], which we also consider here. It is based on the observation that the power of a

© Springer Nature Switzerland AG 2019
F. Dressler and C. Scheideler (Eds.): ALGOSENSORS 2019, LNCS 11931, pp. 119–136, 2019.
https://doi.org/10.1007/978-3-030-34405-4_7

wireless signal decreases as it suffers from the path loss while traveling through the medium. In order to distinguish the signal from noise, the signal to noise energy ratio (SNR) has to be above certain threshold, which leads to the disk shaped model for radio coverage.

For our theoretical analysis, we concentrate on an open space model with no interfering communications. We want to find the theoretical limitations of a collaborative multi-hop broadcast. For this, we are interested in sending a carrier signal with no further modulated information. This signal is sent by the sender node positioned at the center of a disk in which all other nodes are randomly distributed. Thus, in the first round the first sender activates some small number of neighboring nodes. Then, in every subsequent round, all of them try to extend the set of informed nodes as far as possible, who then join in the next round, until all nodes of the disk are informed (or the process cannot reach any further nodes).

Due to space limitations some proofs are omitted. A full version is available as a technical report [30].

2   Related Work

Broadcasting algorithms have been widely optimized for speed, throughput, and energy consumption. A lot of algorithms apply MAC (medium access control) protocols like TDMA (Time Division Multiple Access) [2,8,10,20], CDMA (Code Division Multiple Access) [4,32], FDMA (Frequency Division Multiple Access) [32] to increase spatial reuse. Physical models with high path loss exponent $\alpha > 2$ are beneficial here and increase the spatial reuse with only local interference. With spatial reuse, parallel point-to-point communications are possible which either spread the same broadcast message in the network or pipeline multiple broadcast messages at the same time. The latter can achieve a constant broadcasting rate for path loss exponent $\alpha > 2$. Cooperative transmission with MISO (Multiple Input Single Output) or MIMO (Multiple Input Multiple Output) is applied to increase the transmission range and broadcast speed by a constant factor (where underlying MAC protocols still work).

Broadcasting has been first considered for a graph based model, where interference prevents communication and a choice has to be made which link should be used for propagation. Since we do not consider interference and allow the usage of all links, a simple flooding algorithm achieves the optimal bound of the diameter of the network. So, these works (see [29] for a survey) do not apply here. However, even if interference is considered there is only a constant factor slow down in the Unit-Disk-Graph model [8]. Note that Unit-Disk-Graphs are connected, when the node density of the randomly placed nodes is large enough [35].

Launched by the seminal paper of [9], the SNR (Signal to Noise Ratio) model has gained a lot of interest. Here, signals can be received if the energy of the sending nodes is a constant factor larger than the sum of noise energy and interference. This model leads to a smooth receiver area with near convexity properties [1].

If the energy of each sender is constrained, Lebhar et al. [20] show that the SNR-model does not give much improvement compared to the UDG-model. So, they incorporate the unit disk model into the SINR (Signal to Interference and Noise) model. The focus of their work is finding TDMA scheduling schemes to enhance the network capacity while the path-loss exponent in the SINR model is chosen with $\alpha > 2$ such that interferences have only local effects for unsynchronized transmitters. In this context, the SNR model is used for each sender separately. So, the problem of broadcast mainly reduces to range assignment and scheduling problem, for which the number of rounds approaches the diameter [10].

For the superposition model the problem of point-to-point communication has been considered mostly for beam-forming for senders (MISO/MIMO) or receivers (SIMO/MIMO). For MIMO (Multiple Input Multiple Output), most of the research is concerned with the energy gain and diversity gain, as well as the trade-off. For an excellent survey we refer to [34]. Besides the approach, where sender antennas and receiver antennas are connected to one device and only a one hop communication is considered, a lot of work is dedicated to collaboration of independent senders and receivers, for which we now discuss some noteworthy contributions.

A transmission with cooperative beamforming requires phase synchronization of the collaborating transmitters to produce a beam and sharing the data to transmit. Dong et al. [3] present for this a two phase scheme: in phase one, the message is spread among nodes in a disk in the plane around the node holding the original message. The open-loop and closed-loop approach can be used to synchronize nodes to the destination or a known node position and time synchronization. In phase two, the synchronized nodes jointly transmit the message towards the destination.

In [7] a three phase scheme is presented. In order to save energy for a Wireless Sensor Network, in the first phase, a sensor sends its message via SIMO to a group of nearby nodes. In the second phase the nodes use MIMO beamforming to another group of nodes nearby of the receiver and in the final phase the last group of nodes sends the message via MISO to the recipient.

For the MIMO model in [22,27] the authors give a recursive construction, which provides a capacity of n for n senders using MIMO communication using its diversity gain. Yet, in [6], an upper bound of $\sqrt{n}$ for such a diversity gain has been proved. These seemingly contradicting statements have been addressed in [28], where they address the question whether distributed MIMO provides significant capacity gain over traditional multi-hop in large ad hoc networks with n source-destination pairs randomly distributed over an area A. It turns out that the capacity depends on the ratio $\sqrt{A}/\lambda$, which describes the spatial degree of freedom. If it is larger than n it allows n degrees of freedom [27], if it is less than $\sqrt{n}$ the bound of [6] holds. For all regimes optimal constructions are provided in these papers. While in [27] path loss exponents $\alpha \in (2,3]$ are considered, for $\alpha > 3$ the regularity of the node placement must be taken into account [22].

While this research is largely concerned with the diversity gain, we study the physical limitations of the energy gain in MIMO. In [24,25], a method is presented to amplify the signal by using spatially distributed nodes. They explore the trade-off between energy efficiency and spectral efficiency with respect to network size. In [21], a distributed algorithm is presented in which rectangular collaborative clusters of increasing size are used to produce stronger signal beams.

Janson et al. [15] analyze the asymptotic behavior of the rounds for a unicast in great detail and prove an upper and lower bound of $\Theta(\log \log n)$ rounds. If the nodes are placed on the line it takes an exponential number of rounds [14]. The generalization of these observations for different path loss models can be found in [12]. In [16] it is shown that the sum of all cooperating sender power can be reduced to the order of one sender, while maintaining a logarithmic number of rounds to send a message over an n hop distance.

A practical approach already uses this technology. Glossy [4] is a network architecture for time synchronization and broadcast including a network protocol for flooding, integration in network protocols of the application, and implementation in real-world sensor nodes. If multiple nodes transmit the same packet in a local area, the same symbol of the different transmitters will overlap at a receiver without inter-symbol interference if the synchronization is sufficient. The superposed signals of the same message have random phase shifts and in the expectation add up constructively. Faraway, out of sync, transmitters produce noise-like interference the influence of which is alleviated at the receiver via pseudo-noise codes. While a high node density increases interference in common network protocols, a higher density is beneficial here and increases the transmission range and reduces the number of broadcasting rounds.

Glossy is the underlying technology for the so-called Low-Power Wireless Bus [5], where this multi-hop broadcast allows to flood the network with a broadcasting message. The energy efficiency was further improved in Zippy [33], which is an on-demand flooding technique providing robust wake-up in the network. Unlike Glossy, Zippy uses an asynchronous wake-up flooding. In [19] the problem of Rayleigh fading for synchronized identical signals is addressed by producing a low frequency wake-up signal, which results from the beat frequency of closely chosen frequencies. This allows the usage of a passive receiver technology.

Sirkeci-Mergen et al. [32] propose a multistage cooperative broadcast algorithm similar to our work. Their nodes are also uniformly distributed in a disk. A continuum approximation is used to approximate the behavior of the disk with high node density. A minimum SNR threshold is assumed for successful reception of the message. Their algorithm works in stages, in the first stage, the node at the center of the disk transmits the message. All nodes which receive this message are considered as level one. In the next stage, level one nodes retransmit the message, in this way set of informed nodes keeps growing in radially outward direction. Nodes belonging to same levels form concentric rings. Source node emits single block of data.

A similar problem and a similar algorithm has been considered in [31]. Sirkeci-Mergen et al. consider source node transmitting a continuous message signal. Initially source node which is at the center of the disk, transmits the message signal. In the next round, level one nodes, i.e. the set of nodes that received the message in the previous round, transmit the message signal which is received by next level and the source node does not transmit message. In the following round, the source transmits the next message block. In this way, levels send and receive the message block in alternate rounds. In our work, we consider that in each round, all informed nodes send a single message cooperatively and we prove bounds on the number of rounds needed.

Jeon et al. [18] also consider a system model similar to our work. They use two phase opportunistic broadcasting to achieve linear increase in propagation distance. In phase one, nodes inside a disk of specific radius broadcast message with different random phases while in phase two, a node broadcasts the message to its neighboring nodes. These phases are performed repeatedly to broadcast the message. Improving on this work we obtain better bounds by coordinating the phase of the nodes, while we consider only the path loss factor of $\alpha = 2$.

To our knowledge, no research so far has evaluated the asymptotic number of rounds to cover the disk using cooperative broadcast using MIMO, which is the main focus of this work. While [4,5,19,33] use only simulation and [18,31,32] prove all their statements only for the expectation in the continuum limit, i.e. when the number of nodes approaches infinity. Our results are to our knowledge the first asymptotic results in MIMO that hold for a finite number of nodes n with high probability, i.e. $1 - n^{-\mathcal{O}(1)}$.

Notations. The L_2-norm is denoted by $\|p\|_2 = \sqrt{x^2 + y^2}$ for $p = (x, y) \in \mathbb{R}^2$. For representation of signal waves we use complex numbers $\mathbb{C}$ where the imaginary number is $i = \sqrt{-1}$. For $z = a + bi$ the complex conjugate is $z^* = a - bi$, the absolute value $|z| = \sqrt{z \cdot z^*} = \sqrt{a^2 + b^2}$ and the real part is $\Re(z) = a = \frac{z + z^*}{2}$, the imaginary part is $\Im(z) = b = \frac{z - z^*}{2}$. The exponent for the base of the Euler number e gives $e^{a+bi} = e^a(\cos b + i \sin b)$.

3   The Models

We assume n nodes $v_1, \ldots, v_n \in \mathbb{R}^2$ uniformly distributed in a disk of radius R centered at origin, where the additional node v_0 resides. The density is denoted by $\rho = n/(\pi R^2)$. Each node knows the disk radius $R \geq 1$.

We concentrate on broadcasting a pure sinusoidal signal and leave the problem of broadcasting a complete message to subsequent work. The sinusoidal signal has wavelength λ and we normalize the speed of light as $c = 1$ by choosing proper units for time and space. In our theoretical framework we assume that every node knows its exact position in the plane, is synchronized (well enough in order to emit phase-coordinated signals) and is able to precisely emit the signal at a given point in time with a certain phase shift and a fixed amplitude.

We consider three communication models in our analysis: Unit-Disk-Graph (UDG), the Signal-to-Noise Ratio (SNR), and MIMO/MISO (Multiple Input—Single/Multiple Output) for coordinated senders. The difference between MIMO and MISO is whether we consider a single receiver or multiple receivers. Since, MIMO is the more general term we prefer this term throughout this paper.

The coordination of nodes refers here to synchronized signals allowing a radiation pattern containing strong beams, i.e. a beamforming gain. Many physical properties are covered in the **Multiple Input/Multiple Output (MIMO)** model based on superposition of waves. Every node can serve either as sender or as receiver. A node can demodulate a received signal $rx(t) \in \mathbb{C}$ if the square of the length of the Fourier coefficient over an interval of $\delta \gg \lambda$ is larger than β, i.e.

$$z = \frac{1}{\delta} \int\limits_{t=t_0}^{t_0+\delta} rx(t)\, e^{-i2\pi t/\lambda} dt \ ,$$

$$|z|^2/N_0 \geq \beta \ . \tag{1}$$

with imaginary number $i = \sqrt{-1}$ and t denoting time. In this notation we normalize the energy with respect to the time period and assume δ, N_0 and β are constant. The bound (1) demands that the signal-to-noise energy ratio is large enough to allow a successful signal reception, i.e. SNR $\geq \beta$ for signal power $|z|^2$ and additive white noise with power N_0 over time δ.

Each sending node $j \in \{1, \ldots, n\}$ can start sending at a designated time t_1 and stops at t_2, described by the function

$$s_j(t) = \begin{cases} a \cdot e^{i2\pi(t-t_1)/\lambda} \ , & t \in [t_1, t_2] \ , \\ 0 \ , & \text{otherwise} \ , \end{cases}$$

where $a \in \mathbb{C}$ may encode some signal information, e.g. via Quadrature Amplitude Modulation (QAM). Since we are only interested in transmitting a single signal we choose $a = 1$ or $a = e^{i\varphi}$, when we use a phase shift φ. The total signal received at a node $q \in \mathbb{R}^2$ is modeled by

$$rx(t) = \sum_{j=1}^{n} \frac{s_j(t - \|q - v_j\|_2)}{\|q - v_j\|_2} \ ,$$

which models the free space transmission model with a path loss factor of two for the logarithm of sender and receiver energy ratio. We are aware, that this equation describes only the far-field behavior, which starts at some constant numbers $c_f > 1$ of wavelengths, i.e. $\|q - v_i\|_2 \geq c_f \lambda$. Hence, every time $\|r - v_i\| < c_f \lambda$, we will replace the denominator $\|q - v_i\|_2$ by $c_f \lambda$ in this expression. We assume that $c_f \lambda \leq 1$ and therefore $\lambda < 1$.

For nodes $v_1, \ldots, v_n$, the geometric **Unit Disk Graph** is defined by the set of edges (v_i, v_j) where nodes have distance $\|v_i, v_j\|_2 \leq 1$. In each round a message or signal can be sent from a node to an adjacent node. So, collaborative sending is simply ignored. Yet, we also ignore the negative effect of interference. In this model messages can be sent along edge in parallel, independently from what happens somewhere else.

The following Lemma shows the strong relationship between the single sender MIMO model and the UDG model.

Lemma 1. *If only one sender u sends a signal in the MIMO model with amplitude $a \in \mathbb{R}^+$, then a node v in distance d receives it if and only if $d \leq \frac{a}{\sqrt{\beta N_0}}$.*

This Lemma implies that if $a^2 = \beta N_0$, then the MIMO model is equivalent to the Unit-Disk Graph (UDG) model with sending radius 1, if only one sender is active. In order to fairly compare these two models, we fix $a = 1$ and set $\beta N_0 = 1$.

The **Signal-to-Noise-Ratio (SNR)** model adds the received signal energy of all senders, i.e. a signal is received at q in the SNR model, if for sender energy $S_j := a_j^2$, where a_j denotes the amplitude of sender v_j the sum of the received signal energy is large enough:

$$RS := \sum_{j=1}^{n} \frac{S_j}{(\|q - v_j\|_2)^2} \ , \quad \text{where} \quad \frac{RS}{N_0} \geq \beta \ .$$

If we assume that the senders' starting time is not coordinated but independently chosen at random, then the following Lemma shows that the MIMO model in the expectation is equivalent to the SNR model.

Lemma 2. *At the receiver q the expected signal energy S of senders $v_1, \ldots, v_n$ with random phase shift ϕ_i and amplitude a_i in the MIMO model is*

$$\mathbb{E}[S] = RS = \sum_{j=1}^{n} \frac{a_j^2}{(\|q - v_j\|_2)^2} \ .$$

For the proof we refer to [13, 30]. Unlike in the coordinated MIMO model, in the SNR model signals are sent with random phasing which induces a more regular radiation pattern.

Under the assumption that $\mathbb{E}\left[|z|^2\right]/N_0 \geq \beta$ induces a successful reception, $a_j = 1$ and $\beta N_0 = 1$ we derive the Signal-to-Noise Ratio (SNR) model, where the energy of the uncorrelated received signals add up. Again, this model reduces to the UDG model if only one node is sending.

4   Lower Bounds

We denote the density of nodes by $\rho = \frac{n}{\pi R^2}$. A constant density $\rho = \Theta(1)$ implies that the expected number of nodes in a constant diameter disk is again a constant. However, there is also constant probability that such a disk is void, and by $\mathbb{R}^+$ argument any constant area region may be empty then. So, by this argument the central node (or any other node) in a Unit-Disk-Graphs may be disconnected with constant probability. So, a higher density is necessary to ensure broadcasting.

4.1 UDG

Since in the UDG model every transmission has a maximum reach of one unit, it takes $\lceil R \rceil$ rounds until every possible node position can be reached. However, some areas might be empty. For constant density $\rho > 1$ the disk rim with nodes in distance of at least $R - 1$ from the center is not empty with extremely high probability. So, it takes at least $\lceil R \rceil - 1$ hops to broadcast in the UDG model, where $R^2 = \frac{n}{\pi \rho}$.

Lemma 3. *For $\rho > 1$ in the UDG model, broadcasting needs $\Omega(\sqrt{n/\rho})$ rounds to inform all nodes with high probability.*

Proof. The probability that none of the $n-1$ non centered nodes are at a distance larger than $R - 1$ from the center is for $R > 1$:

$$\left(1 - \frac{2R - 1}{R^2}\right)^{n-1} \leq e^{-\frac{n-1}{R}} = e^{-\Theta(\sqrt{n\rho})}.$$

Hence, with high probability some nodes are in this outer rim, which can be reached only after at least $R - 2 = \Omega(\sqrt{n}\rho)$ rounds.   □

For large enough density $\rho = \Omega(\log n)$ this bound is tight. The probability that $n-1$ nodes are not in a given area of size $\pi/8$ is less than $1/n^c$ for $\rho \geq \frac{8}{\pi} c \ln(n+1)$ for any $c > 1$ and $n \geq 2$. From a simple geometric argument [30], it follows that UDG is connected and that the diameter of the UDG is at most $8R = \mathcal{O}\left(\sqrt{n/\rho}\right)$ (see [35] for a better bound).

Theorem 1. *For $\rho = \Omega(\log n)$ in the UDG model, broadcasting needs $\Theta(\sqrt{n/\rho})$ rounds to inform all nodes with high probability.*

Proof. Consider two nodes v_j and v_k with distance $d \leq R$. We have seen that each subregion around a node depicted in Fig. 1 contains at least a node with high probability. Now, we route starting from v_j along the line L connecting v_j and v_k by choosing a node from a sector which is closer to r_k in a sector which in a corridor of width 2 around L. We pick a node from this sector and observe that the messages advances by a distance of at least $\frac{1}{4}$ in the direction towards v_k.

Hence, it takes at most $4R$ hops, where $R^2 = \frac{n}{\pi \rho}$.   □

4.2 SNR

The expected number of nodes $n(r)$ in a disk of radius r around the origin is sharply concentrated around the expectation $\rho \pi r^2$, if it is at least logarithmic in n, which follows from an application of Chernoff bounds.

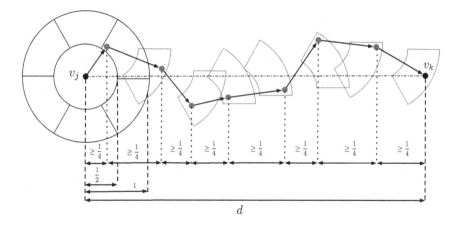

Fig. 1. Routing from v_j to v_k using the unit-disk graph and non-empty sectors.

Lemma 4. *For n randomly distributed nodes in a disk of radius R and a given smaller disk of radius r within this disk, let $n(r)$ denote the number of nodes there within. Then we observe:*

$$\mathbb{E}\left[n(r)\right] = \pi \rho r^2 \ ,$$

$$Prob\left[n(r) \geq (1 + c)\mathbb{E}\left[n(r)\right]\right] \leq e^{-\frac{1}{3}\min\{c,c^2\}\pi \rho r^2} \ ,$$

$$Prob\left[n(r) \leq \tfrac{1}{2}\mathbb{E}\left[n(r)\right]\right] \leq e^{-\frac{1}{8}\pi \rho r^2} \ .$$

These bounds can be used to upper bound the available signal energy in an area and establish a lower bound for collaborative broadcasting in the SNR model.

Theorem 2. *In the SNR-model for $\pi \rho \geq 1$ and $\rho = o(n)$ at least $\Omega\left(\frac{\log n}{\max\{1, \log \rho\}}\right)$ rounds are necessary to broadcast the signal to all n nodes with high probability.*

Proof. We start with the center node in the middle of the disk and denote by r_j the maximum distance of an informed node from the center of the disk. Let n_j denote the number of informed nodes in round j. By definition $r_0 = 0$ and $n_0 = 1$. Then, in round one we have $r_1 = 1$ by applying the SNR model for one sender.

We consider two cases.

1. $\pi \rho \geq k \log n$.
   Then, the expected number of nodes n_1 is $\pi \rho$. By Lemma 4 it is bounded as $n_1 \leq 2\pi \rho$ with high probability by choosing $c = 3k$. Consider a receiver in distance d and assume for the lower bound argument that all nodes $n(r_j)$ in radius r_j send the signal. Since $\pi \rho r_j^2 \geq k \log n$ we have $n(r_j) \geq \frac{1}{2}\pi \rho^2$ with high probability. So, for $d \geq 4\sqrt{\rho}r$ and $\rho \geq 1$ we have $d - r > \sqrt{2\pi \rho}r$. Then,

the received energy is at most $\frac{n(r)}{(d-r)^2} < 1$ with high probability. So, no node farther away than $r_{j+1} = 4\sqrt{\rho}r_j$ is informed in the SNR model in round j. By induction only nodes in distance of at most $r_t = \left(4\sqrt{\rho}\right)^t$ can be informed after t rounds with probability larger than $\frac{1}{n^{O(1)}}$, which only can inform all nodes outside the disk of radius $R - 1 = \frac{n}{\pi\rho} - 1$ if $t \geq \Omega\left(\frac{\log n}{\log \rho}\right)$ for $\rho = o(n)$.

2. $\pi\rho \geq 1$ and $\pi\rho \leq k\log n$.

We overestimate the first radius by $r_1 = \sqrt{\frac{k}{\pi\rho}\ln n}$. Then, $\mathbb{E}\left[n(r_1)\right] = 3k\ln n$ and $n(r_1) \geq 2\mathbb{E}\left[n(r_1)\right]$ only with small probability, i.e. $1/n^k$.

Like in the first case we assume that in round r_j all nodes in this radius send. So, for $d \geq 4\sqrt{\rho}r$ and $\rho \geq 1$ the received energy is less than 1 within a distance of at most $r_{i+1} = 4\sqrt{\rho}r_j$ implying $r_t = (4\sqrt{\rho})^{t-1}r_1$. After t rounds nodes in distance of at most r_t can be informed, which can inform all nodes in the disk of radius $R = \frac{n}{\pi\rho}$ if

$$4(4\sqrt{\rho})^{t-2}\sqrt{\frac{k}{\pi}\ln n} \geq R - 1$$

yielding $t = \Omega\left(\frac{\log n}{\max\{1, \log \rho\}}\right)$ since $\rho = o(n)$.

$\square$

4.3 MIMO

If the unit length amplitudes of all senders in a disk of range r are superpositioned, in the best case, this results in a received absolute amplitude proportional to the number of senders divided by the distance.

Lemma 5. *Assuming that randomly placed senders are in a disk of radius r, then the maximum distance of a node which can be activated is at most $4\pi\rho r^2$ with high probability for $\rho r^2 = \Omega(\log n)$.*

Proof. The expected number of senders in a disk of radius r is $\pi\rho r^2$. Using Lemma 4 and $\rho r^2 = \Omega(\log n)$ one can show that this number does not exceed $2\pi\rho r^2$ with high probability.

Now, in the best case, all waves at a receiver r perfectly add up resulting in a received signal of at most $|\text{rx}| \leq \sum_{i=1}^{2\pi\rho r^2} \frac{1}{\|r - s_i\|_2}$. We overestimate this signal by replacing the denominator with $d - r$, where d is the distance of the receiver from the senders' disk's center. Hence, we receive a signal if $|\text{rx}|^2 = (2\pi\rho r^2)^2 \geq (d-r)^2$ and get $d \leq r + 2\pi\rho r^2 \leq 4\pi\rho r^2$. $\square$

So, the radius of the disk of informed nodes increases by a polynomial recursion.

Corollary 1. *Any broadcast algorithm using MIMO needs at least $\Omega(\log\log n - \log\log \rho)$ rounds to inform all n nodes with high probability.*

Proof. We use Lemma 5 by overestimating the effect of triggered nodes which are bound to disks with radii r_j. We assume that we start with $r_0 = \log n$ for $\rho \geq 1$. Now, let $r_{j+1} = 4\pi \rho r_j^2$ denote the largest distance of a node in the next round.

So $r_j \leq (4\pi \rho \log n)^{2^j}$, which reaches $R - 1 = \sqrt{n/(\pi \rho)} - 1$ at the earliest for some $j = \Omega(\log \log n - \log \log \rho)$. □

This claim also follows from the considerations in [14] and [17] and more extensive in [12] where a lower bound of $\Omega(\log \log n)$ rounds for the unicast problem has been shown. Here, we adapt this argument to include the density ρ.

5 Expanding Disk Broadcasting

For the SNR model a simple flooding algorithm works as well as the algorithm we propose. A straight-forward observation is a monotony property, i.e. every increase in sending amplitude and every additional sending node increases the coverage area. For the upper bound we use Algorithm 1 which is slower, yet still asymptotically tight to the lower bound and easier to analyze. We choose $r_{j+1} = \frac{1}{4}\sqrt{\rho} r_j$, starting with $r_1 = 1$ and prove the following Lemma.

Algorithm *Expanding Disk Broadcast*

   Sender v_0 starts sending ;
   $j \leftarrow 1$;
   while $r_j < R$ **do**
      for all $v \in \{v_1, \ldots, v_n\}$ *which are informed and where* $\|v - v_0\|_2 \leq r_j$
      do
         | Node v starts sending ;
      end
      $j \leftarrow j + 1;$
   end
end

Algorithm 1: Expanding Disk Broadcast

Lemma 6. *If* $\rho = \Omega(\log n)$, *then in round* $j \geq 1$ *all nodes in distance* r_{j+1} *from the origin have been informed with high probability.*

Proof. Lemma 4 states that the expected number of nodes $n(r_j)$ in the disk of radius r_j is $\rho \pi r_j^2$. It also shows that $\mathrm{Prob}\left[n(r_i) \leq \frac{1}{2}\pi \rho r_j^2\right] \leq e^{-\frac{1}{8}\rho \pi r_j^2} \leq e^{-\frac{1}{8}\rho}$, which is a small probability $1/n^c$ for $\rho = \Omega(\log n)$.

The maximum distance from any node in the disk of radius r_{j+1} to a node in this disk is at most $r_j + r_{j+1} \leq 2r_{j+1}$. Hence, the received signal has an expected SNR of at least $\frac{n(r_j)}{(2r_{j+1})^2} \geq \beta = 1$. □

Therefore $r_j = (\rho/16)^{(j-1)/2}$ and for $j \geq 1 + 2\frac{\log n - \log(\pi\rho)}{(\log \rho) - 4} = \Theta(\log n/\log \rho)$ we have $r_j \geq R$ and all nodes are informed.

Corollary 2. *In the SNR-model collaborative broadcasting needs $\mathcal{O}(\log n/\log \rho)$ rounds for $\rho > 16$, if broadcasting starts with at least $\Omega(\log n)$ nodes, or $\rho = \Omega(\log n)$.*

We conjecture that the result of Corollary 2 not only holds for our (line-of-sight, path loss exponent 2) SNR model but also holds for the model proposed in [22,26] where the path loss exponent is $\alpha \leq 2$. Then, the channel from sender v_j to receiver v_k has an contribution of $s_j(t)h_{j,k}(t)$ for emitted signal $s_j(t)$ and $h_{j,k}(t) = \|v_k - v_j\|_2^{-\alpha/2} \cdot e^{i \cdot \theta_{j,k}(t)}$ with random phase shift $\theta_{j,k}(t)$ at time t. We discuss further conjectures about the influence of the path loss factor in the Outlook.

6 MIMO

In MIMO the coverage area is far from being convex. Also adding a sender node might cause destructive wave interference. So, bounding the sending area by a disk, as in the expanding broadcasting algorithm, simplifies the analysis. We use a start radius $r_1 = c_2/\lambda$ and the expansion $r_{j+1} = c_1 \rho r_j^{3/2} \lambda^{1/2}$ for a constant $c_1 > 0$. In the subsequent MIMO rounds, the senders v_k are synchronized with a phase shift $\varphi_\ell = -2\pi\|v_\ell - v_0\|_2/\lambda$ such that the resulting signal of v_ℓ is $e^{i(2\pi t/\lambda + \varphi_\ell)}$. These phases try to imitate the pattern of single sender in the center, the energy of which grows double exponentially in each round.

For the analysis we consider only the signal strength at one receiver and analyze whether MISO works for this sender. We prove that the SNR ratio of the collaborative broadcast signal at every receiver is above the threshold with high probability. So, MISO with high probability results in MIMO with high probability for all receivers in the next disk rim.

Algorithm *MIMO Broadcast*

> Inform all nodes in the disk of radius $15r_1$;
> $j \leftarrow 1$;
> **while** $r_j < R$ **do**
> > **for all** $v \in \{v_1, \ldots, v_n\}$ *which are informed and where* $\|v - v_0\|_2 \leq r_j$
> > **do**
> > > Node v starts sending with phase shift $\varphi = -2\pi\|v - v_0\|_2/\lambda$;
> >
> > **end**
> > $j \leftarrow j + 1$;
>
> **end**

end

Algorithm 2: MIMO Broadcast

Recall that the density is defined as $\rho = \frac{n}{\pi R^2}$ and let $\rho \geq c_3 \log n$.

Theorem 3. *For constant wavelength λ, density $\rho = \Omega(\log n)$ every receiver in distance d can be triggered with high probability, if $15r_j \leq d \leq c_1 \rho r_j^{3/2} \lambda^{1/2}$, for a constant c_1.*

Proof. We consider an arbitrary node q in distance d from the first sender v_0 in the center. We prove that this node is triggered with high probability and thus all receivers in this distance will be triggered likewise with this probability.

First we analyze the expected received signal of a receiver in distance d, which is given by an integral. The complex value of this integral will be asymptotically estimated using a geometric argument over the intersection of ellipses with equal phase shift impact and the sender disk.

Define for $p = (p_x, p_y)$: $\Delta_d(p) := \sqrt{p_x^2 + p_y^2} + \sqrt{(d - p_x)^2 + p_y^2} - d$.

Lemma 7. *For $0 \leq w \leq \tau + \lambda/2$ and senders $v_1, \ldots, v_n \in D(v_0, r)$ the received signal is given as $rx(t) = rx \cdot e^{i2\pi(t-d)/\lambda}$, where*

$$rx = \sum_{j=1}^{n} \frac{e^{-i2\pi\Delta_d(v_j)/\lambda}}{\|q - v_j\|_2} .$$

There is an easy characterization by ellipses E_τ with focal points in $v_0 = (0,0)$ and $q = (d, 0)$, which characterize whether senders help or interfere, see Fig. 2.

$$E_\tau := \{p \in \mathbb{R}^2 \mid \|p\|_2 + \|p - q\|_2 = d + \tau\} .$$

The term $2\pi\tau/\lambda$ describes the phase at which the sender's signal arrives at the receiver q. The main contributor to the received signal comes from the area within $E_{\leq\tau} := \{p \in \mathbb{R}^2 \mid \|p\|_2 + \|p - q\|_2 \leq d + \tau\}$ intersected with D_r for $\tau = \lambda/2$, where we D_r denotes the disk with center $(0,0)$ and radius r. This intersection has an area of $\Theta(r^{3/2}\lambda^{1/2})$, which corresponds to the innermost dark ellipse in Fig. 2. We prove that the other areas cancel themselves out and their sum of signals is much smaller than this area.

To prove this, we give a formula which describes exactly the expected signal at a given point t_0. This expectation will be estimated by carefully chosen bounds.

Lemma 8. *The expected received signal at a receiver in distance d from the center of the sender disk of radius r is the following.*

$$\mathbb{E}[rx] = \frac{1}{d} + \frac{n-1}{2\pi r^2} \iint\limits_{(x,y) \in D_r} \frac{e^{-i\Delta_d(x,y)2\pi/\lambda} \, \mathrm{d}x \, \mathrm{d}y}{\sqrt{(x - d)^2 + y^2}} .$$

In order to estimate this expectation we define for the unit disk D_1:

$$u_{d,\lambda}(w) := \iint\limits_{(x,y) \in E_{\leq w} \cap D_1} \frac{e^{-i\Delta_d(x,y)2\pi/\lambda}}{\sqrt{(x - d)^2 + y^2}} \, \mathrm{d}x \, \mathrm{d}y .$$

The relationship between u with normalized sender radius and expected signal is: $\mathbb{E}[rx] = \frac{1}{d} + \frac{n-1}{2\pi r} u_{d/r, \lambda/r}(2)$. The following lower bound is essential.

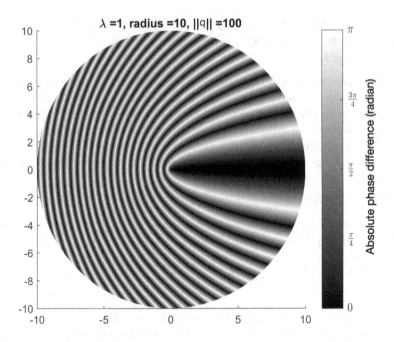

Fig. 2. Senders in a disk of radius 10, colored according to the phase difference perceived by a receiver located at point $(100, 0)$ for wavelength $\lambda = 1$ [23].

Lemma 9. *For $\lambda \leq 2$ and $d > 15$: $\Im(u_{d,\lambda}(2)) \geq \frac{9}{2,240\sqrt{2}} \frac{\sqrt{\lambda}}{d+1}$.*

The main steps of this proof, presented in detail in [30], are the following. In order to evaluate the integral we perform a coordinate transformation, where (x, y) are replaced by the distance to the center $(0, 0)$ and to the receiver $(d, 0)$. For large enough $d \geq 15r$ the influence of the denominator $\sqrt{(x - d)^2 + y^2}$ can be estimated by d. It remains to estimate the areas of positive and negative super-positioned signals.

For this, we analyze the first and second derivative of the area function of the intersecting ellipse with the sender disk $f(\tau, d) := |E_{\leq \tau} \cap D_1|$. We show that the second derivative $f''(x, y) := \frac{d^2 f(x, y)}{d^2 x}$ is negative, i.e. $f''(x, y) < -\frac{1}{8}$. This means that every dark area in Fig. 2 cancels out the next outer light area with opposite signal. It remains to show that the contribution of the combined first dark and light area is large enough. This is done by proving $f'(x, y) \geq \frac{7}{5}f'(x + \lambda/2, d)$ for $f'(x, y) := \frac{d f(x, y)}{d x}$ and $x \leq \lambda/2$. The claim then follows from $\sqrt{x} < f(x, y) < \frac{7}{3}\sqrt{x}$ for all $x \in [0, 2]$.

While there is a closed form for f and its derivatives, they are too involved for a manual analysis. Hence, we use automatized proofs to prove these inequalities. For this, we bounded the input and output values of all terms by interval arithmetics over rational numbers. We divide the input intervals of the functions into small enough partitions and recursively compute lower and upper rational bounds, which comply with the proposed bounds. Since d can be arbitrarily large, the second parameter has been substituted for these proofs with $z = \frac{1}{d}$ and the limit for $d \to z$ has been added for the automatized analysis.

From this we deduce the following Lemma, which lowerbounds the complex component of the received signal in distance d.

Lemma 10. *For $d > 15r$:*

$$\mathbb{E}\left[\Im[rx]\right] \geq \frac{9}{4,480\pi\sqrt{2}} \frac{m\sqrt{\lambda}}{d\sqrt{r}} .$$

Now, we apply the Hoeffding bound (Theorem 2 of [11]) and prove that the received signal has the necessary strength with high probability.

Lemma 11. *For $d \geq 15r$, constant $c, c' > 0$*

$$Prob\left[\Im[rx] \leq c\frac{(n-1)\sqrt{\lambda}}{d\sqrt{r}}\right] \leq \exp\left(-c'\frac{\lambda m}{r}\right) .$$

Note that $\Im(z) \geq a$ implies $|z|^2 = \Im(z)^2 + \Re(z)^2 \geq a^2$. For $r = \Omega(\ln n/\rho)$ we have $n = \Omega\left(\frac{r}{\lambda}\log n\right)$, which implies the following lemma.

Lemma 12. *For $r = \Omega(\log n/\rho)$, constants c, c' and $d > 15r$:*

$$Prob\left[|rx|^2 \geq c\left(\frac{(n-1)\sqrt{\lambda}}{d\sqrt{r}}\right)^2\right] \leq n^{-c'} .$$

The right side is larger than the SNR threshold $\beta = 1$ if $d \leq c(n-1)r^{1/2}\lambda^{1/2}$. Using that $n \geq 1 + \frac{1}{2}\rho\pi r^2$ holds with high probability, the claim follows. □

Theorem 4. *For constant wavelength λ MIMO broadcasting takes $\mathcal{O}(\log\log n - \log\log\rho)$ rounds to broadcast the signal.*

Proof. The algorithm works in two phases. In the first phase, we inform all nodes in radius $r_1 = \mathcal{O}(1)$ using the UDG Broadcast algorithm with single senders. This takes at most $\mathcal{O}(1)$ rounds.

In the second phase we use the phase shift $\varphi_\ell = \|v_\ell - v_0\|_2$ for all senders v_ℓ. Now the radii increase double exponentially with $r_{j+1} = c_1\rho r_j^{3/2}\lambda^{\frac{1}{2}}$. Note that $r_{j+1} \geq 15r_j$ if $r_j \geq \frac{225}{c_1^2\rho^2\lambda} \geq \frac{c_2}{\lambda} = r_1$ which holds for large enough number of nodes n. After $j = \mathcal{O}(\log\log n - \log\log\rho)$ rounds we have reached

$$r_j = r_1^{\left(\frac{3}{2}\right)^j}\left(c_1\rho\lambda^{\frac{1}{2}}\right)^{1+\frac{3}{2}+\ldots+\left(\frac{3}{2}\right)^{j-1}} = r_t^{\left(\frac{3}{2}\right)^j}\left(c_1\rho\lambda^{\frac{1}{2}}\right)^{2\left(\frac{3}{2}\right)^j-2} \geq R = \sqrt{\frac{n}{\pi\rho}}.$$

In the first round nodes in the radius $15r_1$ nodes are informed. So, the minimum distance of $15r_1$ from the senders is upheld. In every other round we increase r_j by a factor of at least 15 to ensure the minimum distance of $15r_j$. □

7   Conclusions and Outlook

We have compared the number of rounds of collaborative broadcasting in three communication models. All of them are derived from the far-field superposition MISO/MIMO model where the signal-to-noise ratio allows a communication range of one unit. For the UDG model the delimiting factor is the diameter of the graph, proportional to $\sqrt{n/\rho}$. For the SNR-model broadcasting takes a logarithmic number of rounds which is caused by the addition of the senders' signal energy. This allows to extend the disk of informed nodes by a factor of $\Theta(\sqrt{\rho})$, where ρ is the sender density.

For the MIMO model it is already known that beamforming increases the energy beyond the SNR model. It is possible to achieve logarithmic number of rounds for unicast on the line [14] and $\mathcal{O}(\log \log n)$ for the plane [15].

We have focused on broadcasting only a single sinusoidal signal and not a message consisting of many different signals. For dealing with inter-signal interference and inter-symbol interference tighter bounds and special encodings might be necessary.

Another question concerns the influence of the path loss exponent α, which we choose as $\alpha = 2$. As an anonymous reviewer pointed out in the SNR model one expects for $\alpha < 2$ a bound of $\mathcal{O}(\log \log n)$ for broadcasting, for $\alpha = 2$ we have proved a bound of $\Theta(\log n)$ and for $\alpha > 2$ we conjecture a bound of $\mathcal{O}(n^{1/2})$.

We conjecture for MIMO that our results can be generalized for $\alpha < 3$ because of area size of around $\Theta(r^{3/2}\lambda^{1/2})$ of nearly synchronous senders. For larger path loss the asymptotic number of rounds increases. For $\alpha = 3$ we conjecture a logarithmic bound and for $\alpha > 3$ the same behavior as in the Unit Disk Graph.

Acknowledgments. We like to thank the organizers of the Dagstuhl Seminar 17271, July 2–7, 2017, Foundations of Wireless Networking, where this research has begun and first results have been found. We would like to thank Alexander Leibold, who performed and checked the automated proofs and anonymous reviewers of a previous version for their detailed and valuable input. We would also like to thank Tigran Tonoyan, Magnús M. Halldórsson and Zvi Lotker for many fruitful discussions.

References

1. Avin, C., Emek, Y., Kantor, E., Lotker, Z., Peleg, D., Roditty, L.: SINR diagrams: convexity and its applications in wireless networks. J. ACM **59**(4), 18 (2012)
2. Clark, B.N., Colbourn, C.J., Johnson, D.S.: Unit disk graphs. Discrete Math. **86**(1–3), 165–177 (1990)
3. Dong, L., Petropulu, A., Poor, H.: A cross-layer approach to collaborative beamforming for wireless ad hoc networks. IEEE Trans. Signal Process. **56**(7), 2981–2993 (2008)
4. Ferrari, F., Zimmerling, M., Thiele, L., Saukh, O.: Efficient network flooding and time synchronization with glossy. In: Proceedings of the 10th ACM/IEEE International Conference on Information Processing in Sensor Networks, pp. 73–84. IEEE, Chicago, April 2011

5. Ferrari, F., Zimmerling, M., Mottola, L., Thiele, L.: Low-power wireless bus. In: Proceedings of the 10th ACM Conference on Embedded Network Sensor Systems, SenSys 2012, pp. 1–14. ACM, New York (2012)
6. Franceschetti, M., Migliore, M.D., Minero, P.: The capacity of wireless networks: information-theoretic and physical limits. IEEE Trans. Inf. Theory **55**(8), 3413–3424 (2009)
7. de Freitas, E.P., da Costa, J.P.C.L., de Almeida, A.L.F., Marinho, M.: Applying MIMO techniques to minimize energy consumption for long distances communications in wireless sensor networks. In: Andreev, S., Balandin, S., Koucheryavy, Y. (eds.) NEW2AN/ruSMART -2012. LNCS, vol. 7469, pp. 379–390. Springer, Heidelberg (2012). https://doi.org/10.1007/978-3-642-32686-8_35
8. Gandhi, R., Mishra, A., Parthasarathy, S.: Minimizing broadcast latency and redundancy in ad hoc networks. IEEE/ACM Trans. Network. (TON) **16**(4), 840–851 (2008)
9. Gupta, P., Kumar, P.R.: The capacity of wireless networks. IEEE Trans. Inf. Theory **46**, 388–404 (2000)
10. Halldórsson, M.M., Tonoyan, T.: Leveraging indirect signaling for topology inference and fast broadcast. In: Proceedings of the 2018 ACM Symposium on Principles of Distributed Computing, PODC 2018, pp. 85–93. ACM, New York (2018)
11. Hoeffding, W.: Probability inequalities for sums of bounded random variables. J. Am. Stat. Assoc. **58**(301), 13–30 (1963)
12. Janson, T.: Energy-efficient collaborative beamforming in wireless ad hoc networks. Ph.D. thesis, University of Freiburg, Germany (2015)
13. Janson, T., Schindelhauer, C.: Analyzing randomly placed multiple antennas for MIMO wireless communication. In: Fifth International Workshop on Selected Topics in Mobile and Wireless Computing (IEEE STWiMob), Barcelona (2012)
14. Janson, T., Schindelhauer, C.: Broadcasting in logarithmic time for ad hoc network nodes on a line using MIMO. In: Proceedings of the 25th ACM Symposium on Parallelism in Algorithms and Architectures, SPAA 2013. ACM, July 2013
15. Janson, T., Schindelhauer, C.: Ad-Hoc network unicast in O(log log n) using beamforming. http://arxiv.org/abs/1405.0417, May 2014
16. Janson, T., Schindelhauer, C.: Cooperative beamforming in ad-hoc networks with sublinear transmission power. In: IEEE 10th International Conference on Wireless and Mobile Computing. Networking and Communications (WiMob), pp. 144–151. IEEE, Larnaca, October 2014
17. Janson, T., Schindelhauer, C.: Self-synchronized cooperative beamforming in ad-hoc networks. In: 16th International Symposium on Stabilization, Safety, and Security of Distributed Systems (SSS 2014), Paderborn, Germany, September 2014
18. Jeon, S.W., Chung, S.Y.: Two-phase opportunistic broadcasting in large wireless networks. In: IEEE International Symposium on Information Theory, ISIT 2007, pp. 2771–2775. IEEE (2007)
19. Kumberg, T., Schindelhauer, C., Reindl, L.: Exploiting concurrent wake-up transmissions using beat frequencies. Sensors **17**(8), 1717 (2017)
20. Lebhar, E., Lotker, Z.: Unit disk graph and physical interference model: putting pieces together. In: IEEE International Symposium on Parallel Distributed Processing (IPDPS 2009), pp. 1–8, May 2009
21. Merzakreeva, A., Özgür, A., Lévêque, O.: Telescopic beamforming for large wireless networks. In: IEEE International Symposium on Information Theory, Istanbul (2013)
22. Niesen, U., Gupta, P., Shah, D.: On capacity scaling in arbitrary wireless networks. IEEE Trans. Inf. Theory **55**(9), 3959–3982 (2009)

23. Oak, A.: Analysis of a collaborative iterative MISO broadcasting algorithm. Master's thesis, University of Freiburg, Freiburg, Germany, March 2018
24. Oyman, O., Paulraj, A.J.: Power-bandwidth tradeoff in dense multi-antenna relay networks. IEEE Trans. Wireless Commun. **6**(6) (2007)
25. Oyman, O., Paulraj, A.J.: Cooperative OFDMA and distributed MIMO relaying over dense wireless networks, uS Patent 8,027,301, 27 September 2011
26. Ozgur, A., Lévêque, O., David, N.: Hierarchical cooperation achieves optimal capacity scaling in ad hoc networks. IEEE Trans. Inf. Theory **53**(10), 3549–3572 (2007)
27. Özgür, A., Leveque, O., Tse, D.: Hierarchical cooperation achieves optimal capacity scaling in ad hoc networks. IEEE Trans. Inf. Theory **53**(10), 3549–3572 (2007)
28. Özgür, A., Lévêque, O., Tse, D.: Spatial degrees of freedom of large distributed mimo systems and wireless ad hoc networks. IEEE J. Sel. Areas Commun. **31**(EPFL-ARTICLE-185421), 202–214 (2013)
29. Peleg, D.: Time-efficient broadcasting in radio networks: a review. In: Janowski, T., Mohanty, H. (eds.) ICDCIT 2007. LNCS, vol. 4882, pp. 1–18. Springer, Heidelberg (2007). https://doi.org/10.1007/978-3-540-77115-9_1
30. Schindelhauer, C., Oak, A., Janson, T.: Collaborative broadcast in O(log log n) rounds. arXiv e-prints arXiv:1906.05153, June 2019
31. Sirkeci-Mergen, B., Gastpar, M.C.: On the broadcast capacity of wireless networks with cooperative relays. IEEE Trans. Inf. Theory **56**(8), 3847–3861 (2010)
32. Sirkeci-Mergen, B., Scaglione, A., Mergen, G.: Asymptotic analysis of multistage cooperative broadcast in wireless networks. IEEE/ACM Trans. Netw. **14**(SI), 2531–2550 (2006)
33. Sutton, F., Buchli, B., Beutel, J., Thiele, L.: Zippy: on-demand network flooding. In: Proceedings of the 13th ACM Conference on Embedded Networked Sensor Systems, pp. 45–58. ACM (2015)
34. Tse, D., Viswanath, P.: Fundamentals of Wireless Communication. Cambridge University Press, New York (2005)
35. Xue, F., Kumar, P.R.: The number of neighbors needed for connectivity of wireless networks. Wireless Netw. **10**(2), 169–181 (2004)

Multi-channel Assignment and Link Scheduling for Prioritized Latency-Sensitive Applications

Shih-Yu Tsai[1]([✉]), Hao-Tsung Yang[1], Kin Sum Liu[1], Shan Lin[2], Rezaul Chowdhury[1], and Jie Gao[1]

[1] Department of Computer Science, Stony Brook University, Stony Brook, USA
{shitsai,haotyang,kiliu,rezaul,jgao}@cs.stonybrook.edu
[2] Department of Electrical and Computer Engineering, Stony Brook University, Stony Brook, USA
shan.x.lin@stonybrook.edu

Abstract. Current wireless networks mainly focus on delay-tolerant applications while demands for latency-sensitive applications are rising with VR/AR technologies and machine-to-machine IoT applications. In this paper we consider multi-channel, multi-radio scheduling at the MAC layer to optimize for the performance of prioritized, delay-sensitive demands. Our objective is to design an interference-free schedule that minimizes the maximum weighted refresh time among all edges, where the refresh time of an edge is the maximum number of time slots between two successive slots of that edge and the weights reflect given priorities. In the single-antenna unweighted case with k channels and n transceivers, the scheduling problem reduces to the classical edge coloring problem when $k \geq \lfloor n/2 \rfloor$ and to strong edge coloring when $k = 1$, but it is neither edge coloring nor strong edge coloring for general k. Further, the priority requirement introduces extra challenges. In this paper we provide a randomized algorithm with an approximation factor of $\tilde{O}\left(\max\left\{\sqrt{\Delta_p}, \frac{\Delta_p}{\sqrt{k}}\right\} \log m\right)$ in expectation, where Δ_p denotes the maximum degree of the unweighted multi-graph, which is formed by duplicating each edge e_i for w_i times (w_i is e_i's integral priority value), and m is the number of required link communications ($f(n) \in \tilde{O}(h(n))$ means that $f(n) \in O\left(h(n) \log^k(h(n))\right)$ for some positive constant k. The results are generalized to the multi-antenna settings. We evaluate the performance of our methods in different settings using simulations).

Keywords: Latency sensitive scheduling · Multi-channel scheduling · Fairness

1 Introduction

Today's communication networks have provided great support to delay-tolerant applications (e.g., web, email). But demands for latency-sensitive applications in

© Springer Nature Switzerland AG 2019
F. Dressler and C. Scheideler (Eds.): ALGOSENSORS 2019, LNCS 11931, pp. 137–157, 2019.
https://doi.org/10.1007/978-3-030-34405-4_8

wireless and mobile networks are rising, with emerging applications from video-conferencing, real-time interactions using Virtual Reality/Augmented Reality (VR/AR), vehicular networking and distributed robotics. These new applications require more stringent delay guarantees. To support latency-sensitive applications, one must develop network control algorithms at various layers with latency guarantees.

In this paper, we look at the MAC layer and consider a TDMA-based (Time-Division Multiple Access) multi-channel link scheduling problem. Multi-radio multi-channel architecture is widely adopted in wireless mesh networks deployments (e.g., in MIT Roofnet, WING [1,4,5,8,24]) and is increasingly supported in IEEE standards (e.g., 02.11 and 802.16) [7,9,11]. We assume that there are k channels of different frequencies to use and each node may have one or multiple radio interfaces, possibly operating on different channels. At each time slot, each of the radio interfaces may be assigned one of the k channels and if two nodes within the same communication range have two radio interfaces on the same channel, the message can be successfully received provided there is no interference in the neighborhood. The general question on channel assignment and scheduling is to decide for each link which channel to use and when, given an optimization objective. In this paper, we examine the following problem.

Min Max Weighted Refresh Time Scheduling. Given k channels and a simple weighted graph $G = (V, E)$ with $|V| = n$ and $|E| = m$ in which edge $e_i \in E$ has integer weight w_i with the minimum edge weight being 1, we would like to design a periodic schedule for all edges in $G,$[1] which specifies a set of edges for each time slot and the channels they use. The channel assignment for an edge (u, v) specifies the channel that the transceivers at u and v adopt. If a node has r radio interfaces, different radio interfaces may operate on different channels. A feasible schedule must follow the following rules to avoid interference:

- There are at most r active edges incident to any node at any given time, since a node has r radio interfaces.
- Two edges that are active at the same time must use different channels if they are within the interference distance from each other, i.e., they have a common endpoint or some of their endpoints are neighbors[2].

Here, we consider interference at the protocol level, leaving the physical model (SINR model) for future exploration. Our goal is to find a feasible schedule of all edges that minimizes

$$\max_{i \in \{1,...,m\}} w_i T_i.$$

Here, T_i denotes the *maximum refresh time* for edge e_i, i.e., the maximum number of time slots until edge e_i appears again in the given schedule. We name this

---

[1] Schedules are restricted to be periodic because each non-periodic infinite schedule with a finite max weighted refresh time can be turned to a periodic schedule with the same refresh time. See Appendix for a proof.

[2] This is the case of ℓ-hop interference model (wireless links $\ell + 1$ or more hops away from one another can be scheduled to transmit data at the same time) when $\ell = 2$.

problem as Min Max Weighted Refresh Time Scheduling problem for the case of non-uniform weights; Min Max Refresh Time Scheduling otherwise.

In this paper, we focus on the algorithmic aspect of the scheduling problem and assume that the networking issues (synchronization, packet loss, and retransmissions) are handled in the standard manner. We assume relatively long streaming traffic flow such that the schedules for traffic demands are updated when traffic demands change substantially.

Motivation and Related Work. A lot of prior work on channel assignment and scheduling focused on maximizing network throughput (i.e., the total number of links one can schedule in a single slot without interference), or makespan (i.e., minimize the time slots to complete a given demand vector), which will be reviewed in the next section. For latency sensitive applications fairness is important as well, in order for traffic flows to experience steady and predictable latency over time. Our problem provides guaranteed share of resources for each edge. Further, we wish to allow prioritized treatment for emergency oriented applications (compared to recreational applications). This can be implemented by edges on the routes of traffic with high priority carrying higher weights. In our problem, these edges are scheduled more frequently.

Mathematically, our problem is closely related to edge coloring and strong edge coloring problems. The problem of edge coloring is to assign a color to each edge such that no two adjacent edges have the same color. The minimum number of colors used is called the *chromatic index*, which is either Δ or $\Delta + 1$, where Δ is the maximum degree in the graph (Vizing's Theorem), although deciding which one is the optimal index is NP-hard [13]. Greedy coloring, i.e., use a color that is not yet used in the neighboring edges, gives a 2-approximation. In strong edge coloring, two edges e, e' cannot have the same color if they share a common endpoint or their endpoints are connected by an edge (Fig. 1). In the wireless network setting, this maps to

Fig. 1. The edges (a, b), (c, d) can be colored the same in edge coloring but cannot be colored the same in strong edge coloring (due to the edge (a, d)).

the scenario when protocol level interference is considered and shall be eliminated in the schedule [3,17,20,21]. The minimum number of colors used is called the *strong chromatic index*. Counting the number of edges that could be in conflict with any edge shows that the strong chromatic index is between Δ and $2\Delta(\Delta - 1) + 1$. Erdös and Nešetřil conjectured that the strong chromatic index is at most $5\Delta^2/4$, which is still open. For a given graph, computing its strong chromatic index is NP-hard [25], and a greedy algorithm gives a $\Theta(\Delta)$ approximation. Closing the gap appears to be a long-standing problem (see [16]).

Our problem adds more complications by considering k possible channels and r radios per node. As we will show in this paper, our scheduling problem includes edge coloring and strong edge coloring as special cases. As far as we are aware, our problem has not been studied before.

Our Contribution. In this paper, we initiate the study of the Min Max Weighted Refresh Time Scheduling problem. We consider the single radio case first, i.e., $r = 1$. When edges have the same weight, our problem reduces to the classical *edge coloring* problem if k is at least $\lfloor n/2 \rfloor$ and the *strong edge coloring* problem if $k = 1$. For a general k, a greedy algorithm that assigns each edge the earliest possible time slot with the first available channel achieves an approximation factor of $\left\lceil \frac{2(\Delta-1)}{k} \right\rceil + 2$, where Δ is the maximum degree of the given graph. Notice that this bound is a smooth transition from the 2-approximation for edge coloring to $\Theta(\Delta)$-approximation for strong edge coloring, when k varies between 1 and $n/2$.

When edges have different priorities/weights, the problem becomes tricky. Intuitively, an edge with a higher weight should be scheduled more frequently. That is, we may want to create multiple copies of this edge so that we can apply the scheduling algorithm for the unweighted setting by treating each duplicate edge as a different edge. But how many copies should we make for an edge of weight w_i? Second, the duplicated copies of the same edge, ideally, shall be spread uniformly in the schedule, avoiding a large gap somewhere. However, it is not clear how to ensure the uniform placement of the duplicated copies of e_i, for every edge e_i, with non-trivial interference patterns to avoid. Last, we need to obtain a lower bound for the optimal refresh time in order to prove approximation factors.

Our insights come from understanding the optimal schedule. Suppose the optimal schedule repeats every T slots. There is a lower bound $\mathbb{L}(S)$ of the optimum maximum refresh time – by simply dividing T by μ_i, the number of times e_i appears in one cycle, for each edge e_i. Next, we show that this lower bound achieves the minimum value ℓ^* if μ_i is Cw_i, for some integer C. This is useful for the algorithm design as we know that the number of copies duplicated for e_i shall be *proportional* to w_i, but we still do not know what C is. By using the probabilistic method, we show that if we set $C = 1$ and take the schedule that minimizes the lower bound $\mathbb{L}(S)$, then the value of $\mathbb{L}(S)$ is at most a factor of $7 \log m$ of ℓ^*, where m is the number of distinct edges to be scheduled. This way we are only losing a factor of $O(\log m)$.

The analysis above suggests the following simple scheduling algorithm for the weighted setting. We first make w_i copies of edge e_i, generate a random permutation of these edges (possibly with duplicates), and partition the permutation into chunks of equal length. For each chunk, run the aforementioned greedy scheduling algorithm and then combine the schedules together. We ensure that the length of each chunk is small enough such that for each edge e, only $O(1)$ edges in expectation may interfere with e. Hence, the greedy schedule uses $O(1)$ time slots for each chunk. Further, in a random permutation, the duplicated edges are likely to be placed evenly – the maximum gap can be bounded by the standard balls and bins problem. In summary, the approximation factor (in expectation) is bounded as

$$O\left(\max\left\{ \sqrt{\Delta_p}, \frac{\Delta_p}{\sqrt{k}} \right\} \log m \frac{\log W_{\max}}{\log \log W_{\max}} \right),$$

where Δ_p denotes the maximum degree of the unweighted multi-graph, which is formed by duplicating each edge e_i for w_i times, and $W_{\max}$ is the highest weight of all edges. Notice that the endpoints of the edge of maximum weight has degree at least $W_{\max}$ in the multi-graph. That is, $\Delta_p \geq W_{\max}$. Hence, the provided approximation factor can be written concisely as $\tilde{O}\left(\max\left\{\sqrt{\Delta_p}, \frac{\Delta_p}{\sqrt{k}}\right\} \log m\right)$.

Finally, both the weighted and unweighted algorithms can be extended to the multi-antenna case, i.e., $r > 1$. We also run simulations empirically (in Appendix) to evaluate the performance of our algorithms. The simulations show that our unweighted algorithm works as efficiently for large graphs as for small graphs when they have similar densities. When we have a reasonable number of channels, our algorithm can efficiently use them for large graphs to keep the latency low. On the other hand, our weighted algorithm can efficiently use only two available channels for graphs with uniform weight distribution. It is approximately two times better than with only one channel.

The rest of this paper is organized as follows. Section 2 discusses related work. We address the single antenna case in Sect. 3 and Sect. 4, and extend our result to the multi-antenna case in Sect. 5. Section 6 concludes this paper.

2   Related Work

Channel assignment and link scheduling with wireless interference have mainly focused on throughput optimization (maximizing the number of edges that can be scheduled at the same time). This problem is closely related to finding the maximum independent set. For a given demand vector, a commonly formulated problem is to minimize the number of slots to meet the demand, called the *makespan*.

For the centralized setting, Hajek and Sasaki [12] considered the problem of minimizing makespan but ignored wireless interference, proposing two polynomial-time algorithms for direct messages and relayed messages. Ramanathan and Lloyd [19] considered wireless interference and focused on trees and planar graphs. Balakrishnan et al. [2] looked at unit disk graphs and proposed PTAS and distributed constant factor polynomial-time approximation algorithms. Sharma [22] considered approximation algorithms for the k-hop interference model.

A few papers [6,15] considered fully distributed scheduling algorithms that optimize for throughput or makespan. For 1-hop interference model, the maximum number of edges that could be scheduled at the same time is the maximum matching. A greedy maximal matching algorithm has at least half of edges of the optimal, and in general has an approximation factor depending on the 'interference degree' [6,14,28].

The results have been generalized to multi-hop communication scenarios. Kumar et al. [15] studied the problem of minimizing makespan for given packets in a wireless setting with 2-hop interference (the same as ours) and proposed a distributed algorithm with an approximation bound of $\Theta(\Delta \log^2 n)$ for arbitrary graphs. They also show that it is hard to approximate the minimum makespan within a factor of $\Delta^{1-\varepsilon}$ for any positive constant $\varepsilon < 1$, even in the centralized setting. On the other hand, with the same greedy idea, Wan et al. [26] scheduled replicated edges (traffic demands on direct-communicated links) in any multi-hop wireless network under any arbitrary interference model. The proposed algorithm achieves a $1 + \mu \ln \alpha$ approximation ratio using a μ−approximate algorithm for finding a maximal set of transmitting edges to greedily schedule the edges, where α is the maximum number of edges that can transmit simultaneously. Furthermore, in the multi-antenna scenario under the binary interference model, they also considered a variant in which traffic demands are given on the node-level links and proposed a constant factor approximation algorithm [27].

Fairness is not considered in the scheduling literature as much as throughput. Shi et al. [23] discussed the existing fairness models of channel assignment and compared them systematically. They also stated several challenges, such as designing fairness strategies under distributed scenarios (since we consider wireless networks), corrective strategies for unfairness, and how to assign weights to nodes and how to allocate resources according to the weights. Most studies have focused on resource allocation but the weight assignment strategies have not received much attention. Chaporkar et al. [6] proposed the use of a token generation mechanism together with maximal scheduling for fairness, but no guarantee is provided.

3   Min Max Refresh Time in the Single-Antenna Setting

We start with the case in which all edges are unweighted and each node has only one antenna ($r = 1$) and show the connection of our problem (i.e., the Min Max Refresh Time Scheduling problem defined in Sect. 1) with other graph problems. For different k, the number of channels, the problem in the single-antenna unweighted case maps equivalently to different graph coloring problems.

- When $k = 1$, this problem is equivalent to the *strong edge coloring* problem. The edges of the same color are scheduled during the same time slot.
- When $k \geq \lfloor |V|/2 \rfloor$, the problem is equivalent to the *edge coloring* problem, where V is the set of transceivers. Again the edges of the same color are scheduled during the same time slot – though they may use different channels.
- In between the problem is neither edge coloring nor strong edge coloring. We show that a greedy algorithm gives a $\lceil 2(\Delta - 1)/k \rceil + 2$ factor approximation to the optimal solution.

Theorem 1. *In the single-antenna case with unit weights, the Min Max Refresh Time Scheduling problem with only one channel available is equivalent to strong edge coloring.*

Proof. In a strong edge coloring problem, the edges of the same color form an induced matching. Let us identify the colors by unique integers from $\{1, \cdots, c\}$. Here c is the number of available colors. We schedule all edges of color i during time slot i, for all $i \in \{1, \cdots, c\}$. We repeat this finite schedule forever to form our final infinite schedule. In each slot, the edges do not cause any interference. Further, the maximum refresh time for any one edge is exactly c in this schedule.

In the other direction, given an infinite schedule solution with the maximum refresh time t, it can be transformed into a periodic schedule by finding the prefix schedule that achieves the maximum refresh time. Focus on this prefix schedule (cycle), it will create an induced matching for each slot and we remove any duplicate edges in this cycle. If we color the edges in the same time slot by the same color, this becomes a valid strong edge coloring solution. The maximum refresh time t implies that the cycle cannot have a length more than t, so the valid strong edge coloring solution has at most t colors. Therefore, the two problems are equivalent. □

Theorem 2. *In the single-antenna case with unit weights, the Min Max Refresh Time Scheduling problem with at least $\lfloor |V|/2 \rfloor$ channels is equivalent to the edge coloring problem.*

Proof. Suppose we are given an edge coloring solution with c colors. Observe that it is a decomposition of the given graph G into c matchings. Assign a new time slot to each matching. In each time slot, assign each edge in the corresponding matching to a different channel. There are at most $\lfloor |V|/2 \rfloor$ edges in a matching of G so we have enough channels to build this schedule. Form a periodic schedule by repeating this schedule of c time slots. The refresh time for any edge is at most c.

On the other hand, given an infinite schedule with maximum refresh time t, it must have a smallest periodic cycle of length at most t. By eliminating any duplicate edges, each edge appears exactly once now, i.e., this cycle partitions the edges into at most t time slots. The edges scheduled for a given time slot cannot share any common vertices – since each node is given only one channel. That means each time slot gives a matching, so this graph is t edge colorable. □

For any k, we show that the following greedy algorithm has an approximation ratio of $\lceil 2(\Delta - 1)/k \rceil + 2$. We examine the edges one by one. For each edge e, we check the first slot with the first channel to see if e can be scheduled without violating any constraints. If not, we move on to the next channel and check again. If we run out of channels, we move on to the next time slot. When we go through all the edges, denote the number of slots used as h. We then repeat the schedule an infinite number of times. The refresh time for all edges is precisely h.

To show the approximation factor, we observe that the optimal schedule for G, for any k, is at least Δ – this is because these Δ edges attached to the common node must be placed in different slots.

Theorem 3. *In the single-antenna unweighted case, the greedy algorithm gives a schedule with a maximum refresh time of at most $\lceil \frac{2(\Delta-1)^2}{k} \rceil + 2(\Delta - 1) + 1$. Therefore, this algorithm is a $\lceil \frac{2(\Delta-1)}{k} \rceil + 2-$approximate algorithm for the Min Max Refresh Time Scheduling problem.*

Proof. We consider the edges that are placed in the last time slot of the generated finite schedule. Take one of these edges, say, edge e. The reason e is placed at the h-th slot, by the greedy rule, is that it cannot be placed anywhere earlier. For each of the previous slot, at least one of the following two events happens: the first event is that an edge incident to one endpoint of e is scheduled and so we cannot schedule e. The second event is that we run out of channels for e. For *each* of the k channels, there is an edge e' that is at most one hop away from e and is scheduled with this channel. (Here, at most one hop away means that edges e and e' have a common endpoint or some of their endpoints are neighbors.)

Since e is incident to at most $2(\Delta - 1)$ edges, the number of slots of the first type is at most $2(\Delta - 1)$. At most $2(\Delta - 1)^2$ edges are one hop away from e. For the second event to happen we need to use k such edges. Therefore, there are at most $\lceil 2(\Delta - 1)^2/k \rceil$ slots of the second type.

The worst case happens if, for each slot, exactly one of the two events happens. This amounts to a total of at most $\lceil 2(\Delta - 1)^2/k \rceil + 2(\Delta - 1) + 1$ slots. Furthermore, the lower bound of optimal max refresh time Δ means that this greedy algorithm produces a $(\lceil 2(\Delta - 1)/k \rceil + 2)$-approximate solution.   □

Remark. When $k = \Theta(\Delta)$, the greedy algorithm is a constant approximation. The upper bound $\lceil 2(\Delta - 1)^2/k \rceil + 2(\Delta - 1) + 1$ is nearly tight – for $k = 1$ there are graphs that require $\Omega(\Delta^2)$ slots. For example, a 5-cycle must use 5 colors for strong edge coloring. If we glue two 5-cycles together as in Fig. 2, the graph requires 20 colors. In general, if we glue l of the 5-cycles together, this amounts to $5\Delta^2/4$, where $\Delta = 2l$.

Remark. The bounds here work for general graphs. Specifically, in the case of unit disk graphs, using packing argument, we can show that the greedy algorithm mentioned above has a $O(1)$ approximation factor [3].

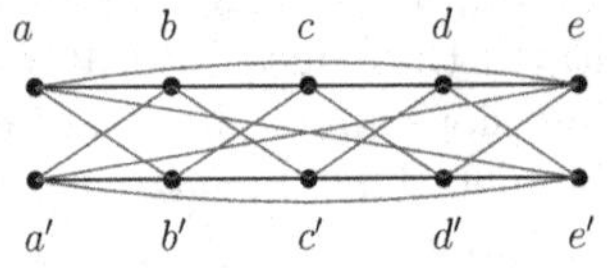

Fig. 2. Two 5-cycles $abcde$ and $a'b'c'd'e'$ glued to each other (by the blue edges). The graph requires 20 colors/slots to schedule if a single channel is used. (Color figure online)

4   Min Max Weighted Refresh Time in the Single-Antenna Setting

In this section, we discuss the Min Max Weighted Refresh Time Scheduling problem under the single-antenna setting. Let $G = (V, E)$ be a weighted graph, where E is the set of m edges $e_1, ..., e_m$ with weights $w_1, ..., w_m$, respectively. We would like to minimize $\max_i w_i T_i$, where T_i is the maximum refresh time for edge e_i. When w_i's are not the same, the algorithm in the previous section does not work. If an edge is more important, then we would like to schedule it more frequently.

4.1   Lower Bound of the Optimal Solution

We first try to understand the structure of the optimal solution. Let us consider the optimal periodic schedule and consider one cycle S^* of the optimal periodic schedule. Suppose S^* has T^* time slots and the maximum refresh time for edge e_i is T_i^* and edge e_i appears μ_i^* times in S^*. We can picture this periodic schedule as wrapping S^* around on a cycle. T_i^* is the maximum gap between adjacent appearances of i on the cycle. Clearly, $T_i^* \geq T^*/\mu_i^*$ by the pigeonhole principle. Define $\mathbb{L}(S^*) = \max_{i \in \{1,\ldots,m\}} w_i T^*/\mu_i^*$. Therefore, the optimal solution is lower bounded as follows.

$$\mathbb{O}(S^*) = \max_{i \in \{1,\ldots,m\}} w_i T_i^* \geq \max_{i \in \{1,\ldots,m\}} w_i T^*/\mu_i^* = \mathbb{L}(S^*). \tag{1}$$

Now let us suppose we have a collection of edges in which edge e_i is duplicated μ_i times and consider a feasible finite schedule S for these edges and denote by $T(S)$ the total number of time slots. For each feasible finite schedule S, let us define

$$\mathbb{L}(S) = \max_{i \in \{1,\ldots,m\}} w_i T(S)/\mu_i.$$

Here, μ_i is the number of occurrences of edge e_i in S. Now, we want to understand when we can get the minimum value of $\mathbb{L}(S)$ among all feasible finite schedules S. Since S^* is one finite feasible schedule, the minimum value of $\mathbb{L}(S)$ is a lower bound of $\mathbb{L}(S^*)$, hence, a lower bound of $\mathbb{O}(S^*)$ as well.

Lemma 1. *Among all possible feasible schedules S, $\mathbb{L}(S)$ is minimized when the schedule has $\mu_i = Cw_i$ for some integer C, for all i.*

Proof. Assume otherwise. Let S be a schedule that achieves the minimum $\mathbb{L}(S)$ but not every μ_i is exactly Cw_i for some integer C. We will create a feasible schedule S' with $\mathbb{L}(S') < \mathbb{L}(S)$, yielding a contradiction.

First, we repeat the schedule D times for some big integer D, which will be determined later. Now we take the edge e_i that has the largest $w_i T(S)/\mu_i$ among all edges (i.e., i realizes the value $\mathbb{L}(S)$). We create a slot that only contains edge e_i and add this slot at the end of the enlarged schedule. In the new schedule S', we have a total of $T(S') = DT(S) + 1$ slots.

Now we calculate the ratio $w_j T(S')/\mu_j'$, for each edge e_j in the new schedule S'. First, for edge e_i, we have

$$\frac{w_i T(S')}{\mu_i'} = \frac{w_i(DT(S) + 1)}{D\mu_i + 1} < \frac{w_i T(S)}{\mu_i} = \mathbb{L}(S)$$

The inequality is true because $\mu_i < T(S)$.

Now consider an edge e_j, $j \neq i$. There are two cases.

– If $w_j T(S)/\mu_j < w_i T(S)/\mu_i$, then we can show that

$$w_j T(S')/\mu_j' < w_i T(S')/\mu_i' = \mathbb{L}(S)$$

by taking

$$D > \frac{w_j}{w_i \mu_j - w_j \mu_i}.$$

– If $w_j T(S)/\mu_j = w_i T(S)/\mu_i = \mathbb{L}(S)$, we repeat the same procedure as above. Notice that in every iteration we remove one edge that realizes $\mathbb{L}(S)$.

At the end we can argue that we find a new schedule S' such that for all edges j, $w_j T(S')/\mu'_j < \mathbb{L}(S)$. Thus $\mathbb{L}(S') < \mathbb{L}(S)$. This is a contradiction to the optimality of S. Hence, the statement of this lemma is true.   □

Therefore, $\mathbb{L}(S)$ is minimized when $\mu_i = C w_i$, for all i and some constant C. Next, we show that it does not hurt too much to consider $\mu_i = w_i$ if we only care about minimizing $\mathbb{L}(S)$.

Suppose we have two scheduling problems, in the first one, each edge e_i is duplicated $\mu'_i = w_i$ times and we take S' to be one of the best finite feasible schedules for these edges that minimize $\mathbb{L}(S')$; while in the second one, each edge e_i is duplicated $\mu''_i = C w_i$ times, for a variable C taking all possible integer values. Let S'' be one of the optimal schedules that minimize $\mathbb{L}(S'')$. Clearly $\mathbb{L}(S'') \leq \mathbb{L}(S')$ by definition. We now argue that,

Lemma 2. $\mathbb{L}(S') \leq 7 \log m\, \mathbb{L}(S'')$, where m is the number of edges of G.

To prove this lemma, we first need the following lemma.

Lemma 3. *Given a bipartite graph with vertex sets X and Y. If all the degree of $y_i \in Y$ is a multiple of C for a fixed constant C and $|X|$ is also a multiple of C, then there is a subset $X' \subseteq X$ such that $|X'| = |X| \cdot \beta/C$ and for each vertex $y \in Y$, the number of neighbors of y in X' is at least $d(y)/C$, where $d(y)$ is the degree of y and $\beta = 7 \log m$ with $m = |Y|$.*

Proof. We will use a probabilistic argument to prove that such an X' exists. Partition the vertex set X into disjoint subsets X_1 and X_2 randomly with $|X_1| = |X|\beta/C$. Hence, each vertex in X has probability β/C to be in X_1. Now, for each vertex $y_i \in Y$, denote by Y_i the number of edges incident to y_i and a vertex in X_1. Clearly the expectation of Y_i is $E(Y_i) = d(y_i) \cdot \beta/C$. By Chernoff bound,

$$\text{Prob}\{Y_i \leq d(y_i)/C\} = \text{Prob}\{Y_i \leq E(Y_i)\big(1 - (1 - 1/\beta)\big)\}$$
$$\leq \exp\{-\beta d(y_i)/C \cdot (1 - 1/\beta)^2/3\}.$$

Since $d(y_i)/C \geq 1$ and $(1 - 1/\beta)^2 > 1/2$ for $\beta = 7 \log m$,

$$\text{Prob}\{Y_i \leq d(y_i)/C\} < \exp\{-\beta/6\}.$$

Therefore, the probability that all nodes in Y have at least $1/C$ fraction of edges in X_1 can be estimated by the union bound.

$$\text{Prob}\{\text{All nodes in } Y \text{ have at least } 1/C \text{ fraction of edges in } X_1\}$$
$$\geq 1 - \sum_i \text{Prob}\{Y_i \leq d(y_i)/C\} > 1 - m/\exp\{\beta/6\} > 0.$$

Thus, the probability that all vertices in Y have at least $1/C$ of their edges in X_1 is positive. This implies that such a partition must exist. Therefore, such X' exists.   □

Now, we are ready to prove Lemma 2.

Proof of Lemma 2. We will prove this by forming a feasible schedule which has edge e_i with occurrence μ_i from schedule S'' and this feasible schedule consists of at most $T(S'')7\log m/C$ time slots, where m is the number of edges of G. (If $T(S'')$ is not a multiple of C, we supplement with empty slots to make it a multiple of C.) Such a feasible schedule exists by Lemma 3. Here, the bipartite graph with vertex set $X \cup Y$ is the following. X consists of $T(S'')$ vertices and each represents a time slot. On the other hand, Y consists of m vertices and each represents an edge in G. We connect a vertex (time slot) in X with a vertex (an edge in G) e_i in Y if the edge e_i in G is scheduled in that time slot. Note that for each vertex $y \in Y$, if its corresponding edge in G is e_i, then the degree of y is exactly Cw_i. Hence, Lemma 3 shows that there is a subset of the time slots in S'' such that each edge e_i appears at least w_i times in these time slots. This generates a scheduling with at most $T(S'')\beta/C$ slots, where $\beta = 7\log m$.

Recall that S' is the optimal schedule with the smallest $T(S')$. Thus, $T(S') \leq T(S'')\beta/C$. On the other hand, $\mu' = w_i$ and $\mu'' = Cw_i$ yield $\mathbb{L}(S') = T(S')$ and $\mathbb{L}(S'') = T(S'')/C$. Combining them, we get $\mathbb{L}(S') \leq \beta\mathbb{L}(S'') = 7\log m \cdot \mathbb{L}(S'')$. $\square$

Now for the first scheduling problem (we duplicate edge e_i exactly w_i times and minimize $\mathbb{L}(S')$), by the same idea of the max unweighted refresh time in Sect. 3, we can get a similar lower bound on $T(S')$. Define an unweighted multigraph $G_m = (V, E_m)$ by duplicating edge e_i for w_i times. Let Δ_p denote the maximum degree of G_m. That is, $T(S') \geq \Delta_p$. Combined with the inequality in Lemma 2, we have $\mathbb{L}(S'') \geq \mathbb{L}(S')/(7\log m) = T(S')/(7\log m) \geq \Delta_p/(7\log m)$. On the other hand, as discussed before, the minimum value of $\mathbb{L}(S)$ among all feasible finite schedules S serves as a lower bound for $\mathbb{O}(S^*)$ and the minimum value occurs when $\mu_i = Cw_i$ for all i, which is the second scheduling problem. Hence, $\mathbb{O}(S^*) \geq \mathbb{L}(S'')$. Now, we get a lower bound on the optimal solution as in Theorem 4.

Theorem 4. *The optimal solution for the Min Max Weighted Refresh Time Scheduling problem has* $\mathbb{O}(S^*) \geq \frac{\Delta_p}{7\log m}$.

4.2   Algorithm

Our algorithm for the Min Max Weighted Refresh Time Scheduling problem works as follows. First, generate a random permutation of the edges in E_m. Second, partition these edges into $g = \lceil W/b \rceil$ buckets of equal length b, where $W = \sum_i w_i$ and b will be determined later. The last bucket may have length less than b and that is alright. For each bucket B_i, consider the induced unweighted multigraph, G_i, which consists of the edges that appear in this bucket and the edges whose two endpoints appear in edges of this bucket. Observe that G_i includes all edges in B_i but may contain other edges, too (e.g., an edge e that is not in B_i but have both vertices appearing in B_i, but we only include one copy of e if it is a duplicate edge). Finally, run the greedy algorithm in Sect. 3 on G_i. (In fact, the greedy algorithm works for unweighted multigraphs.)

This generates a schedule S_i for all the edges in G_i. Keep only the edges in B_i in the schedule S_i to form a new schedule S_i'. Our final schedule will run $S_1', S_2', ..., S_g'$ in sequence and periodically.

4.3 Analysis of the Approximation Ratio

Now we bound the approximation ratio of the aforementioned algorithm. First, we examine how many time slots in expectation are needed for each bucket. Second, we use the balls and bins technique to analyze the maximum weighted refresh time. Let us consider two cases, $k = 1$ and $k > 1$ separately.

Lemma 4. *Suppose $k = 1$ and $b = W/\Delta_p^2$. Then the number of time slots needed for the edges in a specific bucket B_i is $O(1)$ in expectation.*

Proof. The number of time slots needed for a bucket B_i, by the greedy algorithm, depends on the degree of the induced subgraph G_i (Theorem 3). We first analyze the probability that a specific edge $e_j = (u, v)$ falls inside the induced subgraph G_i. In order for this event to happen, either edge e_j is placed in B_i (with probability at most b/W as there are $\lceil W/b \rceil$ buckets in total), or both endpoints u and v of e_j appear in B_j (as other edges incident to u (v) are placed in B_i). We can bound the probability as follows. Recall that $b = W/\Delta_p^2$. By $\lim_{x \to \infty}(1 - 1/x)^x = 1/e$ and Taylor's Formula, we get

$$
\begin{aligned}
\text{Prob}\{e_j \in G_i\} &\leq b/W + (1 - (1 - b/W)^{\Delta_p})^2 \\
&\leq 1/\Delta_p^2 + (1 - (1 - 1/\Delta_p^2)^{\Delta_p})^2 \\
&\leq 1/\Delta_p^2 + (1 - e^{-1/\Delta_p})^2 \leq 2/\Delta_p^2.
\end{aligned}
$$

Let edge e_j be the last edge be added to the last time slot in the schedule for G_i. The number of slots used for G_i depends on the number of edges that can interfere with e_j. Specifically, we have to analyze the following two parameters:

- $\Delta_i(e_j)$: the number of edges in G_i, counting duplication, that share a common vertex with e_j.
- $\Delta_i'(e_j)$: the number of edges in G_i, counting duplication, that are exactly one hop away from e_j. That is, some of their endpoints are neighbors and they don't share any common endpoints.

For bounding $\Delta_i(e_j)$ from above, we consider the edges incident to e_j in G_m, each appearing in G_i with probability at most $2/\Delta_p^2$. The total number of these edges other than e_j is $w_j - 1 + 2(\Delta_p - w_j)$. Therefore,

$$
E[\Delta_i(e_j)] \leq (w_j - 1 + 2(\Delta_p - w_j)) \cdot 2/\Delta_p^2 < 4/\Delta_p \leq 4.
$$

Similarly, $E[\Delta_i'(e_j)] \leq 2\Delta_p^2 \cdot 2/\Delta_p^2 = 4$.

By the linearity of expectation, $E[\Delta_i(e_j) + \Delta_i'(e_j)] = O(1)$. That is, it introduces $O(1)$ edges, in expectation, in the interference range of the last edge e_j. Hence, the number of slots needed to resolve interference for bucket i, in expectation, is bounded by $O(1)$. $\square$

Now, we can analyze the maximum refresh time for each edge e using balls and bins results.

Theorem 5. *With $k = 1$ and $b = W/\Delta_p^2$, the proposed algorithm in Sect. 4.2 , for the Min Max Weighted Refresh Time Scheduling problem, has an approximation factor of $O(\Delta_p \log m \log W_{\max}/ \log \log W_{\max})$ in expectation, where $W_{\max}$ is the highest possible weight and Δ_p is the maximum degree in G_m.*

Proof. For each edge e_i, we would like to evaluate the maximum refresh time T_i, i.e., the maximum number of time slots before edge e_i is scheduled again. Recall that edge e_i is duplicated w_i times and the schedule is produced from a random permutation of all (duplicate) edges. We examine each gap between adjacent appearances of edge e_i in the permutation (wrapped as a cycle).

The number of edges in this gap can be upper bounded by the balls and bins analysis. Here these w_i duplicated edges e_i are placed first on the cycle and each of the $W - w_i$ remaining edges is randomly placed in one of these w_i gaps. We recall the balls and bins results:

Lemma 5. *[10, 18] Throwing R balls independently and uniformly at random into Z bins. If $R = \Omega(Z \log Z)$, then the maximum number of balls in one bin is $O(R/Z)$ with probability $1 - O(1/R)$; if $R = o(Z \log Z)$, then the maximum load of bins is $O(\frac{\log Z}{\log \log Z})$ with probability $1 - O(1/R)$.*

If $W = \Omega(w_i \log w_i)$, the maximum gap among these w_i gaps is bounded by $O(W/w_i)$, with high probability in W. The number of buckets in this gap is $O(\frac{W}{bw_i}) = O(\frac{\Delta_p^2}{w_i})$. w.h.p. in W. Since each bucket uses a constant number of slots in expectation and the maximum load (number of buckets in the maximum gap) is highly concentrated around its mean in the balls and bins setting, we can directly multiply these two expected values to obtain the expected value for the refresh time for edge e_i. That is, the weighted refresh time for e_i is bounded by $w_i T_i = w_i \cdot O(\frac{\Delta_p^2}{w_i}) = O(\Delta_p^2)$ in expectation.

If $W = o(w_i \log w_i)$, a similar argument shows that the weighted refresh time for e_i is bounded by $O(\frac{w_i \log w_i}{b \log \log w_i}) = O(\frac{\Delta_p^2 \log w_i}{\log \log w_i})$ in expectation. Now compared to the lower bound of the optimal solution as in Theorem 4, our algorithm has an approximation factor of $O(\frac{\Delta_p \log m \log W_{\max}}{\log \log W_{\max}})$ in expectation.   □

When the number of channels k is not 1, we will change the size of the buckets b to $\min\{\sqrt{\Delta_p}, \sqrt{k}\}W/\Delta_p^2$. The analysis is similar but a bit more technical.

Theorem 6. *Suppose we have k channels. Take $b = \min\{\sqrt{\Delta_p}, \sqrt{k}\}W/\Delta_p^2$, then the algorithm in Sect. 4.2 has an expected approximation factor of*

$$O\left(\max\left\{ \sqrt{\Delta_p}, \frac{\Delta_p}{\sqrt{k}} \right\} \log m \log W_{\max}/ \log \log W_{\max} \right).$$

Proof. Given k channels, observe that Theorem 4 is for general k, i.e., $\frac{\Delta_p}{7 \log m}$ gives a lower bound of the optimal solution. On the other hand, Lemma 4 also holds for general k and $b = \min\{\sqrt{\Delta_p}, \sqrt{k}\}W/\Delta_p^2$. For convenience, let $h = \min\{\sqrt{\Delta_p}, \sqrt{k}\}$. Hence, $b = hW/\Delta_p^2$.

$$\begin{aligned}
\text{Prob}\{e_j \in G_i\} &\leq b/W + (1 - (1 - b/W)^{\Delta_p})^2 \\
&\leq h/\Delta_p^2 + (1 - e^{-h/\Delta_p})^2 \\
&\leq h/\Delta_p^2 + h^2/\Delta_p^2 \leq 2h^2/\Delta_p^2 \text{ since } h \geq 1.
\end{aligned}$$

$$E[\Delta_i(e_j)] \leq (w_j - 1 + 2(\Delta_p - w_j)) \cdot 2h^2/\Delta_p^2 \leq 4h^2/\Delta_p$$

Similarly, we can get $E[\Delta_i'(e_j)] \leq 2\Delta_p^2 \cdot 2h^2/\Delta_p^2 = 4h^2$.

By the linearity of expectation and the key idea of the proof of Theorem 3, the number of slots for bucket i, in expectation, is bounded by $O(4h^2/\Delta_p + 4h^2/k)$. By $h = \min\{\sqrt{\Delta_p}, \sqrt{k}\}$, $O(4h^2/\Delta_p + 4h^2/k) = O(8)$.

Next, let us analyze the number of edges in the gaps of edge e_i. If $W = \Omega(w_i \log w_i)$, the number of bins in this gap is at most $O\left(\frac{W}{bw_i}\right) = O\left(\frac{\Delta_p^2}{hw_i}\right)$ w.h.p. in W. Because of the high concentration around its mean in the balls and bins problem, we can calculate the expectation of the weighted refresh time directly by multiplying these two values mentioned earlier. That is, in expectation,

$$w_i T_i = w_i O\left(\frac{\Delta_p^2}{hw_i}\right) O(4h^2/\Delta_p + 4h^2/k) = O(h(\Delta_p + \Delta_p^2/k)).$$

Similarly, if $W = o(w_i \log w_i)$, the weighted refresh time in expectation for e_i is at most

$$\begin{aligned}
w_i T_i &= w_i O\left(\frac{\log w_i}{b \log \log w_i}\right) O(4h^2/\Delta_p + 4h^2/k) \\
&= O\left(\frac{w_i \Delta_p^2 \log w_i}{Xh \log \log w_i}\right) O(4h^2/\Delta_p + 4h^2/k) \\
&= O\left(\frac{\log w_i}{\log \log w_i} h(\Delta_p + \Delta_p^2/k)\right)
\end{aligned}$$

Combining these two upper bounds, in expectation, its approximation factor is bounded by $O(\min\{\sqrt{\Delta_p}, \sqrt{k}\} \cdot \Delta_p \log m \log W_{\max}/k \log \log W_{\max})$. Then by case analysis, we get the approximation factor as Theorem 6 states.   □

5   Min Max (Weighted) Refresh Time in the Multi-antenna Setting

In this section, we discuss the multi-antenna case. Since each node has $r > 1$ radios, it now can have at most r adjacent edges that are active in a time slot. The interference rule is the same as in the single-antenna setting: in a time slot, if two active edges are within interference range, then they must use different channels. The only difference is that now j adjacent edges incident to the same vertex v can be active in the same slot if they use different channels and different radio interfaces on v. The problem becomes more complicated than before. Fortunately, our algorithms for the weighted and unweighted problems can be generalized to the multi-antenna case.

Considering these two problems in the multi-antenna scenario, we have the following bounds for the optimal solution and the approximation factor for our scheduling algorithm.

Lemma 6. *In the multi-antenna case, the optimal solution has a maximum refresh time of at least* $\left\lceil \frac{2\Delta-1}{\min\{2r,k\}} \right\rceil$.

Proof. In the multi-antenna scenario, given an arbitrary edge e, at most $\min\{2r,k\}$ edges that are incident to e can appear in the same time slot. The reason is that for each endpoint of e, it can transmit at most $\min\{r,k\}$ messages successfully at the same time. There are at most $2\min\{r,k\}$ possible transmissions in total. They are within the interference area of e so they must use different channels. Hence, the maximum number of successful transmissions in a time slot is $\min\{k, 2\min\{r,k\}\}$, which is equivalent to $\min\{2r,k\}$. Remember that there are at most $2\Delta - 1$ edges in the interference range of edge e, so the maximum refresh time of the optimal solution is bounded from below by $\left\lceil \frac{2\Delta-1}{\min\{2r,k\}} \right\rceil$. □

Theorem 7. *In the multi-antenna case, the greedy algorithm gives a schedule of maximum refresh time at most* $\left\lceil \frac{2(\Delta-1)^2}{k} \right\rceil + \left\lceil \frac{2(\Delta-1)}{\min\{r,k\}} \right\rceil + 1$. *Therefore, this solution for the Min Max Refresh Time Scheduling problem is a* $\left\lceil \frac{\min\{2r,k\}(\Delta-1)}{k} \right\rceil + 2 - approximation$.

Proof. It is similar to the proof of Theorem 3. The event "an edge incident to one endpoint of e is scheduled so we cannot schedule e" now becomes "we run out of channels or radios for one endpoint of e". That means for *each* of the r radios, an edge e' that is adjacent to e is scheduled with this radios or for *each* of the k channels, e' is scheduled with this channel. For this event to happen, we need to use at least $\min\{r,k\}$ such edges. Hence, there are at most $\left\lceil \frac{2(\Delta-1)}{\min\{r,k\}} \right\rceil$ slots of this type. The maximum refresh time now is at most $\left\lceil \frac{2(\Delta-1)^2}{k} \right\rceil + \left\lceil \frac{2(\Delta-1)}{\min\{r,k\}} \right\rceil + 1$. Furthermore, the lower bound of optimal max refresh time $\left\lceil \frac{2\Delta-1}{\min\{2r,k\}} \right\rceil$ implies that this greedy algorithm produces a $\left\lceil \frac{\min\{2r,k\}(\Delta-1)}{k} \right\rceil + 2$-approximation of the optimal. □

Lemma 7. *In the multi-antenna case, the optimal solution for the Min Max Weighted Refresh Time Scheduling problem has* $\mathbb{O}(S^*) \geq \frac{\Delta_p}{7\log m \min\{r,k\}}$.

Proof. First of all, notice that Lemmas 1 and 2 still hold in the multi-antenna scenario. Only the proof of Lemma 1 is different. That is inserting e_i may remove more than one occurrence for any e_j, but no more than $\min\{r,k\}$ occurrences. With at most $\min\{r,k\}$ occurrences, we still can give a sufficiently large D that yields contradiction. Now we get an inequality, $T(S) \geq \Delta_p/\min\{r,k\}$. Combining with Lemma 2, we get $\frac{\Delta_p}{7\log m \min\{r,k\}}$ as a lower bound for optimal.

Before ending this proof, let us clarify why an edge now can appear at most $\min\{r,k\}$ times in the same time slot. It is because that for edges that have common endpoints, if we require these edges appear in the same time slot, then they must use different radios with different channels. Different radios represent different interfaces in the endpoints and different channels mean no interference occurs. Hence, there are at most $\min\{r, k\}$ duplicate edges in a time slot.   □

Theorem 8. *In the multi-antenna case with $b = \min\{\sqrt{\Delta_p \min\{r, k\}}, \sqrt{k}\}$ W/Δ_p^2, our algorithm for the Min Max Weighted Refresh Time Scheduling problem has an expected approximation factor*

- $O(\Delta_p \sqrt{k} \cdot \log m \log W_{max}/ \log \log W_{max})$, *if $k \le r$;*
- $O(r\Delta_p/\sqrt{k} \cdot \log m \log W_{max}/ \log \log W_{max})$, *if $k > r$ and $k \le r\Delta_p$;*
- $O(\sqrt{r\Delta_p} \cdot \log m \log W_{max}/ \log \log W_{max})$, *if $k > r\Delta_p$.*

Proof. In the multi-antenna setting with k channels, Lemma 7 still holds. That is, $\frac{\Delta_p}{7 \log m \min\{r,k\}}$ serves as a lower bound for the optimal solution. On the other hand, Lemma 4 also holds for general k and $b = \min\{\sqrt{\Delta_p \min\{r, k\}}, \sqrt{k}\}W/\Delta_p^2$. The only difference is the following. By the linearity of expectation and the key idea of the proof of Theorem 7, the number of slots for bucket i, in expectation, is bounded by $O\left(\frac{4h^2}{\Delta_p \min\{r,k\}} + \frac{4h^2}{k}\right)$. Using $h = \min\left\{\sqrt{\Delta_p \min\{r, k\}}, \sqrt{k}\right\}$, we get

$$O\left(\frac{4h^2}{\Delta_p \min\{r, k\}} + \frac{4h^2}{k}\right) = O(8).$$

The analysis for the number of edges in gaps of edge e_i remains the same. Hence, when $W = \Omega(w_i \log w_i)$, in expectation,

$$w_i T_i = w_i O\left(\frac{\Delta_p^2}{hw_i}\right) O\left(\frac{4h^2}{\Delta_p \min\{r, k\}} + \frac{4h^2}{k}\right) = O\left(h\left(\frac{\Delta_p}{\min\{r, k\}} + \frac{\Delta_p^2}{k}\right)\right).$$

Similarly, when $W = o(w_i \log w_i)$, $w_i T_i = O\left(\frac{\log w_i}{\log \log w_i} h\left(\frac{\Delta_p}{\min\{r,k\}} + \frac{\Delta_p^2}{k}\right)\right)$. As a result, the expected upper bound is

$$w_i T_i = O\left(\frac{\log W_{max}}{\log \log W_{max}} h\left(\frac{\Delta_p}{\min\{r, k\}} + \frac{\Delta_p^2}{k}\right)\right).$$

Its approximation factor is bounded from above by

$$O\left(\frac{\log W_{max}}{\log \log W_{max}} \min\{\sqrt{\Delta_p \min\{r, k\}}, \sqrt{k}\} \cdot \left(\frac{1}{\min\{r, k\}} + \frac{\Delta_p}{k}\right) \log m \min\{r, k\}\right).$$

Then by case analysis, we get the expected approximation factors, which is stated in Theorem 8.   □

6 Conclusion and Future Work

There are a few directions to explore in future work. One direction is to consider the physical model (SINR model) as our interference model. Another direction is to generalize the problem. In general, the problem of fair scheduling with conflicting constraints (low delay and interference) goes beyond scheduling wireless links. We expect our techniques can be applied to a broader setting.

Acknowledgements. This work was supported in part by NSF grants CCF-1439084, CCF-1535900, CNS-1553510, CNS-1618391, CNS-1553273, and DMS-1737812.

A Appendix: Omitted Proof

A.1 Proof on Schedule Periodicity

Given any infinite schedule S with a finite maximum refresh time, we can find a periodic schedule with max refresh time for each edge e_i no worse than that in S. Let the max refresh time of all edges in S be L. Consider the family of all possible schedules of the edges of G with no interference with length L. The number of these schedules is finite.

Now, let's construct a periodic schedule S' from S. We divide S into subschedules of length L each. Since the configuration of these sub-schedules of length L is finite and S is infinitely long, there exists a subschedule M that repeats at some point in S. Extract the subschedule of S that starts from the first appearance of M and ends right before the second appearance of M. We now repeat this sub-schedule periodically and call it S'.

Since each sub-schedule has length L, any edge e_i appears at least once in each sub-schedule. Thus, all the gap between two successive time slots of the same edge e_i in S' also happens in the original schedule S. Hence, the constructed periodic schedule has a maximum refresh time for each edge e_i which is no worse than that in the original schedule S.   □

B Evaluation

In this section, we evaluate our unweighted and weighted channel assignment algorithms under different scenarios in the single antenna case. Without loss of generality, we can assume that the smallest weight is 1 and all other weights are rounded to integer values. We consider model networks such as random node placement and perturbed grid placement with unit disk communication capacity, and also a real testbed network (denoted the Tmote network) which consists of 48 TMotes in a building that uses the ChipCon CC2420 radio. We vary network parameters such as node degree, the number of channels, weight distributions and measure the performance of our algorithms using the maximum fresh time divided by maximum (weighted) degree and Δ_p as the metric. For each network, we ran our algorithm 50 times to compute the average performance.

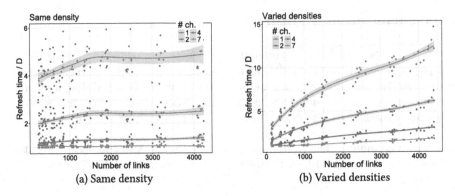

(a) Same density   (b) Varied densities

Fig. 3. Unit disk network with random node placement. The node degree is kept similar or increases when the scale of network increases to thousand of edges.

The network topology in Fig. 3 is constructed by throwing random nodes with a uniform circular range in a 2D unit square. This imitates random node placement in the wild. For each evaluation, we generate 50 networks. In Fig. 3.a, we increase the number of nodes in the unit square from 50 to 600 while keeping the average degrees the same (by scaling down the communication range of each node), so every node continues to have a similar number of interfering counterparts even when the network scale increases. The almost flat slopes of curves indicate that our algorithm still works as efficiently for large graphs as for small graphs when those graphs have similar densities. Besides, the result shows that when we have a reasonable number of channels, our algorithm can efficiently assign channels to a large network while keeping the latency low. In Fig. 3b, we increase the number of nodes but keep the communication range the same, i.e., when the number of nodes increases, the network becomes denser. That means a lot of implicit interferences occur. Therefore, the maximum refresh time increases unavoidably. Still, when we have a reasonable number of channels, our algorithm can keep the max refresh time moderate.

Random node placement often leads to many small holes in the network. To make the network more robust, perturbed grid placement is preferred which gives a more stable node degree among the network while reducing the number of gaps inside. Therefore, we often see an almost grid placement in real-world sensor networks. In order to evaluate on such wireless networks, we use a perturbed 7×7 grid placement network shown in Fig. 4a and also a Tmote network as shown in Fig. 4b. In the Tmote network, these nodes are deployed on walls and ceilings of a building. We collect traces of 3,600,000 packet transmissions using IEEE 802.15.4 standard for each pair of nodes. With the transmission traces, we define two nodes are connected if and only if the packet reception rate of its link is over 90%.

In Fig. 5, we evaluate our algorithm on these two networks when weight distributions are uniform and power-law. In both networks, our algorithm can efficiently use channels to reduce the refresh time. However, when the weight

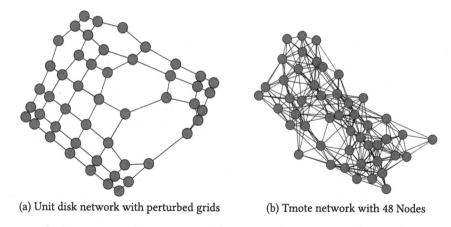

(a) Unit disk network with perturbed grids   (b) Tmote network with 48 Nodes

Fig. 4. Visualization of the network topologies

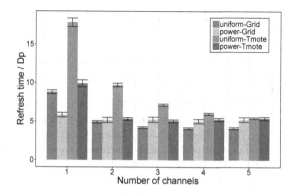

Fig. 5. Performance of weighted channel assignment on perturb grid and Tmote network with varying number of channels and weight distributions.

distribution is power-law, the benefit diminishes because some implicit interference is unavoidable. Note that some edges have very high priorities and they contribute to the weighted degree which makes the maximum weighted degree pretty high. The ratio of the maximum weighted degree to the total weight is 0.32 for the perturbed grid and it is 0.12 for the Tmote network. The node with the maximum weighted degree creates more unavoidable interferences in the perturbed grid. Hence, the performance of the Tmote network is better than the one of the perturb grid. On the other hand, for both networks under the uniform distribution, the ratios are the same, 0.06, which is quite small and leaves room for improvement of our algorithm. When we vary the number of channels from one to two, our algorithm improves the most. It is almost twice as better than the case of only one channel.

References

1. Al Islam, A.A., Islam, M.J., Nurain, N., Raghunathan, V.: Channel assignment techniques for multi-radio wireless mesh networks: a survey. IEEE Commun. Surv. Tutorials **18**(2), 988–1017 (2015)
2. Balakrishnan, H., Barrett, C.L., Kumar, V.S., Marathe, M.V., Thite, S.: The distance-2 matching problem and its relationship to the mac-layer capacity of ad hoc wireless networks. IEEE J. Sel. A. Commun. **22**(6), 1069–1079 (2006)
3. Barrett, C.L., Istrate, G., Kumar, V.S.A., Marathe, M.V., Thite, S., Thulasidasan, S.: Strong edge coloring for channel assignment in wireless radio networks. In: Fourth Annual IEEE International Conference on Pervasive Computing and Communications Workshops (PERCOMW 2006), pp. 105–110, March 2006
4. Bicket, J., Aguayo, D., Biswas, S., Morris, R.: Architecture and evaluation of an unplanned 802.11 b mesh network. In: Proceedings of the 11th Annual International Conference on Mobile Computing and Networking, pp. 31–42. ACM (2005)
5. Chambers, B.: A rooftop ad hoc wireless network (2002). http://www.pdos.lcs.mit.edu/grid/
6. Chaporkar, P., Kar, K., Luo, X., Sarkar, S.: Throughput and fairness guarantees through maximal scheduling in wireless networks. IEEE Trans. Inf. Theory **54**(2), 572–594 (2008)
7. Committee, L.S., et al.: Wireless LAN Medium Access Control (MAC) and Physical Layer (PHY) Specifications: High-Speed Physical Layer in the 5 GHZ Band, vol. 802, no. 1. IEEE Std., Piscataway (1999)
8. CREATE-NET and Technion: WING: wireless mesh network for next-generation internet (2012). http://www.wingproject.org. Accessed 15 June 2019
9. Ghosh, A., Wolter, D.R., Andrews, J.G., Chen, R.: Broadband wireless access with WiMax/802.16: current performance benchmarks and future potential. IEEE Commun. Mag. **43**(2), 129–136 (2005)
10. Gonnet, G.H.: Expected length of the longest probe sequence in hash code searching. J. ACM (JACM) **28**(2), 289–304 (1981)
11. Group, I.W., et al.: Part 11: wireless LAN Medium Access Control (MAC) and Physical Layer (PHY) Specifications: Higher-Speed Physical Layer Extension in the 2.4 GHZ Band. ANSI/IEEE Std 802.11 (1999)
12. Hajek, B., Sasaki, G.: Link scheduling in polynomial time. IEEE Trans. Inf. Theory **34**(5), 910–917 (1988)
13. Holyer, I.: The NP-completeness of edge-coloring. SIAM J. Comput. **10**(4), 718–720 (1981)
14. Joo, C., Lin, X., Shroff, N.B.: Understanding the capacity region of the greedy maximal scheduling algorithm in multi-hop wireless networks. In: IEEE INFOCOM 2008 - The 27th Conference on Computer Communications, pp. 1777–1785, April 2008
15. Kumar, V.S.A., Marathe, M.V., Parthasarathy, S., Srinivasan, A.: End-to-end packet-scheduling in wireless ad-hoc networks. In: Proceedings of the Fifteenth Annual ACM-SIAM Symposium on Discrete Algorithms, SODA 2004, Philadelphia, PA, USA, pp. 1021–1030 (2004)
16. Mahdian, M.: The strong chromatic index of graphs. Dissertation, Department of Computer Science, University of Toronto (2000)
17. Nandagopal, T., Kim, T.E., Gao, X., Bharghavan, V.: Achieving MAC layer fairness in wireless packet networks. In: Proceedings of the 6th Annual International Conference on Mobile Computing and Networking, pp. 87–98. ACM (2000)

18. Raab, M., Steger, A.: "Balls into Bins"—a simple and tight analysis. In: Luby, M., Rolim, J.D.P., Serna, M. (eds.) RANDOM 1998. LNCS, vol. 1518, pp. 159–170. Springer, Heidelberg (1998). https://doi.org/10.1007/3-540-49543-6_13
19. Ramanathan, S., Lloyd, E.L.: Scheduling algorithms for multihop radio networks. IEEE/ACM Trans. Networking 1(2), 166–177 (1993)
20. Ramanathan, S.: A unified framework and algorithm for channel assignment in wireless networks. Wireless Netw. 5(2), 81–94 (1999)
21. Ramanathan, S., Lloyd, E.L.: Scheduling algorithms for multihop radio networks. IEEE/ACM Trans. Network. (TON) 1(2), 166–177 (1993)
22. Sharma, G., Mazumdar, R.R., Shroff, N.B.: On the complexity of scheduling in wireless networks. In: Proceedings of the 12th Annual International Conference on Mobile Computing and Networking, MobiCom 2006, pp. 227–238. ACM, New York (2006)
23. Shi, H., Prasad, R.V., Onur, E., Niemegeers, I.G.M.M.: Fairness in wireless networks: issues, measures and challenges. IEEE Commun. Surv. Tutorials 16(1), 5–24 (2014)
24. Si, W., Selvakennedy, S., Zomaya, A.Y.: An overview of channel assignment methods for multi-radio multi-channel wireless mesh networks. J. Parallel Distrib. Comput. 70(5), 505–524 (2010)
25. Stockmeyer, L.J., Vazirani, V.V.: NP-completeness of some generalizations of the maximum matching problem. Inf. Process. Lett. 15(1), 14–19 (1982)
26. Wan, P.J., Frieder, O., Jia, X., Yao, F., Xu, X., Tang, S.: Wireless link scheduling under physical interference model. IEEE (2011)
27. Wan, P.J., Jia, X., Dai, G., Du, H., Wan, Z., Frieder, O.: Scalable algorithms for wireless link schedulings in multi-channel multi-radio wireless networks. In: INFOCOM, 2013 Proceedings IEEE, pp. 2121–2129 (2013)
28. Wu, X., Srikant, R., Perkins, J.R.: Scheduling efficiency of distributed greedy scheduling algorithms in wireless networks. IEEE Trans. Mob. Comput. 6(6), 595–605 (2007)

Throughput and Packet Displacements
of Dynamic Broadcasting Algorithms

Mark de Berg[1(✉)], Corrie Jacobien Carstens[2], and Michel Mandjes[2]

[1] Department of Mathematics and Computer Science, TU Eindhoven,
Eindhoven, The Netherlands
M.T.d.Berg@tue.nl
[2] Korteweg-de Vries Institute for Mathematics, Amsterdam, The Netherlands
{c.j.carstens,m.r.h.mandjes}@uva.nl

Abstract. Most dynamic broadcasting algorithms focus on maximizing throughput. We present several broadcasting algorithms focusing on low maximum displacement, that is, that limit how far out of order packets may be received. Experiments show that in many settings our algorithms have smaller displacement than existing algorithms, while still guaranteeing high throughput. As a result of independent interest, we show that modelling decisions on the order of edge activations in one round of a broadcasting algorithm can have substantial impact on the throughput.

1 Introduction

Background. Traditionally communication networks were wired and changed slowly over time. Nowadays wireless ad-hoc networks, which have little to no infrastructure [1,10,18], play an important role as well. Such networks can be used to extend a network in areas where there is no infrastructure or to allow for communication between mobile agents. There are many new challenges in the transition from wired to wireless networks. In particular routing policies need to be adapted in order to work efficiently in the wireless case.

There are many different (application specific) requirements and difficulties in designing good routing policies. Here we focus on policies for packet broadcasting. Broadcasting is a fundamental network functionality and is often used for management, control, and data exchange purposes in self-organising wireless networks [4,16,17]. Another application of broadcasting is the simultaneous streaming of packets to all nodes in a network, for instance to stream live video footage of a sports event or to share tactical information to deployed army troops connected by a mobile ad-hoc network [2,12].

Previous Work. One of the most common performance measures of a routing policy is its throughput, i.e. the rate at which packets are delivered at their destinations. In their seminal work, Tassiulas and Ephremides introduced the backpressure algorithm and proved that it is throughput optimal [14]. It was

Funded by the NWO Gravitation project NETWORKS, grant no. 024.002.003.

© Springer Nature Switzerland AG 2019
F. Dressler and C. Scheideler (Eds.): ALGOSENSORS 2019, LNCS 11931, pp. 158–174, 2019.
https://doi.org/10.1007/978-3-030-34405-4_9

designed for the anycast/unicast setting (where a packet is delivered when it reaches a single target node) in a static setting, but it can be adapted to dynamic networks in which it has been shown to be throughput optimal as well [9].

Recently Sinha et al. [12] extended the idea of the backpressure algorithm to the broadcast setting, overcoming the difficulty of dealing with packet duplication required in broadcasting. They introduced a policy for directed acyclic graphs [11,13] and for general directed graphs [12], proved that their algorithms are throughput optimal, and extended their algorithms for dynamic networks. Another approach that surprisingly leads to throughput optimal routing on directed networks, is the random useful packet forwarding algorithm [8]. This policy has also been extended to the dynamic setting, including throughput optimality under certain assumptions [15]. A main focus in all these works was on obtaining high throughput, which indeed is an important requirement for a good broadcasting algorithm. Less attention has been paid to the order of packet arrivals, which is important for applications such as video streaming (as a packet can only be 'used' when all preceding packets have been received). In this article, we explicitly focus on the order in which packets arrive.

Our Contribution. We quantify the level of disorder in packet arrivals at a node by the *displacement*, defined as the difference between (the indices of) the oldest missing packet and the newest received packet of the node. The displacement has implications for the required buffer size and the time delay before content can be played, since packets need to be stored until they can be used.

Section 2 describes our network model, several existing broadcasting policies, and our new policies that limit the displacement to a user-specified value. To fairly analyze these policies, Sect. 3 focuses on the impact of the precise modelling assumptions on the throughput, showing that assumptions on the edge-activation order in each round in which packets are sent have a crucial effect. Section 4 analyzes low-displacement policies, showing (i) that many broadcast algorithms are throughput optimal for networks with at most a single spanning tree, (ii) that greedy in-order routing has zero-displacement, and (iii) that there are fixed displacement policies with relatively low displacement and high throughput. We then focus on the storage requirements and delays of policies with high broadcast rate in Sect. 5, identifying a trade-off between storage requirements and the broadcast rate and the delay. Section 6 provides a discussion and directions for future research.

2   Model and Algorithms

Following Sinha et al. [12] we analyze the performance of dynamic broadcasting algorithms on static graphs. It simplifies the simulations and allows us to talk about throughput optimal broadcast algorithms: for static graphs the broadcast capacity is known to equal the maximum number of edge-disjoint spanning trees [3], whereas the broadcast capacity of dynamic graphs is not known [6].

Model and Definitions. We model a communication network as a directed graph $G = (V, E)$, and define $n := |V|$ and $m := |E|$. Packets arrive at a source node s according to a Poisson arrival process $A(t)$ of rate λ. All packets are indexed by consecutive integers and we often refer to a packet by its index (i.e. "packet i"). Packet transmissions take place in synchronized timeslots (rounds), that is, at each timeslot $t \in \mathbb{N}$ certain packets are sent over the links. Packets are duplicated whenever they are sent. We assume each edge sends at most a single packet in a timeslot. Within this model there are still different choices for the order in which transmissions take place within a timeslot; see Sect. 3.

For each vertex v we define $P_v(t)$ as the set of packets it has received up to time t and we write $\mathbf{P}(t) := \{P_v(t)\}_{v \in V}$ for the state of the network. Let $R^\pi(t) := |\cap_{v \in V} P_v^\pi(t)|$ be the number of packets received by all vertices at time t under policy π. A broadcast policy π has a *broadcast rate or throughput* of λ if for a packet arrival rate of λ we have $R^\pi(t)/t = \lambda$ as $t \to \infty$, in probability (i.e., for any $\epsilon > 0$, $P(|R^\pi(t)/t - \lambda| > \epsilon) \to 0$ as $t \to \infty$). The *broadcast capacity* λ^* of a network G is the supremum of arrival rates λ for which there exists a policy π with broadcast rate λ. A policy is *throughput optimal* if it has broadcast throughput $\lambda^* - \epsilon$ for any $\epsilon > 0$. The *delay*, or latency, $L(p)$ of a packet p is the difference between its time of arrival at the source node and the time that it is successfully broadcast, i.e. the first time that all vertices have received p. Finally, we introduce a measure for how much out-of-order packets are received.

Definition 1. *The* displacement $\Delta_v(t)$ *at vertex v at time t is the difference between the largest index $p^{\max}(v, t)$ of any packet received by v at t and the smallest index $p^{\mathrm{miss}}(v, t)$ of any packet not yet received by v at t. More precisely,*

$$\Delta_v(t) := \begin{cases} 0 & \text{if } P_v(t) = \emptyset \text{ or } p^{\mathrm{miss}}(v, t) > p^{\max}(v, t) \\ p^{\max}(v, t) - p^{\mathrm{miss}}(v, t) & \text{otherwise} \end{cases}.$$

Routing Algorithms. We compare (i) a generalisation of the well-known back-pressure policy π^* [12], (ii) the random useful packet forwarding policy π^{rnd} [8], and (iii) two fixed-displacement policies $\tilde{\pi}_\ell^*$ and $\tilde{\pi}_\ell^{\mathrm{rnd}}$ that we introduce.

The original back-pressure algorithm uses *queue lengths*, the number of packets present at nodes, to make routing decisions for packets in the *anycast*[1] setting. In this setting packets do not get duplicated. Due to packet duplications in broadcasting, it is not straightforward to define queues and packet weights in this setting. We use the following definitions to describe virtual queues that can be used to define packet weights [12]. Let $G = (V, E)$ be a directed network, let $\mathcal{P}(t)$ denote the set of packets in the network at time t and let $F \subset V$ be a subset of the vertices of the network. A packet $p \in \mathcal{P}(t)$ is called a class-F packet at time t if it is present at all vertices in F and nowhere else. The size, $Q_F(t)$, of a virtual queue at F, is defined as the number of class-F packets at time t. Thus $Q_F(t) := |\{p \in \mathcal{P}(t) | p \in P_v(t) \iff v \in F\}|$. Finally define the following weight function: given an edge $e = (u, v)$ and a packet $p \in P_u(t) \backslash P_v(t)$, let $w_{p,e}(t) := Q_{F_p}(t) - Q_{F_p \cup \{v\}}(t)$ where F_p is the class of packet p.

---

[1] In the anycast setting packets have a set of one or more destination nodes and leave the network when they reach any one of these nodes.

We now describe the routing decisions of the different broadcasting policies, that is, we describe how each policy decides *which* packet to send over an edge $e = (u, v)$ given the current state of the network $\{P_v(t)\}_{v \in V}$. Following Sinha *et al.* [12] we focus on routing decisions only. We refer to Sect. 6 for a discussion on scheduling decisions in the wireless case.

Broadcast Policy π^*. The policy π^* proposed by Sinha *et al.* [12] uses packet weights to determine which packet to send. Let $w := \max_{p \in P_u(t) \setminus P_v(t)} w_{p,e}(t)$. If w is non-negative, then send a packet p over e for which $w_{p,e}(t) = w$. If there are multiple packets with maximum weight, select one of these uniformly at random. If $w < 0$, then send nothing. Note that to run the policy π^*, detailed state-information needs to be maintained as we need to keep track of the F classes and the packets present in each class.

Broadcast Policy π^{rnd}. The random useful packet forwarding policy introduced by Towsley and Twigg [15] simply transmits, for each edge (u, v), a packet chosen uniformly at random from the set $P_u(t) \setminus P_v(t)$.

Low-Displacement Policies $\tilde{\pi}_\ell^*, \tilde{\pi}_\ell^{\mathrm{rnd}} \in \tilde{\Pi}_\ell$. We introduce a new class of broadcast policies, denoted by $\tilde{\Pi}_\ell$. Algorithms in this class ensure that packets are delivered with at most displacement ℓ. Formally, under any policy $\pi \in \tilde{\Pi}_\ell$, a node can only receive packet p if it has already received packets $1, \ldots, p - \ell$. For policies $\pi \in \tilde{\Pi}_\ell$ the network state is simplified. For each node, the packets it has received can be stored by the integer p^{miss} (see Definition 1) together with a set of packets of size at most $\ell - 1$, corresponding to the packets that have been received by the node with index larger than p^{miss}.

We introduce two policies in the policy space $\tilde{\Pi}_\ell$: $\tilde{\pi}_\ell^*$ and $\tilde{\pi}_\ell^{\mathrm{rnd}}$. We first define $\tilde{P}_e(t)$ for the edge $e = (u, v)$ as the subset of packets in $P_u(t) \setminus P_v(t)$ that are allowed to be send to v under a policy $\pi \in \tilde{\Pi}_\ell$. The policy $\tilde{\pi}_\ell^* \in \tilde{\Pi}_\ell$ computes the weights $w_p := w_{p,e}(t)$ for all packets $p \in P_e(t)$. If $w = \max_p w_p > 0$ a randomly selected packet p is transmitted for which $w_p = w$. The policy $\tilde{\pi}_\ell^{\mathrm{rnd}} \in \tilde{\Pi}_\ell$ randomly selects a packet $p \in P_e(t)$ and sends it to v.

When ℓ is large enough, the requirement that the packet displacement is smaller than ℓ is always satisfied and the policies $\tilde{\pi}_\ell^*$ and $\tilde{\pi}_\ell^{\mathrm{rnd}}$ effectively do the same as π^* and π^{rnd}. In Sect. 4 we show experimentally that the parameter ℓ gives a trade-off between displacement and throughput. Note that $\tilde{\Pi}_1$ contains *in-order policies*, which send packets in the exact order of arrival.

3 Effect of Modelling Assumptions on Throughput

Before analyzing the performance of the above broadcasting policies we show that assumptions on the order in which edges are activated in each round severely affect the throughput. Previously, it was shown that for any in-order policy the broadcast rate on the graph D_4 shown in Fig. 1 is at most $\frac{5}{3}$ [11, Lemma 1]. The proof implicitly relies on a specific model, namely the regular slotted model below. We show (see Example 1) that under different edge activation assumptions an in-order policy can obtain broadcast rate 2 for D_4. We also show that in the regular slotted model, any *locally deterministic policy* has broadcast rate $\lambda \leq 1$ regardless of the underlying network. However, this result does not hold under different modelling assumptions; see Lemma 2(ii) and (iii).

Edge Activation Models. For static graphs it is commonly assumed that in a given timeslot, each edge makes a routing decision based on the state of the network $\mathbf{P}(t)$ at the start of the time-slot. Hernce in this edge activation model, a *regular slotted* model, there are instantaneous edge activations.

In the *mini-slot model* each time-slot is divided into m mini-slots; a routing decision is made for a single randomly chosen edge based on the network state *at the start of that mini-slot*. [12, Lemma 1] shows its equivalence to the regular slotted model in terms of throughput, which seems to indicate we may as well work in the mini-slot model. However, Example 1 below shows that, when updating the state after each packet transmission, we can construct an edge activation pattern such that in-order routing is a throughput optimal policy on D_4.

Example 1. Let D_4 be the directed graph on four nodes $\{s, x, y, z\}$ as displayed in Fig. 1. We choose to activate the edges, during every timeslot, in the following order: $(s, x), (x, y), (y, z)$ followed by $(s, y), (s, z), (z, x)$. Routing packets in-order using the updated network state after each packet transmission then corresponds to routing packets round-robin over the two edge-disjoint spanning trees. It is well-known that this has broadcast rate 2.

Even though the edge activation model in this example is artificial, it illustrates the importance of explicitly stating the edge-activation model. We will also investigate a third model, the *random sequential* model, which is a version of the mini-slot model where each edge is activated exactly once in a time-slot and the order of edge activations is chosen uniformly at random. Routing decisions are made based on the state of the network *at the start of that mini-slot*.

Throughput of Locally Deterministic Policies. We now show that in the regular slotted model some randomness or non-local information is needed to get a broadcast rate of more than 1. We define a *locally deterministic routing policy* to be a routing policy that, given an edge (u, v), makes a deterministic decision about which packet to route from vertex u to v based only on the set of packets P_u received by vertex u and the set of packets P_v received by vertex v.

Lemma 1. *In the regular slotted model, any locally deterministic policy has broadcast rate at most 1, for any network G and arrival process $A(t)$.*

Proof. By definition of the broadcast rate it suffices to show a node $v \in V$ exists for which $|P_v(t)| \leq t$ for all t. We use induction to show that this is true for all $v \in N^{\text{out}}(s)$, where $N^{\text{out}}(s)$ is the set of out-neighbours of the source s.

Assume that for t the following holds: (1) the sets $P_v(t)$ are identical for all $v \in N^{\text{out}}(s)$, (2) $|P_v(t)| \leq t$ for all $v \in N^{\text{out}}(s)$ and (3) for any $u \in V \setminus \{\{s\} \cup N^{\text{out}}(s)\}$ and $v \in N^{\text{out}}(s)$ we have $P_u(t) \subseteq P_v(t)$.

Clearly (1)–(3) hold for $t = 0$. Now assuming they hold for t, two things can happen. Firstly, if $P_s(t) > P_v(t)$, then all nodes $v \in N^{\text{out}}(s)$ receive the same packet from s since the policy is locally deterministic and $P_v(t)$ is equal for all $v \in N^{\text{out}}(s)$. Furthermore no node in $N^{\text{out}}(s)$ can receive a packet via incoming edges from nodes y in $V \backslash \{\{s\} \cup N^{\text{out}}(s)\}$, since $P_u(t) \subseteq P_v(t)$, so that at $t + 1$ (1) and (2) hold. Secondly, if $P_s(t) = P_v(t)$ the nodes v in $N^{\text{out}}(s)$ receive no packets at all, so that (1) and (2) hold trivially. Note that (3) holds for $t + 1$ in both cases, because any packet that arrives in the network at node s has to travel through the nodes $N^{\text{out}}(s)$ before it can reach other nodes in the network. Now $P_u(t) \subseteq P_v(t)$ holds for all $u \in V \backslash \{\{s\} \cup N^{\text{out}}(s)\}$ and $v \in N^{\text{out}}(t)$ because the sets $P_v(t)$ are identical for all v. This finishes the proof.   □

Influence of Edge-Activation Model on the Broadcast Rate. We now show that Lemma 1 does not hold under the mini-slot model and the random sequential model. We illustrate the differences that can occur using a small network D_3 (see Fig. 1) and the *greedy in-order* broadcasting policy π_1^g. This policy routes packets in order of arrival (i.e. first packet 1 then packet 2 etc.) and transmits a packet whenever possible. For this policy, we can describe the packets received by a node v at time t by a single number, namely the index of the last packet received, which we will denote by $L_v(t)$.

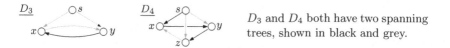

D_3 and D_4 both have two spanning trees, shown in black and grey.

Fig. 1. The directed graphs D_3 and D_4.

Note that the broadcast capacity λ^* of D_3 equals 2, since its edges can be decomposed into two edge-disjoint spanning trees. For simplicity, we assume that there is an infinite number of packets at the source node s and that at time zero there are no packets at vertices x and y. Lemma 2 implies shows that the broadcast rate of the greedy in-order routing policy differs for significantly for the various edge-activation models. In the remainder of the article we use the regular slotted time model.

Lemma 2. *The broadcast rate of π_1^g on D_3 equals 1 for the regular slotted model, while its expected broadcast rate on D_3 equals $\frac{4}{3}$ for the mini-slot model and 1.26333 for the random sequential model.*

Proof. We prove the three cases mentioned in the lemma separately.

– We prove the first case by induction on t, in particular we show that $L_x(t) = L_y(t) = t$ for all $t \in \mathbb{N}$. For $t = 0$ this is true by assumption. Now if $L_x(t) =

$L_y(t) = t$ at time t, then both edge (s, x) and (s, y) will send packet $t + 1$ to vertex x and vertex y respectively. Neither edge (x, y) nor edge (y, x) will send a packet since $L_x(t) = L_y(t)$. Hence $L_x(t + 1) = L_y(t + 1) = t + 1$.

- We can describe the state of the packets in the entire network by the numbers $L_x(t)$ and $L_y(t)$. Due to the symmetry of D_3, the states $L_x(t) = k$, $L_y(t) = \ell$ and $L_x(t) = \ell$, $L_y(t) = k$ are equivalent, hence we can describe the system by two integers (k, ℓ). We only distinguish between qualitatively different states (i, i), $(i, i+1)$, etc. We can now describe the policy π_1^g in the mini-slot model as a discrete-time Markov chain. In each mini-slot a single, randomly chosen, edge is activated. When we are in state (i, i) selecting edge (x, y) or (y, x) results in staying in the state (i, i) and happens with probability $\frac{1}{2}$. With probability $\frac{1}{2}$ the selected edge is (s, x) or (s, y) and we move to the state $(i, i + 1)$. It is not hard to see that when we are in state $(i, i + j)$ we have a probability of $\frac{1}{4}$ of moving to state $(i, i + j + 1)$ and a probability $\frac{1}{2}$ of moving to $(i + 1, i + j) = (i, i + j - 1)$. This leads to the birth-death Markov chain displayed in Fig. 2(a). This Markov chain has stationary distribution $\pi_0 = \frac{1}{3}$ and $\pi_j = \frac{2}{3}\frac{1}{2}^j$ for $j > 0$, where π_j is the probability of finding the Markov chain in state $(i, i + j)$. This implies that the Markov chain spends two thirds of the time in states $(i, i + j)$ with $j > 0$ and $\frac{1}{3}$ of the time in state (i, i). When the chain is in state $(i, i + j)$ there is a probability $\frac{1}{2}$ of moving to the state $(i + 1, i + j)$ which increases the broadcast rate by 1. When the chain is in state (i, i) the broadcast rate can not go up. Hence we find that on average the broadcast rate increases by $\frac{2}{3} \times \frac{1}{2} \times 1 = \frac{1}{3}$ per mini-slot. There are four mini-slots in each timeslot, hence the expected broadcast rate is $\frac{4}{3}$.

- For the random sequential model we take full timeslots as our time unit. In each slot, all edges are activated once. It is not hard to see that the difference between $L_x(t)$ and $L_y(t)$ can be at most one at any time. Hence the state of this system is either (i, i) or $(i, i + 1)$. We derived the transition probabilities between these two states by recording the effect of the 24 different edge activation orders, each occurring with probability $\frac{1}{24}$, see Fig. 2(b). Note that there is a probability of $\frac{2}{3}$ to stay in state (i, i) and the broadcast rate to go up by 1 (e.g. when the edges are activated in order $(x, y), (y, x), (s, x), (s, y)$) and also a probability of $\frac{1}{12}$ to remain in state (i, i) and for the broadcast rate to go up by 2 (e.g. when the edges are activated in order $(s, x), (x, y), (s, y), (y, x)$). Similarly there is a probability of remaining in state $(i, i + 1)$ with the broadcast rate going up by one, and a probability of remaining in this state where the broadcast rate goes up by two. The stationary distribution is $\pi_{i,i} = 0.76$ and $\pi_{i,i+1} = 0.24$. We find an expected broadcast rate of $0.76 \left(\frac{2}{3} + \frac{1}{4} + 2\frac{1}{12} \right) + 0.24 \left(\frac{1}{6} + 2(\frac{1}{24} + \frac{19}{24}) \right) = 1.26333$.

$\square$

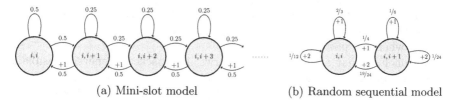

(a) Mini-slot model   (b) Random sequential model

Fig. 2. Markov chains that describe the network state under greedy in-order routing on D_3.

4 Broadcast Rate of Low-Displacement Policies

A good broadcasting policy should have a high throughput. Both π^* and π^{rnd} have previously been shown to be throughput optimal (though the former in a mini-slot setup) and suited to routing on dynamic networks. We will study the trade-off between low packet displacement and high throughput. The broadcast capacity of a network equals the maximum number of edge-disjoint spanning trees in the network. In most real networks this number is not very high (at most the edge-connectivity of the network) whereas in planar networks there can at most be two edge-disjoint spanning trees [7].

We will show that in a network with at most a single spanning tree, there are many throughput optimal routing strategies. In particular, the greedy in-order routing policy is throughput optimal and has zero displacement. When a network contains more than a single spanning tree, there no longer exists a throughput optimal policy with zero displacement. We show that in this case, the static algorithm which routes packets round-robin over disjoint spanning trees has bounded displacement. We then show experimentally that π^* and π^{rnd}, developed specifically for dynamic networks, do not appear to share this property. Instead, the maximum displacement seems to keep growing over time and both have relatively high displacement. Our fixed-displacement policies provide a trade-off between low displacement and high throughput, and are capable of reaching a high throughput while keeping the maximum displacement low.

Networks with Broadcast Capacity 1. On networks that do not have two edge-disjoint spanning trees—networks that consists of a single spanning tree, possibly with some 'redundant' edges—any policy which forwards a packet over an edge (u, v) whenever possible (i.e. when $P_u(t) \backslash P_v(t)$ is non-empty) is throughput optimal. To see this, first assume that the graph is a tree. Note that an immediate neighbour of the source receives a packet whenever there are more packets at the source than at the node itself. The source node can be modelled as a discrete queue and is expected to always have more packets than its neighbours [19, Chapter 15]. This implies that neighbours of the node receive a packet at each time step. Nodes that are further removed from the source node receive the packets that their parent node has received in the previous time slot. Thus, all nodes are expected to receive packets at rate 1. Since packets are arriving at the source node at rate 1, all nodes receive the same packets eventually, hence the policy has broadcast rate 1 and is throughput optimal. Adding redundant edges to a tree can only improve the broadcast rate for a policy which forwards a packet whenever possible.

We conclude that any policy which forwards a packet whenever possible is throughput optimal for any graph which contains just a single spanning tree. We may then choose such a policy with other desirable properties. For instance, the greedy in-order routing policy is throughput-optimal, has *zero displacement* and minimal delay.

Networks with Higher Broadcast Capacity. We now consider the more complicated setting of networks that contain multiple edge-disjoint spanning trees. In this case it is impossible to find throughput optimal policies with zero displacement: if we require zero-displacement for each node, then all out-neighbours of the source have to receive packets in-order, limiting the broadcast rate to one. But do there exist throughput optimal policies with low displacement in this setting? We first show that the policy which routes packets round-robin over spanning trees always has bounded displacement. We then show that π^* and π^{rnd} may have large maximum displacement even for relatively small graphs.

Lemma 3. *Let $G = (V, E)$ be a network with $c > 1$ edge-disjoint spanning trees $T_1, \ldots, T_c$. Let π^r be a policy routing packets round-robin (in some order) over these trees. The displacement of packets at any node is bounded by $d_{\max}c - 1$ under the policy π^r, where $d_{\max}$ is the biggest difference in distance from the source s to any node via distinct spanning trees. That is, $d_{\max} := \max_{v \in V} \max_{T_i \neq T_j} |d_i(v) - d_j(v)|$, where $d_i(v)$ is the hop distance from s to v via spanning tree T_i.*

Proof. We will assume that during every round (time slot) there are enough packets at the source (at least c) to route a unique packet over each spanning tree, because we can only obtain the maximum displacement if this is the case. Given an order of the spanning trees $(i_1, \ldots, i_c)$, the policy π^r in round t routes packet $1 + c(t - 1)$ over tree T_{i_1}, packet $2 + c(t - 1)$ over tree T_{i_2} and so on.

We will show that it is possible to obtain a displacement of $d_{\max}c - 1$ at a node v for which there exists a pair of spanning trees T_{red} and T_{blue} such that $d_{\mathrm{red}}(v) - d_{\mathrm{blue}}(v) = d_{\max}$. Note that $d_{\mathrm{red}}(v)$ is the longest distance and $d_{\mathrm{blue}}(v)$ is the shortest distance from s to v on spanning trees.

Let p be a packet leaving the source in round t over the spanning tree T_{red}. It will take $d_{\mathrm{red}}(v)$ rounds until this packet arrives at node v, that is p arrives at node v in round $t + d_{\mathrm{red}}(v) - 1$. Let p' be the packet that gets routed over spanning tree T_{blue} in round t, then $p' + c$ will get routed over T_{blue} in round $t + 1$, $p' + 2c$ will get routed over T_{blue} in round $t + 2$ and so on. All packets p', $p' + c, \ldots, p' + (d_{\max} - 1)c$ will arrive at v before p does (i.e. prior to round $t + d_{\mathrm{red}}(v) - 1$). We know that $p^{\mathrm{miss}} \leq p$ in round $t + d_{\mathrm{red}}(v) - 2$, and hence we find $\Delta_v(t + d_{\mathrm{red}}(v) - 2) \geq p' + (d_{\max} - 1)c - p$. This value is maximized when p is the first packet routed in round t and p' the last, that is when $p' = p + c - 1$. This leads to a displacement of $p + c - 1 + (d_{\max} - 1)c - p = d_{\max}c - 1$ at v if $p^{\mathrm{miss}} = p$. In fact, p^{miss} has to equal p since all packets with index smaller than p have been sent prior to round t and must have arrived at v by round $t + d_{\mathrm{red}}(v) - 1$ since $d_{\mathrm{red}}(v)$ is the longest distance from s to v over all spanning trees. Figure 3 illustrates the above construction.

Note that this construction explicitly maximises the displacement at v. Since $d_{\max}$ is maximised over all nodes the value $d_{\max}c - 1$ is an upper bound on the displacement for all nodes.   □

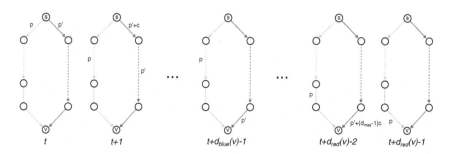

Fig. 3. An illustration of the packets routed from s to v by π^{r}. Only a subset of the edges of the network G is depicted; the paths from s to v on the red and the blue spanning tree. In round t packets p and p' are routed over spanning trees T_{red} and T_{blue} respectively. In round $t + 1$ packet $p' + c$ is routed over T_{blue}. In round $t + d_{\mathrm{blue}}(v) - 1$ packet p' arrives at v, and in all the subsequent rounds packets $p' + c, p' + 2c, \ldots$ arrive at v. Round $t + d_{\mathrm{red}} - 2$ is the latest round for which p has not yet arrived at v; in this round packet $p' + (d_{\max} - 1)c$ arrives via the blue spanning tree. Finally in round $t + d_{\mathrm{red}}(v) - 1$ packet p arrives at node v. (Color figure online)

Round-robin routing is impractical in a dynamic setting as it requires computing the spanning trees after each network change. Hence, we consider π^* and π^{rnd}, which were designed to run on dynamic networks. Figure 4 illustrates that the maximum displacement of both π^* and π^{rnd} seems to be growing over time. The maximum displacement of π^* grows much more rapidly than that of π^{rnd}. This can be explained by the way weights are assigned to packets. The displacement at a node v grows rapidly when $p^{\mathrm{miss}}(v)$ remains constant for a while. This happens when the weight of $p^{\mathrm{miss}}(v)$ is negative or when it is low and there are other packets with higher weight. Note that all edges (u, v) over which the packet p^{miss} can be routed (i.e. all such edges for which p^{miss} is present at u) have equal weight $w_{p,(u,v)}$. If it is negative for a single edge then it is negative for all.

We furthermore found that there are more nodes that have relatively high maximum displacement under π^* than for π^{rnd} as is illustrated in Fig. 4(b) and (c). Notice that for both algorithms nodes in the centre of the network have lower maximum displacement than nodes in the periphery.

We next explore the behaviour of our fixed-displacement policies $\tilde{\pi}^*_\ell$ and $\tilde{\pi}^{\mathrm{rnd}}_\ell$ for different ℓ, focusing on the trade-off between ℓ and the achieved broadcast rate

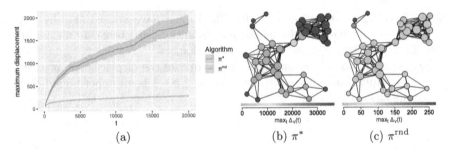

(a)   (b) π^* (c) π^{rnd}

Fig. 4. (a) Maximum displacement $\Delta_{\max}(t) := \max_{v \in V} \Delta_v(t)$ of π^* and π^{rnd} averaged over 100 runs on geometric random graphs on 20 vertices with two edge-disjoint spanning trees. Packets arrive according to a Poisson process of rate 1.8 (90% of the broadcast capacity); both algorithms broadcast at this rate. (b) and (c): Distribution of the maximum displacement over nodes for a single geometric graph with 50 nodes and two edge-disjoint spanning trees. The grey node is the source node. The colour of the other nodes corresponds to the largest displacement at the node over time (shown on the horizontal scale). These scales are very different for π^* and π^{rnd}: the nodes that have the highest maximum displacement under π^* have a maximum displacement of roughly a hundred times as high as the nodes that have the maximum displacement under π^{rnd}. The size of each node corresponds to its degree (number of connections). (Color figure online)

for low values of ℓ. We compare the performance of $\tilde{\pi}_\ell^*$ and $\tilde{\pi}_\ell^{\mathrm{rnd}}$ on three different types of directed networks, chosen to assess the impact of the broadcast capacity λ^* and the effect of redundant edges on throughput and displacement. We expect that networks with higher broadcast capacity will have higher displacement due to packets having to arrive at a node via an increasing number of distinct routes, and hence potentially being further apart. We also expect that adding edges will reduce the displacement, because this may introduce 'short cuts' in the network.

The simplest networks for which we can fix the broadcast capacity are disjoint unions of k trees ($G_k^{\mathrm{st}}(n)$). We create these by generating random trees on n vertices, until we have found k edge-disjoint trees which we merge into a network (which has $k(n-1)$ edges). The second family of networks is $G_k^{\mathrm{st}+}(n)$, made by adding $k(n-1)$ edges to $G_k^{\mathrm{st}}(n)$. These networks are used to explore the effect of redundant edges. The third family $G_k^{\mathrm{geo}}(n)$ consists of disk graphs, which are geometric networks commonly used to model ad-hoc networks [5]. We choose n points uniformly at random in the unit square and connect each pair of vertices that is at most a distance ε apart (using Euclidean distance). We choose ε as the smallest radius such that the graph has k edge-disjoint spanning trees.

To assess the impact of ℓ on the broadcast rate we run $\tilde{\pi}_\ell^{\mathrm{rnd}}$ and $\tilde{\pi}_\ell^*$ for different ℓ. We measure the difference between the arrival rate $\lambda = 0.9\lambda^*$ and achieved broadcast rate after 20,000 time slots. We keep ℓ below 200 because we are interested in policies with relatively low displacement. Figure 5 shows that for $\tilde{\pi}_\ell^{\mathrm{rnd}}$ to achieve a broadcast rate of $0.9\lambda^*$, a value of $\ell < 200$ suffices (remaining packet rate equals zero). For $\tilde{\pi}_\ell^*$ this is only true for networks with

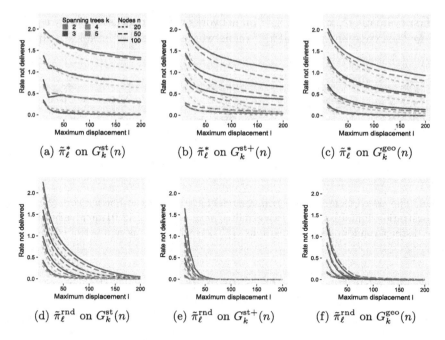

(a) $\tilde{\pi}_\ell^*$ on $G_k^{\mathrm{st}}(n)$ (b) $\tilde{\pi}_\ell^*$ on $G_k^{\mathrm{st}+}(n)$ (c) $\tilde{\pi}_\ell^*$ on $G_k^{\mathrm{geo}}(n)$

(d) $\tilde{\pi}_\ell^{\mathrm{rnd}}$ on $G_k^{\mathrm{st}}(n)$ (e) $\tilde{\pi}_\ell^{\mathrm{rnd}}$ on $G_k^{\mathrm{st}+}(n)$ (f) $\tilde{\pi}_\ell^{\mathrm{rnd}}$ on $G_k^{\mathrm{geo}}(n)$

Fig. 5. Average remaining packet rate (i.e., difference between the arrival rate of a Poisson process with rate $0.9\lambda^*$ and the broadcast rate after $20,000$ time slots) for a set of 100 random networks.

two edge-disjoint spanning trees, or networks with many redundant edges and few nodes (Fig. 5(b)). It is unclear if there always exists a large ℓ for which $\tilde{\pi}_\ell^*$ achieves a broadcast rate of $0.9\lambda^*$, since π^* itself has not been proven to be throughput optimal in the regular slotted model. Furthermore, the number of network nodes only slightly affects the value of ℓ for $\tilde{\pi}_\ell^{\mathrm{rnd}}$, whereas for $\tilde{\pi}_\ell^*$ the required value of ℓ increases when the network grows. The required value of ℓ for $\tilde{\pi}_\ell^*$ also seems to increase more than that of $\tilde{\pi}_\ell^{\mathrm{rnd}}$ when the number of spanning trees increases. As expected, the broadcast rate improves for both policies when there are redundant edges in the grap; see Figs. 5(b–c) and (e–f). This effect is strongest for $\tilde{\pi}_\ell^{\mathrm{rnd}}$.

We conclude that fixing the maximum displacement of the policy $\tilde{\pi}_\ell^{\mathrm{rnd}}$ is an effective way to achieve a high broadcast rate while ensuring low displacement. For $\tilde{\pi}_\ell^*$ this strategy is only suited to networks that contain at most two edge-disjoint spanning trees. In the next section, we compare high-throughput, low-displacement policies in more detail, based on additional performance measures.

5   Comparing High-Throughput Policies

We now study π^*, $\tilde{\pi}_\ell^*$, π^{rnd} and $\tilde{\pi}_\ell^{\mathrm{rnd}}$ for networks with multiple spanning trees in terms of other performance measures (storage requirements, packet delays).

We first evaluate π^*, π^{rnd}, $\tilde{\pi}_\ell^*$, $\tilde{\pi}_\ell^{\mathrm{rnd}}$ on networks with broadcast capacity equal to two; we then compare π^{rnd} and $\tilde{\pi}_\ell^{\mathrm{rnd}}$ on networks with higher broadcast capacity.

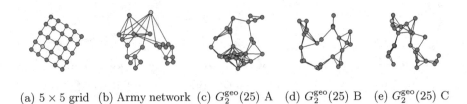

(a) 5×5 grid   (b) Army network   (c) $G_2^{\mathrm{geo}}(25)$ A   (d) $G_2^{\mathrm{geo}}(25)$ B   (e) $G_2^{\mathrm{geo}}(25)$ C

Fig. 6. The networks are a 5×5 grid, a model for a military ad-hoc network (Based on an illustration found on http://www.miltechmag.com/2012_12_01_archive.html.) and three distinct random geometric graphs $G_2^{\mathrm{geo}}(25)$ with varying number of edges.

Networks with Broadcast Capacity 2. Figure 6 shows the networks with broadcast capacity 2 that are used for the experiments in this section.

The edges in these networks are bidirectional and all networks have roughly 25 nodes. We run π^*, π^{rnd}, $\tilde{\pi}_\ell^*$ and $\tilde{\pi}_\ell^{\mathrm{rnd}}$ on these networks for 20,000 time slots. The values of ℓ are such that the fixed-displacement policies have (almost) optimal throughput: the difference between the arrival rate $0.9\lambda^*$ and the broadcast rate at the end of the simulation is less than 0.01. For all networks the maximum displacement grows over time for both π^* and π^{rnd}; after 20,000 time slots both are still increasing. Not surprisingly, the maximum displacement is much higher for π^* and π^{rnd} than for the fixed displacement policies $\tilde{\pi}_\ell^*$ and $\tilde{\pi}_\ell^{\mathrm{rnd}}$. For the policies $\tilde{\pi}_\ell^*$ and $\tilde{\pi}_\ell^{\mathrm{rnd}}$ there is always at least one node which has the maximum packet displacement ℓ at some point in the simulation.

In practice, a high displacement could imply high storage needs, because if we do not want to drop any packets, nodes need to store packets until they can be used. We assume a packet can be used as soon as all its preceding packets have been received. Thus, the number of packets to be stored at a given node can never exceed the displacement. However, it is possible that only very few packets need to be stored even though the displacement is high. For instance, a node which has received packets 1 and 10000 has displacement 9998 but only stores a single packet. We investigate if the storage requirements of π^* and π^{rnd} exceed those of our fixed displacement policies or if, even though the maximum displacement of π^* and π^{rnd} is much higher than that of $\tilde{\pi}_\ell^*$ and $\tilde{\pi}_\ell^{\mathrm{rnd}}$, they require a similar amount of storage space per node.

To do so we keep track of the maximum number of packets stored at each node for a complete run of each routing policy. We find that on average (over all nodes and 100 runs) the required storage is lowest for $\tilde{\pi}_\ell^{\mathrm{rnd}}$ and highest for π^*; see Table 1 (mean storage per node). For the average maximum storage requirement the differences are much larger. It is hard to know which nodes will

Table 1. The average over 100 runs of (left) the mean storage requirements per node and (right) the maximum storage requirement over all nodes. The storage requirement of a node is the largest observed queue at the node during a simulation. The values of ℓ for $\tilde{\pi}_\ell^*$ are 170, 250, 30, 50 and 300; the values of ℓ for $\tilde{\pi}_\ell^{\text{rnd}}$ are 20, 80, 20, 20 and 50 (both from top to bottom).

Networks			Mean storage				Maximum storage			
	n	m	π^*	$\tilde{\pi}_\ell^*$	π^{rnd}	$\tilde{\pi}_\ell^{\text{rnd}}$	π^*	$\tilde{\pi}_\ell^*$	π^{rnd}	$\tilde{\pi}_\ell^{\text{rnd}}$
5×5 grid	25	80	638.96	156.15	87.16	20	1429.21	170	161.43	20
Army network	23	74	1102.38	233.22	184.64	72.91	2276.95	250	321.12	80
$G_2^{\text{geo}}(25)$ A	25	146	398.20	29.88	50.76	19.54	1000.51	30	151.71	20
$G_2^{\text{geo}}(25)$ B	25	104	488.13	49.99	76.5	20	1326.65	50	137.83	20
$G_2^{\text{geo}}(25)$ C	25	74	1459.65	253.49	126.22	42.4	3159.31	300	293.61	50

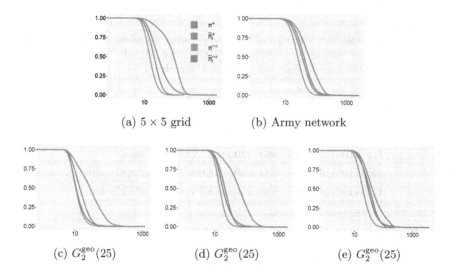

(a) 5×5 grid   (b) Army network

(c) $G_2^{\text{geo}}(25)$ (d) $G_2^{\text{geo}}(25)$ (e) $G_2^{\text{geo}}(25)$

Fig. 7. Cumulative frequency of packet delays (i.e., fraction of packets with delay below the given value). Delay (horizontal axis) is given on a logarithmic scale.

require most storage, and hence we would either have to drop packets (when giving each node the mean storage) or waste storage (when giving each node the maximum storage). For dynamic networks the storage requirements would differ over time, as the topology of the network changes. Then our fixed displacement policies behave much nicer; we can assign ℓ storage spaces to each node and be guaranteed that no packet is dropped while maintaining a high broadcast rate.

Now focus on packet delays under the different routing policies. For each packet we record the difference between the time between it arrived at the root and the time it has been delivered to all nodes. Packets that have not been delivered at the end of the simulation have delay ∞. Random policies have lower delay than weighted policies. Also, fixing the displacement leads to longer delays (Fig. 7). Thus, even when the fixed-displacement policies have high throughput, there is still a trade-off between low displacement and packet delay.

Networks with Higher Broadcast Capacity. We compare π^{rnd} and its fixed displacement variant $\tilde{\pi}_\ell^{\mathrm{rnd}}$ for four random geometric networks on 100 nodes, two with three edge-disjoint spanning trees and two with four. Table 2 shows the average storage requirements for π^{rnd} and $\tilde{\pi}_\ell^{\mathrm{rnd}}$ for 100 simulation runs. Here ℓ is chosen such that the broadcast rate of $\tilde{\pi}_\ell^{\mathrm{rnd}}$ is at least the arrival rate minus 0.01. We see that the mean storage requirement of nodes is again lower for the fixed displacement policy $\tilde{\pi}_\ell^{\mathrm{rnd}}$ than for the policy π^{rnd}, but this difference reduces when the number of spanning trees increases. The maximum storage requirement is again much better for $\tilde{\pi}_\ell^{\mathrm{rnd}}$ than for π^{rnd}. Note that under $\tilde{\pi}_\ell^{\mathrm{rnd}}$, packets have higher delays than under π^{rnd}, in line with what we observed for networks with two edge-disjoint spanning trees.

Table 2. The average over 100 runs of the mean storage requirements per node (left), and of the maximum storage requirement over all nodes (right). The storage requirement of a node is the largest observed queue at the node.

Networks				Mean storage		Max storage	
	n	m	ℓ	π^{rnd}	$\tilde{\pi}_\ell^{\mathrm{rnd}}$	π^{rnd}	$\tilde{\pi}_\ell^{\mathrm{rnd}}$
$G_3^{\mathrm{geo}}(100)$ A	100	1248	30	58.72	29.99	240.38	30
$G_3^{\mathrm{geo}}(100)$ B	100	960	130	139.55	98.19	506.63	130
$G_4^{\mathrm{geo}}(100)$ A	100	926	60	54.99	48.80	320.81	60
$G_4^{\mathrm{geo}}(100)$ B	100	936	310	128.45	78.76	865.17	310

6   Discussion and Concluding Remarks

The main conclusions from our experiments can be summarized as follows.

- There are *many* throughput optimal broadcasting policies for networks with a *single spanning tree*. Then the greedy in-order routing policy is a good choice: it is throughput-optimal, has zero displacement and minimal delay.
- For networks with higher broadcast capacity, i.e. networks with *multiple edge-disjoint spanning trees*, round-robin routing has bounded maximum displacement. Our results suggest that policies designed for broadcasting on dynamic networks (π^* and π^{rnd}) have unbounded maximum displacement.
- For networks with *broadcast capacity 2*, policies $\tilde{\pi}_\ell^*$ and $\tilde{\pi}_\ell^{\mathrm{rnd}}$ have low displacement and high throughput. These fixed displacement policies require less storage but deliver packets with higher delays than π^* and π^{rnd}.
- When a network has *broadcast capacity 3 or more*, we recommend using either policy π^{rnd} or $\tilde{\pi}_\ell^{\mathrm{rnd}}$ depending on what is more important: fixed displacement and low storage or high throughput and low delays.

We also showed that it is crucial to explicitly state the edge activation model when assessing the throughput, as it has a significant impact. In particular, we showed that for the regular slotted model, any locally deterministic policy has broadcast rate $\lambda \leq 1$, which does not hold under different modelling assumptions.

Random useful packet forwarding, being implementable in a distributed way, often performs very well. It only needs *local* information (i.e. to decide which packet to send over the edge (u, v) only knowledge of the packets present at nodes u and v is needed). For π^* however, knowledge about the F-sets is needed to compute the packet weights (i.e. *global* knowledge). There are issues with π^{rnd} when scheduling decisions need to be made; in this case π^* is preferred [12].

We have analyzed broadcasting policies on static networks, even though they are designed for dynamic networks. This allowed us to compare the throughput achieved by the policies to the broadcast capacity of the network, and it reduced the number of parameters in our simulations. To make recommendations for specific applications, it would be useful to perform experiments on dynamically evolving networks from those applications.

References

1. Conti, M., Giordano, S.: Mobile ad hoc networking: milestones, challenges, and new research directions. IEEE Commun. Mag. **52**(1), 85–96 (2014)
2. Deshpande, H., Bawa, M., Garcia-Molina, H.: Streaming live media over peers. Technical report 2002–21, Stanford InfoLab (2002)
3. Edmonds, J.: Edge-disjoint branchings. In: Rustin, R. (ed.) Combinatorial Algorithms, pp. 91–96. Algorithmics Press (1972)
4. Gandhi, R., Mishra, A., Parthasarathy, S.: Minimizing broadcast latency and redundancy in ad hoc networks. IEEE/ACM Trans. Netw. **16**(4), 840–851 (2008)
5. Haenggi, M., Andrews, J.G., Baccelli, F., Dousse, O., Franceschetti, M.: Stochastic geometry and random graphs for the analysis and design of wireless networks. IEEE J. Sel. Areas Commun. **27**(7), 1029–1046 (2009)
6. Keshavarz-Haddad, A., Ribeiro, V., Riedi, R.: Broadcast capacity in multihop wireless networks. In Proceedings of the 12th Annual International Conference on Mobile Computing and Networking, pp. 239–250 (2006)
7. Kundu, S.: Bounds on the number of disjoint spanning trees. J. Comb. Theory **17**, 199–203 (1974)
8. Massoulié, L., Twigg, A., Gkantsidis, C., Rodriguez, P.: Randomized decentralized broadcasting algorithms. In: Proceedings of the 26th IEEE International Conference on Computer Communications, pp. 1073–1081 (2007)
9. Neely, M.J.: Stochastic Network Optimization with Application to Communication and Queueing Systems, vol. 3. Morgan & Claypool Publishers, San Rafael (2010)
10. Rajaraman, R.: Topology control and routing in ad hoc networks: a survey. SIGACT News **33**(2), 60–73 (2002)
11. Sinha, A., Paschos, G., Li, C., Modiano, E.: Throughput-optimal broadcast on directed acyclic graphs. In: Proceedings of the IEEE Conference on Computer Communications, INFOCOM 2015, pp. 1248–1256 (2015)
12. Sinha, A., Paschos, G., Modiano, E.: Throughput-optimal multi-hop broadcast algorithms. In: Proceedings of the 17th ACM International Symposium on Mobile Ad Hoc Networking and Computing, pp. 51–60 (2016)

13. Sinha, A., Tassiulas, L., Modiano, E.: Throughput-optimal broadcast in wireless networks with dynamic topology. In: Proceedings of the 17th ACM International Symposium on Mobile Ad Hoc Networking and Computing, pp. 21–30 (2016)
14. Tassiulas, L., Ephremides, A.: Stability properties of constrained queueing systems and scheduling policies for maximum throughput in multihop radio networks. IEEE Trans. Autom. Control **37**(12), 1936–1948 (1992)
15. Towsley, D., Twigg, A.: Rate-optimal decentralized broadcasting: the wireless case. In: International Technology Alliance, pp. 323–333 (2008)
16. Williams, B., Camp, T.: Comparison of broadcasting techniques for mobile ad hoc networks. In: Proceedings 3rd ACM International Symposium on Mobile Ad Hoc Networking and Computing, pp. 194–205 (2002)
17. Zanella, A., Pierobon, G., Merlin, S.: On the limiting performance of broadcast algorithms over unidimensional ad-hoc radio networks. In: Proceedings of WMPC, pp. 165–169 (2004)
18. Zhang, Z.: Routing in intermittently connected mobile ad hoc networks and delay tolerant networks: overview and challenges. IEEE Commun. Surv. Tutor. **8**(1), 24–37 (2006)
19. Zukerman, M.: Introduction to Queueing Theory and Stochastic Teletraffic Models. https://arxiv.org/abs/1307.2968 (2018)

Faulty Robots

Chauffeuring a Crashed Robot from a Disk

Debasish Pattanayak$^{(\boxtimes)}$, H. Ramesh, and Partha Sarathi Mandal●

Indian Institute of Technology Guwahati, Guwahati, India
{p.debasish,ramesh_h,psm}@iitg.ac.in

Abstract. Evacuation of robots from a disk has recently attained a lot of atten-tion. We visit the problem from the perspective of fault-tolerance. We consider two robots trying to evacuate from a disk via a single hidden exit on the perime-ter of the disk. The robots communicate wirelessly. The robots are susceptible to crash faults, after which they stop moving and communicating. We design the algorithms for tolerating one fault. The objective is to minimize the worst-case time required to evacuate both the robots from the disk. When the non-faulty robot chauffeurs the crashed robot, it takes $\alpha \geq 1$ amount of time to travel unit distance. With this, we also provide a lower bound for the evacu-ation time. Further, we evaluate the worst-case of the algorithms for different values of α and the crash time.

Keywords: Evacuation · Mobile robots · Crash faults · Distributed algorithms

1 Introduction

Searching has always been a classical problem, and by extension, the search of a hidden object in a domain has piqued the interest. In particular, a variant of search problem introduced by Czyzowicz et al. [5] as the *evacuation* problem, which tries to minimize the time required for the last searcher to reach the target. The searchers, in this case, are mobile robots which can move around in the domain. The domain con-sidered can be a convex shape like a disk, a circle or a triangle [2–4], while the target is hidden on the boundary. Another variant of the problem considers the domain as lines and rays [1] with faulty robots [11,13]. The objective is to minimize the *compet-itive ratio* between the time required for the robot to reach the exit and the distance from the exit.

The recent literature has focused on the aspect of collective-collaborative search. Czyzowicz et al. [5] introduced two robots trying to search for an exit located on the perimeter of a unit disk. A robot can locate the exit only when it is at the exit. There are two models of communication between the robots, namely, *wireless* and *face-to-face*. In face-to-face, the robots can exchange messages if they are collocated at the same point at the same time. They showed that the evacuation time for two robots in the wireless model was $1 + 2\pi/3 + \sqrt{3} \approx 4.826$, which was optimal. In the same paper, they achieved an upper bound of 5.740 and lower bound 5.199 for two robots in the face-to-face model. In a subsequent paper, Czyzowicz et al. [10] improved the upper and lower bounds to 5.628 and 5.255, respectively. Later Brandt et al. [2], fur-ther improved the upper bound to 5.625 with the introduction of a linear detour.

© Springer Nature Switzerland AG 2019
F. Dressler and C. Scheideler (Eds.): ALGOSENSORS 2019, LNCS 11931, pp. 177–191, 2019.
https://doi.org/10.1007/978-3-030-34405-4_10

Recently, Disser et al. [12] improved the upper bound to 5.6234 by introducing a second detour.

Further, Czyzowicz et al. [7] studied priority evacuation of a particular robot from the disk, namely the Queen, while other servant robots search for the exit. This paper established the upper and lower bounds for evacuation for one, two, and three servants. Another paper by Czyzowicz et al. [8] presented the bounds for $n \geq 4$.

Another aspect of this evacuation problem deals with fault-tolerance. The two types of faults considered are *crash fault* and *byzantine fault*. The type of crash fault considered in [6, 11] does not detect the target when it passes through or does not communicate when it finds the target. The robots with byzantine faults in [6, 9] even lie about the position of the target. Czyzowicz et al. [6] focused on minimizing the evacuation time for the latest non-faulty robot. They achieved a lower bound of 5.188 and upper bound 6.309 for three robots out of which at most one is susceptible to crash fault with wireless communication. We initiate the study on a type of crash fault, where the robot stops moving and sending messages altogether (unlike [6]). Instead of abandoning the crashed robot, our objective is to chauffeur it to the exit in the least time. As a natural outcome, we consider the robot which chauffeurs the crashed robots incurs an extra cost. The chauffeur carrying the crashed robot travels at a fraction of its original speed.

Our Contributions: In this paper, we consider a variant of the crash fault where the affected robot stops moving and communicating after it has crashed. We address the problem of evacuation for two robots out of which at most one can be faulty. We propose three evacuation algorithms in the wireless communication model, where the non-faulty robot chauffeurs the crashed robot.

- We present a lower bound for evacuation time.
- We rigorously analyze our algorithms to provide the worst-case evacuation time corresponding to the crash time w at which a robot becomes faulty.
- We compare the performance of the algorithms given particular values of the crash time (w) and the chauffeuring cost (α).

The rest of the paper is organized as follows. First, we delve into the model and notations in Sect. 2. We establish a lower bound for evacuation time in Sect. 3. Next, we describe three algorithms, namely, the trivial Algorithm $\mathscr{A}_0$ in Sect. 4.1, Algorithm $\mathscr{A}_1$, where robots start from the same point on the perimeter in Sect. 4.2 and Algorithm $\mathscr{A}_2$, where robots start at the endpoints of an arc of length ζ on the perimeter in Sect. 4.3. Finally, we compare the algorithms in Sect. 5 before concluding in Sect. 6.

2   Model and Preliminaries

We consider the evacuation of two robots from a unit disk, i.e., a disk with radius one. Let R_1 and R_2 be the robots. The disk contains an exit located on its perimeter. Both robots have to evacuate the disk. Initially, the robots are situated at the center of the disk and start moving at the same time towards the perimeter of the disk. A robot can find an exit only when it reaches the position of that exit.

We follow a convention that $\overset{\frown}{AE}$ denotes the arc along the perimeter on the disk starting at A and ending at E moving in the counter-clockwise direction. Accordingly, $\overset{\frown}{EA}$ is the complement of the arc $\overset{\frown}{AE}$. We abuse the notation $\overset{\frown}{AE}$ to denote the length of the arc and $\overline{AE}$ to denote the length of the chord corresponding to the arc $\overset{\frown}{AE}$. Note that, the length of a chord corresponding to an arc of length ζ is $2\sin(\zeta/2)$.

Both robots travel at a uniform speed of one unit distance per unit time. We consider that the robots are susceptible to *crash faults*. A crashed robot stops moving and communicating after the crash. At most a single robot is faulty. Suppose, R_1 has crashed, R_2 can still chauffeur R_1 to the exit. A non-faulty robot chauffeuring the crashed robot travels at speed $1/\alpha$ times the original speed. In other words, it takes α time to travel unit distance, where $\alpha \geq 1$.

The robots can communicate by sending messages wirelessly. The communication is reliable. For analytical purposes, we ignore the message propagation delay. The robots frequently communicate with each other. Without loss of generality, let w be the time after which R_1 crashes. So $w - 1$ is the distance traveled by the robot after reaching the perimeter at a speed of one unit distance per unit of time before it crashes at time w. We also follow a convention that x is the distance of the exit in the counter-clockwise direction, starting from the point where R_1 has reached the perimeter. So, $\overset{\frown}{AE} = x$ as shown in Fig. 2. We assume that O is the origin and $\overline{OA}$ is the positive x-axis.

Evacuation Problem (2, 1)-Crash Fault: The objective is to minimize the time required by the latest robot to evacuate from the unit disk via an exit located on the perimeter of the disk starting from the center of the disk, where both robots travel at uniform speed of one unit distance per unit time and at most one robot is faulty out of the two. Chauffeuring the faulty robot increases the time for movement by a factor $\alpha \geq 1$ for the non-faulty robot.

3 Lower Bounds for Wireless Communication

The lower bound for wireless communication model without faults is $1 + 2\pi/3 + \sqrt{3} \approx 4.826$ [5]. Hence, the lower bound is applicable to the crash fault model if the crash time $w \geq 1 + 2\pi/3 + \sqrt{3}$. We have the following theorems if the robot crashes before evacuation.

Theorem 1. *The lower bound for evacuation with crash fault for crash time $w < 1$ is $2\pi + w + \alpha(1 - w)$.*

Proof. Consider the simple case where the robot crashes at the center of the disk immediately after it is activated. As the adversary can always place the exit at a position which is still unexplored, it requires at least 2π time to search for the exit on the perimeter by the non-faulty robot. Additionally, α is the minimum time required for the faulty robot to be carried to the exit from the center. Since the non-faulty robot can also travel to the perimeter while carrying the faulty robot, it does not need additional time to reach the perimeter. Then the worst-case time for evacuation for the faulty robot is always greater than $2\pi + \alpha$. Similarly, if $0 < w \leq 1$, we have the lower bound for evacuation at

$$2\pi + w + \alpha(1 - w) \tag{1}$$

where the robots travel together for a distance w, and the non-faulty robot chauffeurs the faulty robot rest of the $1 - w$ distance to the perimeter.   □

Lemma 1 (Lemma 5 from[5]). *Consider a perimeter of a disk whose subset of total length $u + \epsilon > 0$ has not been explored for some $\epsilon > 0$ and $\pi \geq u > 0$. Then there exist two unexplored boundary points between which the distance along the perimeter is at least u.*

Intuitively, the proof follows from this argument. If u is the unexplored part of the perimeter and it is a continuous arc, then the endpoints of the arc are separated by at least the same distance along the perimeter. Otherwise, the unexplored part is separated into multiple arcs, and the distance between two farthest endpoints of the multiple arcs are at least separated by a distance which is greater than the unexplored part $u \leq \pi$. A detailed proof is available in [5].

Theorem 2. *The lower bounds for evacuation with crash fault for crash time $w > 1 + 2\pi/3$ are*

$$1 + 2\pi/3 + \sqrt{3} \qquad\qquad\qquad\qquad\qquad\text{for } w \geq 1 + 2\pi/3 + \sqrt{3}$$

$$1 + 2\pi/3 + (\alpha + 1)(1 + 2\pi/3 + \sqrt{3} - w) \qquad\text{for } w \in [1 + 2\pi/3, 1 + 2\pi/3 + \sqrt{3}/2]$$

$$1 + 2\pi/3 + \sqrt{3} + (\alpha - 1)(1 + 2\pi/3 + \sqrt{3} - w) \quad\text{for } w \in [1 + 2\pi/3 + \sqrt{3}/2, 1 + 2\pi/3 + \sqrt{3}]$$

Proof. If $w > 1 + 2\pi/3 + \sqrt{3}$, then we claim that the robots evacuate before any of them fails. By the time $1 + t$, two robots can explore at most $2t$ on the perimeter. The unexplored part is $2\pi - 2t$. According to Lemma 1, there exist two unexplored points such that the smallest arc between them is at least $2\pi - 2t$. If a robot is at one of the unexplored points, then the adversary can place the exit at the other unexplored point, and the exit is found. The robot, which does not find the exit, can receive a message and travel to the exit along a straight line through the disk. The evacuation time in that case is $1 + t + 2\sin(t)$ over all possible values of $\pi/2 < t < \pi$. This results in a worst-case at $t = 2\pi/3$, which is $1 + 2\pi/3 + \sqrt{3} \approx 4.826$. Since the crash time w is more than the worst-case evacuation time, both robots evacuate before the fault occurs and the lower bound for evacuation is $1 + 2\pi/3 + \sqrt{3}$.

If $w < 1 + 2\pi/3 + \sqrt{3}$, the robot can fail at any moment before the evacuation occurs. For this part of the proof, consider that the exit is found at time $1 + 2\pi/3$ by R_2. In the worst-case R_1 travels a distance $\sqrt{3}$ from its position towards the exit in a straight line. The distance between the two robots is $\sqrt{3}$, so the robots can meet at the midpoint of that chord at time $1 + 2\pi/3 + \sqrt{3}/2$. If R_1 fails before the midpoint, then R_2 has to travel extra distance to chauffeur R_1. Otherwise, they meet at the midpoint and travel together. In that case, if R_1 fails, R_2 chauffeurs the remaining distance. The following two cases present the evacuation time if the robot fails before or after the midpoint.

Fault before the midpoint $(1 + 2\pi/3 < w < 1 + 2\pi/3 + \sqrt{3}/2)$: R_2 has to travel extra distance of $1 + 2\pi/3 + \sqrt{3}/2 - w$ to reach R_1 from midpoint and chauffeur it for a distance $1 + 2\pi/3 + \sqrt{3} - w$. The evacuation time is $1 + 2\pi/3 + (\alpha + 1)(1 + 2\pi/3 + \sqrt{3} - w)$.

Fault after the midpoint $(1+2\pi/3+\sqrt{3}/2 < w < 1+2\pi/3+\sqrt{3})$: R_1 and R_2 have already met and are travelling together. The distance R_2 needs to chauffeur R_1 is $1+2\pi/3+\sqrt{3}-w$. The chauffeuring distance adds the cost by a factor of $(\alpha - 1)$ since the robots were already travelling towards the same destination. The evacuation time is $1+2\pi/3+\sqrt{3}+(\alpha-1)(1+2\pi/3+\sqrt{3}-w)$. $\qquad\square$

Theorem 3. *The lower bound for evacuation with crash fault for crash time* $w \in [1, 1+ 2\pi/3]$ *is* $\max_{w-1\le t\le 2\pi-2(w-1)} \left(1+t+2(\alpha+1)\cos(t/4)\right)$ *where* $1+t$ *is the time for finding the exit and* $w-1$ *is the part of the perimeter explored by the crashed robot.*

Proof. The lower bounds we describe are irrespective of the points where the robots hit the perimeter starting from the center of the disk. There can be two cases depending on the relation between crash time w and the time an exit is found $(1 + t)$ by one of the robots.

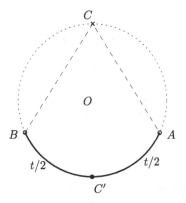

Fig. 1. The exit lies in $\widehat{BA}$ with respect to crash position C

Case 1: If a robot crashes after the exit is found, i.e., $w \ge 1 + t$, then the robot not near the exit position is already traveling towards the exit. So, the worst-case time of evacuation would happen if and only if the robot crashes at the moment the exit is found, i.e., $w = 1 + t$. The worst-case distance from the crash position to exit is the diameter. If the robot covers part of the perimeter around the antipodal position (C') of the crashed robot position (C), then the maximum distance between the crashed position and exit is at most $\overline{CB} = \overline{AC} = 2\sin((2\pi - (w-1))/4)$ as shown in Fig. 1. The worst-case evacuation time is

$$w + 2(\alpha + 1)\sin((2\pi - (w-1))/4)$$

Case 2: Suppose the exit is found at time $1 + t > w$. By the time the faulty robot crashes at w, it has covered at most $w - 1$ on the perimeter. Consider two points A and B as shown in Fig. 1 which are at a distance $w - 1 + \epsilon$ from the crashed position C for some small value of $\epsilon > 0$. If the adversary places the exit in the $\widehat{BA}$, then it would take at least $2\pi - 2(w - 1)$ to explore the arc. The distance from any point on the arc is greater than $2\sin((w - 1)/2)$. The time required for evacuation is at least

$$1 + t + 2(\alpha + 1)\sin((w - 1)/2)$$

For a value of $t < 2\pi - 2(w - 1)$, this still holds. Then the time for evacuation is

$$1 + t + 2(\alpha + 1)\cos(t/4) \tag{2}$$

The above expression holds as a lower bound since the robot which finds the exit at time $1 + t$ has to be at the exit, and we show the linear distance between exit and crash position is at least $2\cos(t/4)$. As the robot has already crashed, the optimal path is to go to the crashed robot and pick up along the chord.   □

Remark 1. For $w - 1 = 2\pi/3$, expression 2 results in evacuation time $1 + 2\pi/3 + (\alpha + 1)\sqrt{3}$ for $t = 2\pi/3$.

4   Upper Bound for Wireless Communication

The upper bound for evacuation in the wireless communication model is $1 + 2\pi/3 + \sqrt{3}$. This is the worst-case evacuation time of the algorithm proposed by Czyzowicz et al. [5]. In this paper, we also present evacuation strategies which determine the upper bound with chauffeuring. First, we present a simple strategy to put a ceiling on the upper bound. Next, we present two algorithms which provide us a tighter upper bound corresponding to the crash time.

4.1   Trivial Upper Bound (Algorithm $\mathscr{A}_0$(MoveTogether))

Since at most one robot can be faulty, a trivial strategy is to move both robots along the same path on the perimeter of the disk. Even if one of the robots becomes faulty, the other robot can chauffeur it and continue its search along the perimeter until it finds the exit. Then both the robots can evacuate via the exit, as shown in Fig. 2.

The time required for this evacuation algorithm is at most $1 + 2\pi$ in the case where both robots are free of fault until the evacuation, where the time required to reach the perimeter is 1 and to search the perimeter is 2π. If a robot becomes faulty after time w from the activation, then the execution of the algorithm requires the following time

$$z_0 = w + \alpha(1 + 2\pi - w) \tag{3}$$

where z_0 denotes the trivial upper bound with respect to the crash time w and $\alpha \geq 1$.

4.2   Evacuation Algorithm $\mathscr{A}_1$ (MoveOpposite)

We start with a base algorithm which works with robots without faults. Both robots move together to an arbitrary point A on the perimeter starting from the center O and then move in opposite directions, i.e., clockwise and counter-clockwise as shown in Fig. 3. Once a robot finds the exit, it sends a message to the other robot.

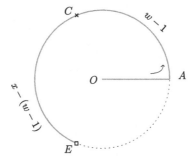

Fig. 2. R_1 and R_2 start from O, hit the perimeter at A and move together until they find exit at E and evacuate.

On receiving the message, the other robot finds the position of the sender, which is also the position of the exit by the time of arrival of the message, knowledge of other robot's path and speed. Then it proceeds for evacuation along the straight line joining its current position and the exit.

As one of the robots can be faulty, it cannot communicate after it crashes. To determine the position of the crashed robot, we assume that the robots communicate with each other regularly in small intervals. If a robot crashes and then it fails to send a message, which determines the position of the crashed robot. There can be two simple strategies in the aftermath of the crash. The non-faulty robot can carry the faulty robot and search together, or the non-faulty robot searches for the exit without carrying the faulty robot. If both robots are traveling together, then they evacuate the moment the exit is found. Otherwise, the robot which finds the exit sends a message and both robots meet on the chord joining them. When the fault occurs, the non-faulty robot meets the faulty robot, and then it chauffeurs the faulty robot to the exit. It increases the time required by a factor of α. We describe the two strategies SearchTogetherAfterCrash and SearchAloneAfterCrash, where the exit is found after a robot has crashed. An intermediate strategy, where the robot does not immediately pick up the robot after crash and searches for some distance on the perimeter, performs worse than the two aforementioned strategies. Please refer Sect. 4.2 for more details.

SearchTogetherAfterCrash: Two robots start together at the same time from the center O as shown in Fig. 3. Suppose the robot R_1 crashes at C after a time w at a distance $w - 1$ along the arc from the point A, where the robots reach the perimeter of the disk, i.e., $\widehat{AC} = w - 1$. R_2 is at D when R_1 crashes at C. R_2 moves to C along the chord $\overline{DC}$ and continues the search starting from C on $\widehat{CD}$. Suppose the exit is located at E and according to the convention, A is the closest point in the clockwise direction from E where a robot has reached the perimeter, so $\widehat{AE} = x$. By extension, $\widehat{CE} = x - w + 1$. The time taken for the evacuation is $\overline{OA} + \widehat{DA} + \overline{DC} + \alpha\widehat{CE}$, i.e.,

$$w + 2\sin(w - 1) + \alpha(x - w + 1) \tag{4}$$

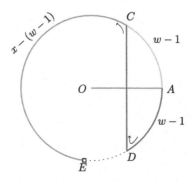

Fig. 3. R_1 crashes at C and then R_2 carries R_1 to continue searching for exit until E.

The worst-case position of exit for which the evacuation time is maximum when E is at an infinitesimally small distance from D in the clockwise direction, i.e., $x = 2\pi - (w-1)$. Then the worst-case evacuation time for this strategy is

$$z_{11} = w + 2\sin(w-1) + \alpha(2\pi - 2(w-1)) \tag{5}$$

The worst-case evacuation time would be the maximum time over all possible values of w. For $w \in [1, 1+\pi]$, the critical point is obtained at $\partial z_{11}/\partial w = 0$, i.e.,

$$\partial z_{11}/\partial w = 1 - 2\alpha + 2\cos(w-1) = 0 \implies w = \arccos((2\alpha-1)/2) + 1 \tag{6}$$

Since, $\partial^2 z_{11}/\partial w^2 = -2\sin(w-1) < 0 \,\forall w \in [1, 1+\pi]$, the critical point is a local maximum. The worst-case evacuation time is obtained at $w - 1 = \arccos(\alpha - 1/2)$. As the value of $\cos(w-1)$ ranges between -1 and 1, the maximum value of α for which the critical point acts as the maximum is $(2\alpha-1)/2 = 1$, i.e., $\alpha = 1.5$.

Remark 2. For $w \le 1$, the `SearchTogetherAfterCrash` strategy has the same worst-case evacuation time as algorithm $\mathscr{A}_0$.

`SearchAloneAfterCrash`: Similarly, the robots R_1 and R_2 start at the center of the disk at the same time and move towards the perimeter. R_1 crashes at C. But R_2 continues to move along its path until it finds the exit at E. Let x be the distance along the arc to the exit from the point where the robots have hit the perimeter, i.e., $\widehat{AE} = x$. Then the distance from the crashed position of R_1 at C to the exit at E is $\widehat{CE} = x - (w-1)$ as shown in Fig. 4. The time required for R_2 to reach the exit is $2\pi - x$. The time for evacuation would be,

$$z_{12} = 1 + 2\pi - x + 2(1+\alpha)\sin((x-(w-1))/2) \tag{7}$$

Suppose the crash position of robot R_1 is fixed. Then the worst-case location of exit would be a critical point of z_{12}, i.e., $\partial z_{12}/\partial x = 0$.

$$(1+\alpha)\cos((x-(w-1))/2) = 1 \implies x = w - 1 + 2\arccos(1/(1+\alpha)) \tag{8}$$

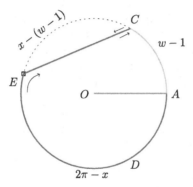

Fig. 4. R_1 crashes at C, but R_2 continues searching for exit until E and then picks up R_1 from C and goes back to E.

Note that, $\partial z_{12}/\partial w < 0$, so z_{12} is a monotonically decreasing function with respect to w. Failure of a robot is not dependent on the position of the exit. So the variables x and w are independent. Hence, the worst-case evacuation time is obtained at $w = 1$. The worst-case evacuation time is $1 + 2\pi - 2\arccos(1/(1+\alpha)) + 2\sqrt{\alpha^2 + 2\alpha}$. Now let us determine the value of α for which the worst-case evacuation time of algorithm $\mathcal{A}_0$ exceeds the worst-case of `SearchAloneAfterCrash` strategy. The worst-case evacuation time of algorithm $\mathcal{A}_0$ from Eq. 3 is $1 + 2\pi\alpha$ for $w = 1$. So,

$$1 + 2\pi\alpha = 1 + 2\pi - 2\arccos(1/(1+\alpha)) + 2\sqrt{\alpha^2 + 2\alpha}$$
$$\implies (1+\alpha)\cos(\pi(1-\alpha) + \sqrt{\alpha^2 + 2\alpha}) - 1 = 0 \tag{9}$$

The solution to Eq. 9 is the value of α for which the worst-case of `SearchAloneAfterCrash` strategy coincides with algorithm $\mathcal{A}_0$. The corresponding α is 1.30346. Hence, for values of $\alpha \le 1.30346$, algorithm $\mathcal{A}_0$ has a better worst-case evacuation time compared to `SearchAloneAfterCrash` strategy.

For the case where a robot becomes faulty before it reaches the perimeter, the non-faulty robot searches for the exit and then it picks up the faulty robot. Let $(w, 0)$ be the position of faulty robot and $(\cos(x), \sin(x))$ be the position of the exit.

$$z_{13} = 1 + x + (1+\alpha)\sqrt{(w - \cos(x))^2 + \sin^2(x)} \tag{10}$$

Remark 3. If the exit is found before a robot crashes, then the worst-case would occur when it crashes on the perimeter.

R_1 and R_2 start moving towards each other as soon as the exit is found; and if R_1 finds the exit, then R_2 moves towards the exit moving along the line joining them. Hence, if R_2 crashes on the perimeter, that would result in the worst-case. Conversely, if R_2 finds the exit, it moves towards R_1 along the line joining them. R_2 would move at most to the midpoint of the line joining them. If R_2 becomes faulty at the midpoint of the line, then the evacuation time is less compared to when it failed at the perimeter.

For $\alpha < 1.30346$, both strategies perform worse compared to the trivial algorithm at $w = 0$. Both the strategies can be combined into one since the path of the robots remain the same until one of them crashes. Note that, the evacuation time has a local maximum at $w = 1 + \arccos((2\alpha - 1)/2)$ for SearchTogetherAfterCrash strategy for $\alpha < 1.5$, while it monotonically decreases for SearchAloneAfterCrash strategy. Since the evacuation time for $w = 1$ is the same for both strategies at $\alpha = 1.30346$, the SearchAloneAfterCrash strategy performs better for all value of w.

Now, let us determine the value of w for which both strategies perform the same, i.e., $z_{11} = z_{12}$. We have the following.

$$w - 1 + 2\sin(w - 1) + \alpha(2\pi - 2(w - 1)) = 2\pi - 2\arccos(1/(1 + \alpha)) - (w - 1) + 2\sqrt{\alpha(\alpha + 2)}$$

$$\implies (w - 1)(1 - \alpha) + \sin(w - 1) = \pi(1 - \alpha) - \arccos(1/(1 + \alpha)) + \sqrt{\alpha(\alpha + 2)} \tag{11}$$

For $\alpha < 1.30346$, we have the solution for w from Eq. 11. Let $\overline{w}$ be a solution to Eq. 11. If $w < \overline{w}$, then the other robot follows SearchTogetherAfterCrash, otherwise it follows SearchAloneAfterCrash strategy. For $\alpha \geq 1.30346$, the SearchAloneAfterCrash strategy performs better than the algorithm $\mathscr{A}_0$, where the worst-case of the SearchTogetherAfterCrash strategy is always greater than or equal to worst-case of algorithm $\mathscr{A}_0$. Hence, combination of the strategies yields a better result for $\alpha \leq 1.30346$.

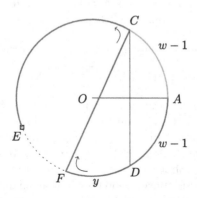

Fig. 5. R_2 goes to pick R_1 at F after travelling a distance y and search along

Comparison Between Strategies in Wireless Communication. Two robots start together from the center O at the same time as shown in Fig. 5. Let R_1 be the robot that crashes at C. R_2 is at the point D at the same time. R_2 travels up to the point F at a distance y along the arc before it decides to pick up R_1.

Then the worst-case evacuation time appears if the exit is at a small distance $\epsilon(> 0)$ from F in the unexplored part. The time for evacuation is $f = w + y + 2\sin(w - 1 + y/2) + \alpha(2\pi - 2(w - 1) - y)$. The function is f is monotonically increasing with respect to y up to $w + y/2 = \arccos(\alpha - 1)$ and then monotonically decreases. So if

$w > \arccos(\alpha - 1)$, then it is better to maximize y. And if $w <= \arccos(\alpha - 1)$, then it is better to have $y = 0$.

Remark 4. Going for meet-up immediately when the other robot fails is better compared to going for the crashed robot later if the exit is not found.

4.3 Evacuation Algorithm $\mathscr{A}_2$ (MoveSameDirection)

In this section, we describe an algorithm where the robots start from the center of the disk at the same time at an angle ζ with each other, where $0 \le \zeta \le 2\pi$. After reaching the perimeter, both robots start traveling in the counter-clockwise direction. Without loss of generality, let us assume that R_1 crashes at time w. We measure the angle ζ in the counter-clockwise direction from the faulty robot R_1.

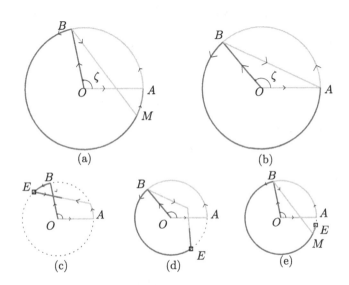

Fig. 6. Path of the robots (red color for R_1 and blue for R_2) in Algorithm $\mathscr{A}_2$ without faults

The base strategy divides the perimeter into two arcs of length ζ and $2\pi - \zeta$. Each robot explores its own arc after reaching the perimeter from the center. For $\zeta < \pi$, R_1 would finish exploring its part of the arc. Then it will try to meet the other robot. Let us determine a meeting point M (ref. Fig. 6(a)) such that $\widehat{AB} + \overline{BM} = \widehat{BM}$. The length, m, of $\overline{BM}$ can be determined from the following equation.

$$\zeta + 2\sin((\zeta + m)/2) = \zeta + m \tag{12}$$

We can determine that the points A and M coincide for $\zeta = 2.24123$. So R_1 would move along $\overline{BM}$ for $\zeta < 2.24123$ (ref. Fig. 6(a)) and along $\overline{BA}$ for $\zeta \ge 2.24123$ (ref. Fig. 6(b)). For $\zeta > \pi$, a similar path is followed by R_2.

Now, we describe the action a robot takes if it finds an exit. On finding the exit, a robot messages the other robot. Then both robots start moving towards each other along the line joining them and meet at the midpoint (ref. Fig. 6(c) and (d)). Thenceforth both robots move towards the exit. If both robots are already traveling together, they evacuate via the exit (ref. Fig. 6(e)).

When R_1 crashes, it stops moving and stays there. Once R_2 has completely explored its arc on the perimeter, then it moves to the position of R_1, and they explore the remaining part of the perimeter together if the exit is not found by that time. Since we assume that R_1 is the robot which crashes, we claim that if the exit is found by R_1, then it would never result in the worst-case. The claim can be proved by the fact that if R_2 crashes, then the evacuation time would be higher. By symmetricity, there exists a situation where R_1 crashes corresponding to an exit found by R_2. So, in the following cases, we only explain the scenarios with R_2 finding the exit.

Case 1: If R_1 crashes before the exit is found, then R_2 explores its own arc to search for the exit.

– If exit lies on R_2's arc, then R_2 picks up R_1 from its crash position. The evacuation time is

$$z_{21} = 1 + x - \zeta + (\alpha + 1)d \tag{13}$$

where d is the distance from the exit to the crash position and x is the distance of the exit from the point where R_1 reaches the boundary in the counterclockwise direction. The coordinates of exit position E are $(\cos(x), \sin(x))$. The coordinates of the crash position C are given by

$(w, 0)$ for $w < 1$

$(\cos(w - 1), \sin(w - 1))$ for $1 \le w \le 1 + \zeta$

$(\lambda \cos(2\zeta + m) + (1 - \lambda) \cos(\zeta), \lambda \sin(2\zeta + m) + (1 - \lambda) \sin(\zeta))$ for $1 + \zeta < w$

where $\lambda = \frac{w - \zeta - 1}{m}$ if $\zeta < \pi$. Equation 13 has two values of $x \in [\zeta, 2\pi]$, such that $\partial z_{21}/\partial x = 0$. The critical point may be a local maximum according to second derivative test. Hence the value of x which provides the worst-case evacuation time for a given value of w may be a critical point or a boundary point of domain of x depending on the value of ζ and α.

– If exit lies on R_1's arc, R_2 picks up R_1 by travelling along a line joining the crash position and current position of R_2 and they explore the remaining part together. The evacuation time is

$$z_{22} = w + d + \alpha(x - w - 1) \tag{14}$$

where d is the distance between crash position $(\cos(w - 1), \sin(w - 1))$ and position of R_2 at time w determined similar to the previous case. In this case, the worst-case position of exit is just before the point where R_2 hits the perimeter, i.e., $x = \zeta - \epsilon$ for an $\epsilon \to 0$.

Case 2: If R_1 crashes after the exit is found, then R_2 is already moving towards R_1 along the line joining them. The evacuation time is

$$z_{23} = w + (\alpha + 1)d \tag{15}$$

where the distance d between the crash position and position of R_2 at time w determined similar to Case 1.

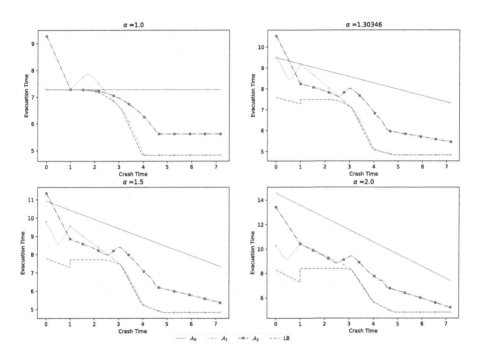

Fig. 7. Comparison between algorithms and the lower bound for different values of α

5 Comparison Between Algorithms

We numerically evaluate the behavior of proposed algorithms. The evaluation includes worst-case evacuation time corresponding to the crash time w for specific values of α. $\{1, 1.30346, 1.5, 2\}$ are chosen as values of α since at these points, the behavior of the algorithms changes according to the analysis in Sect. 4. The crash time w is varied in $[0, 2\pi + 1]$ because it takes $2\pi + 1$ amount of time for a single non-faulty robot to evacuate from the disk. The evacuation times are evaluated at discrete values of w with a gap of $\pi/120$. For each value of w, all possible worst-case positions of the exit are considered for Algorithms $\mathscr{A}_0$, $\mathscr{A}_1$ and $\mathscr{A}_2$.

As shown in Fig. 7, Algorithm $\mathscr{A}_0$ performs better than $\mathscr{A}_1$ for $\alpha < 1.30346$. For $w > 1 + 2\pi/2 + \sqrt{3}/2$, Algorithm $\mathscr{A}_1$ is optimal. Observe that, $\mathscr{A}_2$ performs better compared to $\mathscr{A}_1$ for $w \in [1, 1 + \pi/2]$. The lower bound is dominated by $t = 4\arcsin(2/(\alpha + 1))$ for

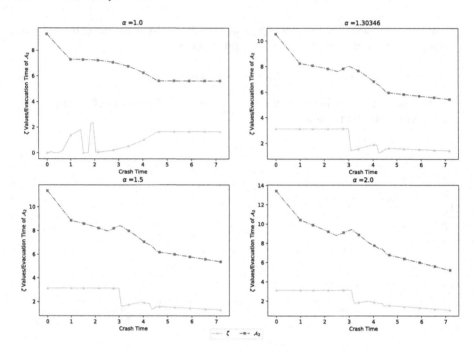

Fig. 8. Value of ζ with respect to the least worst-case evacuation time of $\mathscr{A}_2$

$\alpha = 2$ for crash time $w < 1 + 2\pi/3$. Also, for $\mathscr{A}_2$, the smallest worst-case evacuation time is found for discrete values of $\zeta \in [0, \pi]$ with a step size of $\pi/600$. We also evaluate the lower bound at the same values of w. Figure 8 shows the corresponding value of ζ for which the worst-case evacuation time is obtained for $\mathscr{A}_2$ and the four values of α. Observe that, for $\alpha > 1.30346$, $\zeta = \pi$ performs the best for algorithm $\mathscr{A}_2$ when crash time $w < 1 + 2\pi/3$.

6   Conclusion

In this paper, we have introduced and analyzed evacuation algorithms for two robots, out of which one can be faulty. Along with this, we also provide a lower bound for the evacuation time. For chauffeuring cost $\alpha = 1$ the worst-case evacuation time is equal to the lower bound for crash time $w = 0$. This makes Algorithm $\mathscr{A}_0$ optimal. As the value of crash time w increases beyond $1 + 2\pi/3$, the gap between the lower bound and evacuation time of $\mathscr{A}_1$ is minimal for all values of α. For $\alpha = 1$, the lower bound is very close to the minimum evacuation time of $\mathscr{A}_1$ and $\mathscr{A}_2$, which says that the lower bound is tight. But the same does not happen for larger values of α, where the lower bound is not very close.

This paper revisits the evacuation problem from a fault-tolerance aspect with one of the classical crash fault scenarios. The model can be further extended for generalized crash fault model with k robots out of which f are faulty. Also, it is interesting to design algorithms which can tighten the bounds presented in this paper.

References

1. Brandt, S., Foerster, K., Richner, B., Wattenhofer, R.: Wireless evacuation on m rays with k searchers. In: SIROCCO, Porquerolles, France, pp. 140–157 (2017). https://doi.org/10.1007/978-3-319-72050-0_9
2. Brandt, S., Laufenberg, F., Lv, Y., Stolz, D., Wattenhofer, R.: Collaboration without communication: Evacuating two robots from a disk. In: CIAC, Athens, pp. 104–115 (2017). https://doi.org/10.1007/978-3-319-57586-5_10
3. Chuangpishit, H., Georgiou, K., Sharma, P.: Average case - worst case tradeoffs for evacuating 2 robots from the disk in the face-to-face model. In: Algorithms for Sensor Systems - 14th International Symposium on Algorithms and Experiments for Wireless Sensor Networks, ALGOSENSORS 2018, Helsinki, Finland, August 23–24, 2018, Revised Selected Papers, pp. 62–82 (2018). https://doi.org/10.1007/978-3-030-14094-6_5
4. Chuangpishit, H., Mehrabi, S., Narayanan, L., Opatrny, J.: Evacuating an equilateral triangle in the face-to-face model. In: OPODIS, Lisbon, Portugal, pp. 11:1–11:16 (2017). https://doi.org/10.4230/LIPIcs.OPODIS.2017.11
5. Czyzowicz, J., Gasieniec, L., Gorry, T., Kranakis, E., Martin, R., Pajak, D.: Evacuating robots via unknown exit in a disk. In: DISC, USA, 12–15 October 2014, pp. 122–136 (2014). https://doi.org/10.1007/978-3-662-45174-8_9
6. Czyzowicz, J., et al.: Evacuation from a disc in the presence of a faulty robot. In: SIROCCO, Porquerolles, France, pp. 158–173 (2017). https://doi.org/10.1007/978-3-319-72050-0_10
7. Czyzowicz, J., et al.: God save the queen. In: 9th International Conference on Fun with Algorithms, FUN 2018, 13–15 June 2018, La Maddalena, Italy, pp. 16:1–16:20 (2018). https://doi.org/10.4230/LIPIcs.FUN.2018.16
8. Czyzowicz, J., et al.: Priority evacuation from a disk using mobile robots - (extended abstract). In: Structural Information and Communication Complexity - 25th International Colloquium, SIROCCO 2018, Ma'ale HaHamisha, Israel, 18–21 June 2018, Revised Selected Papers, pp. 392–407 (2018). https://doi.org/10.1007/978-3-030-01325-7_32
9. Czyzowicz, J., et al.: Search on a line by byzantine robots. In: ISAAC, Sydney, Australia, pp. 27:1–27:12 (2016). https://doi.org/10.4230/LIPIcs.ISAAC.2016.27
10. Czyzowicz, J., Georgiou, K., Kranakis, E., Narayanan, L., Opatrny, J., Vogtenhuber, B.: Evacuating robots from a disk using face-to-face communication (extended abstract). In: CIAC, Paris, France, pp. 140–152 (2015). https://doi.org/10.1007/978-3-319-18173-8_10
11. Czyzowicz, J., Kranakis, E., Krizanc, D., Narayanan, L., Opatrny, J.: Search on a line with faulty robots. In: PODC, Chicago, IL, USA, pp. 405–414 (2016). https://doi.org/10.1145/2933057.2933102
12. Disser, Y., Schmitt, S.: Evacuating two robots from a disk: a second cut. In: Proceedings of the Structural Information and Communication Complexity - 26th International Colloquium, SIROCCO 2019, L'Aquila, Italy, 1–4 July 2019, pp. 200–214 (2019). https://doi.org/10.1007/978-3-030-24922-9_14
13. Kupavskii, A., Welzl, E.: Lower bounds for searching robots, some faulty. In: Proceedings of the 2018 ACM Symposium on Principles of Distributed Computing, PODC 2018, Egham, United Kingdom, 23–27 July 2018, pp. 447–453 (2018). https://dl.acm.org/citation.cfm?id=3212745

Optimal Circle Search Despite the Presence of Faulty Robots

Konstantinos Georgiou[1], Evangelos Kranakis[2], Nikos Leonardos[3], Aris Pagourtzis[4([⊠])], and Ioannis Papaioannou[4]

[1] Department of Mathematics, Ryerson University, Toronto, ON, Canada
konstantinos@ryerson.ca
[2] School of Computer Science, Carleton University, Ottawa, ON, Canada
kranakis@scs.carleton.ca
[3] Department of Informatics and Telecommunications,
National and Kapodistrian University of Athens, Ilissia, Greece
nikos.leonardos@gmail.com
[4] School of Electrical and Computer Engineering,
National Technical University of Athens, Zografou, Greece
pagour@cs.ntua.gr, ipapaioannou@corelab.ntua.gr

Abstract. We consider (n, f)-*search on a circle*, a search problem of a hidden exit on a circle of unit radius for $n > 1$ robots, f of which are faulty. All the robots start at the centre of the circle and can move anywhere with maximum speed 1. During the search, robots may communicate wirelessly. All messages transmitted by all robots are tagged with the robots' unique identifiers which cannot be corrupted. The search is considered complete when the exit is found by a non-faulty robot (which must visit its location) and the remaining non-faulty robots know the correct location of the exit.

We study two models of faulty robots. First, crash-faulty robots may stop operating as instructed, and thereafter they remain nonfunctional. Second, Byzantine-faulty robots may transmit untrue messages at any time during the search so as to mislead the non-faulty robots, e.g., lie about the location of the exit.

When there are only crash fault robots, we provide optimal algorithms for the (n, f)-search problem, with optimal worst-case search completion time $1 + \frac{(f+1)2\pi}{n}$. Our main technical contribution pertains to optimal algorithms for $(n, 1)$-search with a Byzantine-faulty robot, minimizing the worst-case search completion time, which equals $1 + \frac{4\pi}{n}$.

Keywords: Adversary · Byzantine · Circle · Exit · Perimeter · Robot · Search · Speed · Wireless communication

1 Introduction

Search is a problem of vital importance because of its numerous critical applications in various branches of mathematics and theoretical computer science.

K. Georgiou and E. Kranakis—Research supported in part by NSERC Discovery grant.

© Springer Nature Switzerland AG 2019
F. Dressler and C. Scheideler (Eds.): ALGOSENSORS 2019, LNCS 11931, pp. 192–205, 2019.
https://doi.org/10.1007/978-3-030-34405-4_11

Several linear search models concerning non-communicating agents have been the focus of investigation in numerous research publications, e.g. see the books Ahlswede and Wegener [1], Alpern and Gal [2], and Stone [15].

In this paper we consider searching for an exit placed at an unknown location on the perimeter of a unit radius disk by dimensionless robots (also referred to as mobile agents) that may communicate wirelessly, some of which are either crash-faulty or Byzantine-faulty. Crash-faulty robots may stop operating, in which case they can transmit no information. Byzantine robots are malicious in that they may falsify the information they transmit to peers by misleading them and thus delaying the overall worst-case search time of the system. Our approach differs from traditional models to search with mobile agents whereby the faults were restricted to the underlying search domain (e.g., graph, continuous infinite line, plane, etc.), in that we are interested in completing the search successfully when one of the mobile agents is faulty thus placing an additional strain on the mobile agents. Before giving details of our main results we formally describe the capabilities of the mobile agents and the computation model.

1.1 Computation Model

Our overall purpose is to design search algorithms which find the exit and whose running time, as measured by the time it takes the first robot to find the exit and convince the rest of the robots, is worst-case optimal. In this subsection we define the main parameters of the model which include communication, robot movement, crash and Byzantine faults, and the power of the adversary.

Communication. The robots can communicate wirelessly and instantaneously (no delay) at any time and regardless of their distance from each other. A typical message may involve information about their location, how far they have moved from their starting location, whether or not they found the exit, etc. Robots can deduce their current relative location from each other's messages, they are equipped with a pedometer (to measure distances) but otherwise have no need for GPS. Each message is tagged with the robot's unique identifier which cannot be altered by any robot.

Robot Movement. Robots start their movement at the centre of a unit radius disk. Their maximum speed is 1, and this is the same for all the robots. During their movement, they may recognize the perimeter of the disk and the exit if they are at its location as well as move along the perimeter. They are also allowed to take "shortcuts" by moving in the interior of the disk.

Fault Types. In our algorithms, robots agree on the specific trajectory that they are supposed to traverse, and in particular they know each others' trajectories. Thus, the location of a robot may be deduced by other robots based on the timing of a message transmission (and the type of the message). A crash-faulty robot may at any time stop functioning, meaning that it permanently remains idle and/or fails to communicate any messages, i.e. it crashes. A Byzantine robot is malicious in that it may alter its trajectory and provide (or hide) information whose purpose is to confuse the rest of the robots on the location of the exit. Note that a Byzantine robot may exhibit the behavior of a crash-faulty robot.

Adversary. For the worst case analysis of our algorithms, we consider an adversary who controls the location of the exit and the behaviour of the malicious robot (its trajectory as well as the messages it will broadcast) so as to maximize the resulting search completion time. A search is complete if the exit has been visited by a non-faulty robot and the rest of the agents, if any, can be convinced (provably) of the (correct) location of the exit.

1.2   Related Work

There has been extensive literature on line search starting with the seminal papers of Beck and Bellman [4,5] and Baeza-Yates et al. [3]. Both cases are concerned with linear search: a single mobile agent searching for an exit placed at an unknown location on an infinite line; in the former case the setting is stochastic and in the latter deterministic. This line of research continued by several authors and culminated with the seminal books by Ahlswede and Wegener [1], Alpern and Gal [2], and Stone [15]. Several other models for line search algorithms were subsequently investigated, e.g., by Kao et al. [14] for randomized line search and Demaine et al. [12] for taking into account the turn cost, just to mention a few. An interesting variant to the linear search above has to do with the presence of faulty robots. The two main papers in this line of research are [10] for crash-faulty robots and [9] for Byzantine-faulty robots.

The circle search model (considered in our paper) for n non-faulty robots was introduced as an evacuation problem (completion time with respect to the last finder of the hidden exit) in [6] and analyzed in both the wireless and face-to-face communication models. Since then there have been numerous related research papers mainly on evacuation, e.g. [13] in the face -to-face model, [11] in equilateral triangles, etc. The interested reader could consult the recent survey [8] for additional related literature.

Directly related to our current work is [7]. In this paper, authors investigate *evacuation* of robots in the presence of crash and/or Byzantine faults. Evacuation is different from search in that it measures completion of the algorithm by the time it takes the last non-faulty robot to find the exit (i.e., all the robots have to go to the exit), unlike search as studied in our current paper which measures success by the time it takes the first non-faulty robot to find the exit so that all non-faulty robots are convinced (provably) that the exit has been found and also know its location. To the best of our knowledge, the circle search model with a Byzantine-faulty robot has not been considered in the past.

1.3   Preliminaries and Notation

Assume that n is the number of robots, f of which are faulty. Robots are dimensionless and are initially located on the centre of a unit radius disk. The exit is located on the *unit circle*, which is the circumference of the disk. Robots can move with maximum speed 1. In our algorithms, all honest agents move at the maximum speed, therefore at each time point all agents know the location of every agent that follows the protocol. The n mobile agents are denoted by $a_0, a_1, \ldots, a_{n-1}$ and exactly f of them are faulty. The indices are treated as elements of $\mathbb{Z}_n$; in particular, index addition and subtraction are performed modulo n. Throughout the paper, we call our problem (n, f)-search, meaning search for $n > 1$ robots, f of which are faulty. Robots will be searching the unit circle either clockwise (cw) or counter-clockwise (ccw). It is assumed throughout that whenever an honest agent finds the exit it announces this fact, and whenever it realizes that an announcement of another agent is faulty it also announces this to everybody.

Our main contribution pertains to the $(n, 1)$-search problem with a Byzantine-faulty robot. By $S(n)$ we denote the infimum, over all algorithms, of the time required for the first non-faulty robot to reach the exit so that all robots also know (provably) the correct location of the exit. Similarly, for the (n, f)-search problem with crash-faulty robots, we denote the optimal search completion time by $S_c(n, f)$.

1.4   Results of the Paper

For $n \geq 2$, we give optimal algorithms for problem $(n, 1)$-search. Our main result is that $(n, 1)$-search on a circle admits a solution with search completion time $1 + \frac{4\pi}{n}$ and this is worst-case optimal. In Sect. 2 we prove a lower bound for f crash-faulty robots, hence for Byzantine robots too. In Sect. 3 we match the previous lower bound for crash-faulty robots with a tight upper bound. Then in Sect. 4 we focus on the upper bounds for searching with 1 Byzantine robots. In particular, in Subsect. 4.1 we analyze the case of 3 robots, in Subsect. 4.2 the case of 4 robots, and in Subsect. 4.3 the general case of n robots. In Sect. 5, we conclude with a relevant discussion and open problems.

2   Lower Bound

In this section we give a lower bound for our search problem. This result builds on the work in [7]; we extend their arguments to the case of f crash-faulty robots (hence, Byzantine too).

Theorem 1 (Lower Bound for (n, f)-Search). *The worst-case search time $S_c(n, f)$ for $n \geq f + 1$ robots exactly f of which are crash-faulty satisfies*

$$S_c(n, f) \geq 1 + (f + 1)\frac{2\pi}{n}.$$

Proof (Theorem 1). Since the maximum speed of the robots is 1, it takes at least time 1 for a robot to reach the perimeter of the disk. Further, every point on the perimeter must be traversed by at least $f + 1$ robots; for if not, the adversary will make the at most f robots visiting this point all faulty in that they remain silent and therefore the non-faulty robots will miss the exit.

Let ℓ_i be the perimeter lengths explored by exactly i robots, where $0 \leq i \leq n$. It is clear from the above discussion that $\ell_0 = \ell_1 = \cdots \ell_f = 0$ and $\ell_{f+1} + \ell_{f+2} + \cdots + \ell_n = 2\pi$. The sum of the parts of the perimeter explored by the robots is $(f + 1)\ell_{f+1} + (f + 2)\ell_{f+2} + \cdots + n\ell_n$. If the robots accomplish this task by exploring the perimeter for time t (after the perimeter of the disk is reached for the first time), then it must be true that

$$
\begin{aligned}
nt &\geq (f + 1)\ell_{f+1} + (f + 2)\ell_{f+2} + \cdots + n\ell_n \\
&\geq (f + 1)(\ell_{f+1} + \ell_{f+2} + \cdots + \ell_n) \\
&= (f + 1)2\pi.
\end{aligned}
$$

It follows that $t \geq (f + 1)2\pi/n$. This completes the proof. □

Since $S(n) \geq S_c(n, 1)$, we immediately obtain the following corollary.

Corollary 1 (Lower Bound for Byzantine $(n, 1)$-Search). *The worst-case search time $S(n)$ for $n \geq 2$ robots exactly one of which is Byzantine-faulty satisfies $S(n) \geq 1 + \frac{4\pi}{n}$.*

3   Searching with Crash Faults

In this section we match the lower bound of Theorem 1 when we search with crash-faulty robots.

Theorem 2 (Upper Bound for (n, f)-Search with Crash Faults). *The worst-case search time $S_c(n, f)$ for $n \geq 2$ robots exactly f of which are prone to crash failures satisfies*

$$
S_c(n, f) \leq 1 + (f + 1)\frac{2\pi}{n}.
$$

Proof. Let $\theta := 2\pi/n$. Our algorithm is as follows. For each $k = 0, \ldots, n - 1$, agent a_k moves to the point $k\theta$ of the unit circle and searches ccw for $(f + 1)\theta$ radians. When (and if) exit is found, it is reported instantaneously.

Clearly, every sector S_j of the circle would be visited by $f + 1$ robots if they all followed the protocol. Since there are at most f faulty robots, there must be at least one honest robot that will visit S_j and announce the correct location. As there can only be crash failures there will not be any contradicting announcements. □

4 Search with One Byzantine Fault

In this section we analyze upper bounds for our search problem with a Byzantine agent. Our main theorem is the following.

Theorem 3 (Upper Bound for $(n, 1)$-Search). *The worst-case search time $S(n)$ for $n \geq 2$ robots exactly one of which is faulty satisfies*

$$S(n) \leq 1 + \frac{4\pi}{n}.$$

Thus, combining Corollary 1 with Theorems 3, we conclude that the worst-case search completion time for $(n, 1)$-search satisfies $S(n) = 1 + \frac{4\pi}{n}$.

First observe that it is trivial to prove $S(2) = 1 + 2\pi$, for $(2, 1)$-search since one of the two robots is faulty and the other non-faulty, hence the non-faulty has no other option but to search the entire perimeter.

In the next two Subsects. (4.1 and 4.2) we show the upper bound for the cases $(3, 1)$-search and $(4, 1)$-search. Although the algorithms for these cases can be seen as special cases of the algorithm for the general case (Subsect. 4.3), this is not the case for their analysis. In addition, presenting them separately allows to better clarify and illustrate the techniques and notions that we employ.

4.1 $(3, 1)$-Search with a Byzantine-Faulty Robot

Lemma 1 ((3,1)-Search). *The worst-case search time for 3 robots exactly one of which is faulty satisfies*

$$S(3) \leq 1 + \frac{4\pi}{3}$$

Proof. We will prove the claim by presenting an algorithm for this case. Consider agents a_0, a_1, a_2 and set $\theta = 2\pi/3$. We describe below the agents' actions in phases (time intervals) $[0, 1)$, $[1, 1 + \theta)$ and $[1 + \theta, 1 + 2\theta)$ and we explain why all agents know the location of the exit at time $1 + 2\theta$.

Phase $[0, 1)$: Each agent a_k, $k \in \{0, 1, 2\}$, moves along a radius to the point $k\theta$ of the unit circle.
Phase $[1, 1 + \theta)$: Agent a_k searches ccw the arc $[k\theta, (k + 1)\theta)$.
Phase $[1 + \theta, 1 + 2\theta)$:

(i) If no announcements were made in time interval $[1, 1 + \theta)$ then in time interval $[1 + \theta, 1 + 2\theta)$ either there will be one correct announcement or two announcements. In the latter case the third agent, say a_k, is honest and the correct announcement is the one by a_{k+1} (otherwise, a_k would have seen in time interval $[1, 1 + \theta)$ the exit announced by a_{k-1}).

(ii) If exactly one announcement was made in time interval $[1, 1 + \theta)$, say by agent a_{k-1}, then agent a_k moves directly (along a chord) to the location of the announcement and a_{k+1} searches ccw for another θ radians. This takes time at most $2 < \frac{2\pi}{3}$. If a_k or a_{k+1} confirms the announcement then it is correct; otherwise, a_{k+1} in this time interval announces the correct exit point. This case is depicted in Fig. 1.[1]

(iii) If two announcements were made in time interval $[1, 1+\theta)$, then they are in consecutive sectors. The silent agent is certainly non-faulty and will visit one of these sectors in this phase and will thus be able to determine which announcement was the correct one.

This completes the description of the algorithm and the proof.   □

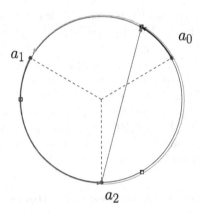

Fig. 1. $(3,1)$-search: robot trajectories in case $t < \frac{2\pi}{3}$.

4.2 $(4,1)$-Search with a Byzantine-Faulty Robot

We will first describe an algorithm for this case. Let $\theta = \pi/2$. Each agent a_k moves with speed one to its *starting point* $k\theta$ and then continues ccw. We call the arc from one starting point to the next a *sector*. We think of each agent being responsible for the arc of length π that begins at its starting point and covers at most two consecutive sectors ccw.

Let t denote the length of the arc from the point of the first announcement to the starting point that corresponds to the agent that made the announcement

---

[1] Figures in this paper depict robot trajectories during the execution of our search algorithm. They restrict to cases where the first announcement is made while robots search their first sector of length $\theta = \frac{2\pi}{n}$, and no other announcement is made until time $1+\theta$. It is assumed that agent a_0 makes the first announcement. A black square shows the location of the announcement; a white square shows the locations of other agents at that time. A solid dot shows the starting positions of the robots on the unit circle (starting from the center of the circle, they move directly, in time 1, to their starting positions). Recall that the arc length between the starting position of a_0 and the point of the announcement is denoted by t (hence, the announcement takes place in time $1 + t$).

(note, there is always an announcement for some $t \leq \pi$). If $t \geq \frac{\pi}{2}$, then each robot checks both sectors that are assigned to it. Otherwise, set $y = \pi - 2$ and suppose an announcement is made by a_0 (w.l.o.g.) at $t < \frac{\pi}{2}$. We consider two cases.

If $t < y$, then a_1 and a_3 will search the two sectors that each is responsible for and a_2 will move along the diameter to check the announcement. This case is depicted in Fig. 2.

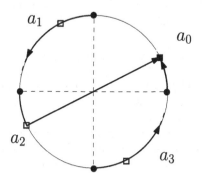

Fig. 2. $(4,1)$-search: robot trajectories in case $t < y$.

If $y \leq t < \frac{\pi}{2}$, then a_1 continues to cover distance $\sqrt{2}$ (unless $t \geq \sqrt{2}$) and then moves along a chord to check the announcement; a_2 finishes its first sector and then moves back along a chord to its starting point and continues cw to check the arc that a_1 didn't check; a_3 continues searching its two sectors. This case is depicted in Fig. 3.

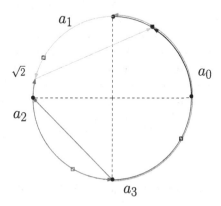

Fig. 3. $(4,1)$-search: robot trajectories in case $y \leq t < \frac{\pi}{2}$.

This completes the description of the algorithm. We will now prove the correctness and the upper bound on the execution time.

Lemma 2 ((4, 1)-Search). *The search time for* 4 *robots exactly one of which is faulty satisfies*

$$S(4) \leq 1 + \pi.$$

Proof. Recall that we denote by t the length of the arc searched on the circle by the agent who made the first announcement, at the time of the announcement.

For $t \geq \frac{\pi}{2}$ we argue that when every robot has checked the sectors it is responsible for (at time $1 + \pi$), all of them know the location of the exit. First, note that if only one announcement is made, then it has to be a valid one. Therefore, assume two announcements are made (note that both are no earlier than $\frac{\pi}{2}$). Observe that they have to come from consecutive sectors: the exit must be at the first sector of the faulty robot, say a_3 since nobody spoke earlier than $\frac{\pi}{2}$, and it is discovered by a_2, while searching its second sector, who makes a correct announcement. The only other announcement can be made by a_3 and is faulty. Therefore, all agents know that the location is at the first of the two sectors in the ccw direction.

For $t < \frac{\pi}{2}$ suppose the first announcement was made by a_0. We claim that in this case the first announcement is checked by two more agents (namely, by a_3 and either a_1 or a_2) and every point of the perimeter is searched by one of the three other agents (unless a second announcement is made in which case it is not necessary to search the whole circle as one of the two must be correct). Assuming this claim, if the first announcement is verified by any other agent, then clearly it is valid. If not, then two agents reject it, thus it must be fake. It follows that another announcement was made which has to be valid. We next verify the claim and the execution time.

Consider the case $t < y$. Note that y was defined so that a_2 reaches the announcement in time less than $1 + y + 2 = 1 + \pi$. Thus, the announcement is checked by a_2 and a_3 in time, while a_1 and a_3 search every point of the perimeter.

Consider now $y \leq t < \frac{\pi}{2}$. First, to see that every sector was searched by the first three agents by time $1 + \pi$, we need to argue that a_1 and a_2 covered the first sector. Indeed, a_2 searched an arc of length $\frac{\pi}{2}$ to finish his first sector, a chord of length $\sqrt{2}$ to go back to his starting point, and an arc of length at most $\frac{\pi}{2} - \sqrt{2}$ that was left uncovered by a_1; this sums up to at most $\frac{\pi}{2} + \sqrt{2} + \frac{\pi}{2} - \sqrt{2} = \pi$ as desired. Next, we need to argue that the announcement location was reached by a_1 in time $1 + \pi$. This is clear if $t \geq \sqrt{2}$. Otherwise, it is not hard to see that the worst case is $t = y$. In this case, the chord a_1 walks corresponds to an arc of length $\phi = \sqrt{2} + \frac{\pi}{2} - y = 2 + \sqrt{2} - \frac{\pi}{2}$. Thus, the total time it needs is $1 + \sqrt{2} + 2\sin\frac{\phi}{2} < 1 + \pi$. $\qquad\square$

4.3 $(n, 1)$-Search with a Byzantine-Faulty Robot, $n \geq 5$

We will first give the description of the algorithm for this case. For each $k \in \mathbb{Z}_n$, agent a_k moves to the k-*th starting point* P_k located at $k\theta$, $\theta = 2\pi/n$, and then continues ccw. We denote the arc of size θ from the k-th starting point to the next by S_k and call it the k-*th sector*. We think of sectors S_k and S_{k+1} as being *assigned* to agent a_k, who is supposed to search them in the ccw direction.

Let t denote the length of the arc from the point of the first announcement to the starting point that corresponds to the agent that made the announcement. We now describe the trajectories of agents for the case that agent a_0 makes the first announcement. We will argue later (in the proof of Theorem 3) that the information they exchange is enough for all agents to learn the exit location.

If $t \geq \theta$, then each agent checks both sectors that are assigned to it. Otherwise, set

$$y = 2\theta - 2\sin\theta$$

and suppose an announcement is made by a_0 at $t < \theta$. Consider two cases.

If $t < y$, then each agent a_k with $k \notin \{0, 2\}$ will search its two sectors, while a_2 will start at time $1 + t$ to move along a chord towards the announcement in order to verify it.

If $y \leq t < \theta$, define arc-lengths x_k (in S_k but not to be searched by a_k) recursively as follows.

$$x_{n-2} = 0; \quad x_k = \theta + x_{k+1} - 2\sin\left(\frac{\theta - x_{k+1}}{2}\right), \text{ for } 0 < k < n - 1. \quad (1)$$

Agent a_1 continues to cover distance $\theta - x_1$ (unless $t \geq \theta - x_1$) and then moves along a chord towards the announcement in order to verify it; for $1 < k < n - 1$, agent a_k continues to cover distance $\theta - x_k$ (unless $t \geq \theta - x_k$), then moves along a chord back to its starting point, and finally searches in the cw direction the arc (of length at most x_{k-1}) that agent a_{k-1} didn't search; agent a_{n-1} continues with its two sectors. This case is depicted in Fig. 4.

This completes the description of the algorithm. We next show its correctness and the upper bound on its running time.

Lemma 3 ($(n, 1)$-Search, for $n \geq 5$). *The worst-case search time for $n \geq 5$ robots exactly one of which is faulty satisfies*

$$S(n) \leq 1 + \frac{4\pi}{n}.$$

Proof (Lemma 3). We are going to argue about the correctness and the execution time of the algorithm described above.

If $t \geq \theta$, then all agents have searched the sectors assigned to them by time $1 + 2\theta$. We need to show that all of them know the location of the exit. First, note that if only one announcement is made, then it has to be a valid one. Thus, assume two announcements are made. Observe that they have to come from consecutive sectors: one of them is the true one and was discovered by an honest agent, say a_k, while searching sector S_{k+1}. It follows that a_{k+1} is faulty (because it didn't make the announcement) and the other announcement must come from it. Therefore, the agents know that the location is at the first announcement encountered in the ccw direction.

Otherwise ($t < \theta$), suppose the first announcement was made by a_0. We claim the following.

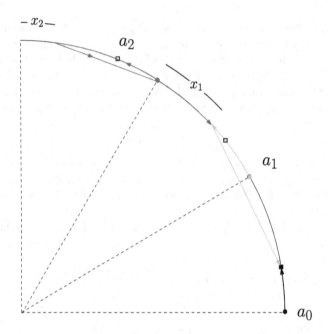

Fig. 4. $(n, 1)$-search: robot trajectories in case $y \leq t < \theta$.

The first announcement is checked by two more agents and every point of the perimeter is searched by at least one agent different from a_0, unless a second announcement is made.

Note first that if the first announcement is verified by one more agent, then it is proved valid to all. If not, then—assuming the claim—two agents reject it and a_0 is proved faulty to all. Furthermore, every point of the perimeter will be searched by at least one honest agent. It follows—by the second part of the claim—that another announcement will be made and will be recognized by all as valid. We next verify the claim and the execution time for the two cases on t.

Consider the case $t < y$. Note that y was defined so that a_2 reaches the announcement in time less than $1 + y + 2 \sin \theta = 1 + 2\theta$. This is because it will spend less than time y on its first sector and then move along the chord that corresponds to two sectors. Thus, the announcement is checked by a_2 and a_{n-1} in time, while the other agents set forth to search every point of the perimeter.

Consider now $y \leq t < \theta$. First, we verify that every sector was searched by one of the agents $a_1, \ldots, a_{n-1}$ by time $1 + 2\theta$. It is clear that a_{n-1} searched sectors S_{n-1} and S_0. Next, we argue that, for $0 < k < n - 1$, agents a_k and a_{k+1} covered sector S_k. Note that x_k is the length of S_k that was not searched by agent a_k. However, x_k is defined so that a_{k+1} has sufficient time to travel back to P_{k+1} and aid a_k. Indeed, the worst case for a_{k+1} is when $t \leq \theta - x_k$. (It is not hard to see that when $t > \theta - x_k$ he will have time to spare.) In this case, after reaching point $\theta - x_{k+1}$ of S_{k+1}, it must search a chord corresponding to an arc of $\theta - x_{k+1}$ radians and an arc of length x_k. Since it has $\theta + x_{k+1}$ time left, the definition of x_k is such that he can manage its task. Finally, we need to argue that the announcement was reached by a_1 in time $1 + 2\theta$. This is clear if $t \geq \theta - x_1$. Otherwise, it is not hard to see that the worst case is $t = y$. In this case, the chord a_1 searches corresponds to an arc of length $2\theta - x_1 - y$. Thus, the total time a_1 needs is

$$T = 1 + (\theta - x_1) + 2\sin\left(\frac{2\theta - x_1 - y}{2}\right).$$

In the sequel we will make use of the following simple facts.

Fact 1. *For* $x \in (0, \frac{\pi}{2})$, $\sin x < x$.

Fact 2. *For* $x \in (0, \frac{\pi}{2})$, $\sin x < 2\sin\frac{x}{2}$.

Fact 3. *For* $x \in (0, \frac{\pi}{4})$, $\sin x < x - \frac{x^3}{7}$.

Since, for $n \geq 4$, $2\theta - x_1 - y < \pi$, using Fact 1 (twice) and substituting $y = 2\theta - 2\sin\theta$ we obtain

$$T \leq 1 + (\theta - x_1) + (2\theta - x_1 - y) \leq 1 + 2\theta - 2x_1 + \sin\theta.$$

To provide a lower bound on x_1, apply Fact 1 on the recursive definition to obtain

$$x_{n-3} = \theta - 2\sin\frac{\theta}{2}; \quad x_k \geq 2x_{k+1}, \text{ for } 0 < k < n - 1. \tag{2}$$

It follows that

$$x_1 \geq 2^{n-4}\left(\theta - 2\sin\frac{\theta}{2}\right).$$

Combining with the upper bound on T, to show $T \leq 1 + 2\theta$, it suffices to argue that

$$2^{n-3}\left(\frac{2\pi}{n} - 2\sin\frac{\pi}{n}\right) \geq \sin\frac{2\pi}{n}.$$

Using Fact 2, $\sin\frac{2\pi}{n} \leq 2\sin\frac{\pi}{n}$. Substituting this and rearranging, it suffices to show that

$$2^{n-3} \cdot \frac{\pi}{n} \geq \left(2^{n-3} + 1\right)\sin\frac{\pi}{n}.$$

In view of Fact 3, the sufficient condition simplifies further to

$$2^{n-3} \geq \left(2^{n-3} + 1\right)\left(1 - \frac{\pi^2}{7n^2}\right) \iff \left(2^{n-3} + 1\right)\pi^2 \geq 7n^2,$$

which holds for all $n \geq 9$.

Finally cases $n \in \{5, 6, 7, 8\}$ have been verified computationally as follows. In the table below we list values $y, x_1, \ldots, x_{n-3}$ for $n \in \{5, 6, 7, 8\}$. These values determine the algorithm for these cases. To verify the table, it suffices to verify $y \leq 2\theta - 2\sin\theta$, $T \geq 1 + (\theta - x_1) + 2\sin(\frac{2\theta - x_1 - y}{2})$, $S(n) \leq 1 + 2\theta$, and $x_k \leq \theta + x_{k+1} - 2\sin(\frac{\theta - x_{k+1}}{2})$ (for $0 < k < n - 2$). With respect to the x_k values, note

n	x_5	x_4	x_3	x_2	x_1	y	T	$S(n)$
5				0.0810	0.2285	0.611	3.51327	3.51327
6			0.047	0.135	0.3	0.36	3.07	3.09
7		0.029	0.085	0.17*	0.34*	0.2	2.74	2.79
8	0.02	0.04*	0.08*	0.16*	0.32*	0.1	2.56	2.57

that those which are double the previous one (marked with an asterisk) need not be verified in view of inequality (2).

This completes the proof of the lemma. $\qquad\Box$

Now we can complete the rest of the proof of Theorem 3.

Proof (Theorem 3). Lemmas 1 and 2 prove the upper bound for $n = 3, 4$ robots respectively, and cases $n \geq 5$ are covered by Lemma 3. $\qquad\Box$

5   Conclusion

In this paper we considered search on a circle with n robots, where either $f \geq 1$ of them are crash-faulty, or one of them is Byzantine-faulty, and we proved that the optimal worst-case search times are exactly $1 + \frac{(f+1)2\pi}{n}$ and $1 + \frac{4\pi}{n}$, respectively. The optimality for the Byzantine case is quite surprising given that there are very few tight bounds for search on a circle even for the wireless model. Extending the results either to multiple Byzantine-faulty robots or to the evacuation problem are two challenging open problems in the context of circle search.

References

1. Ahlswede, R., Wegener, I.: Search Problems. Wiley, Hoboken (1987)
2. Alpern, S., Gal, S.: The Theory of Search Games and Rendezvous, vol. 55. Springer, Heidelberg (2003). https://doi.org/10.1007/b100809
3. Baeza-Yates, R., Culberson, J., Rawlins, G.: Searching in the plane. Inf. Comput. **106**(2), 234–252 (1993)
4. Beck, A.: On the linear search problem. Israel J. Math. **2**(4), 221–228 (1964)
5. Bellman, R.: An optimal search. Siam Rev. **5**(3), 274–274 (1963)
6. Czyzowicz, J., Gąsieniec, L., Gorry, T., Kranakis, E., Martin, R., Pajak, D.: Evacuating robots via unknown exit in a disk. In: Kuhn, F. (ed.) DISC 2014. LNCS, vol. 8784, pp. 122–136. Springer, Heidelberg (2014). https://doi.org/10.1007/978-3-662-45174-8_9
7. Czyzowicz, J., et al.: Evacuation from a disc in the presence of a faulty robot. In: Das, S., Tixeuil, S. (eds.) SIROCCO 2017. LNCS, vol. 10641, pp. 158–173. Springer, Cham (2017). https://doi.org/10.1007/978-3-319-72050-0_10
8. Czyzowicz, J., Georgiou, K., Kranakis, E.: Group search and evacuation. In: Flocchini, P., Prencipe, G., Santoro, N. (eds.) Distributed Computing by Mobile Entities. LNCS, vol. 11340, pp. 335–370. Springer, Cham (2019). https://doi.org/10.1007/978-3-030-11072-7_14

9. Czyzowicz, J., et al.: Search on a line by byzantine robots. In: ISAAC, pp. 27:1–27:12 (2016)
10. Czyzowicz, J., Kranakis, E., Krizanc, D., Narayanan, L., Opatrny, J.: Search on a line with faulty robots. In: PODC, pp. 405–414. ACM (2016)
11. Czyzowicz, J., Kranakis, E., Krizanc, D., Narayanan, L., Opatrny, J., Shende, S.: Wireless autonomous robot evacuation from equilateral triangles and squares. In: Papavassiliou, S., Ruehrup, S. (eds.) ADHOC-NOW 2015. LNCS, vol. 9143, pp. 181–194. Springer, Cham (2015). https://doi.org/10.1007/978-3-319-19662-6_13
12. Demaine, E.D., Fekete, S.P., Gal, S.: Online searching with turn cost. Theor. Comput. Sci. **361**(2), 342–355 (2006)
13. Czyzowicz, J., Georgiou, K., Kranakis, E., Narayanan, L., Opatrny, J., Vogtenhuber, B.: Evacuating using face-to-face communication. CoRR, abs/1501.04985 (2015)
14. Kao, M.-Y., Reif, J.H., Tate, S.R.: Searching in an unknown environment: an optimal randomized algorithm for the cow-path problem. Inf. Comput. **131**(1), 63–79 (1996)
15. Stone, L.: Theory of Optimal Search. Academic Press, New York (1975)

Author Index

Printed in the United States
By Bookmasters